MACRO ECONOMIC ANALYSIS

For
B.B.M. (Semester - II)
As Per Savitribai Phule Pune University's New Syllabus,
Effective from June 2013

Mrs. Kiran Jotwani
M.A. (Economics), B.Ed.

Macro Economic Analysis ISBN 978-93-83750-38-2

Third Edition : June 2015
© : Author

The text of this publication, or any part thereof, should not be reproduced or transmitted in any form or stored in any computer storage system or device for distribution including photocopy, recording, taping or information retrieval system or reproduced on any disc, tape, perforated media or other information storage device etc., without the written permission of Author with whom the rights are reserved. Breach of this condition is liable for legal action.

Every effort has been made to avoid errors or omissions in this publication. In spite of this, errors may have crept in. Any mistake, error or discrepancy so noted and shall be brought to our notice shall be taken care of in the next edition. It is notified that neither the publisher nor the author or seller shall be responsible for any damage or loss of action to any one, of any kind, in any manner, therefrom.

Published By :
NIRALI PRAKASHAN
Abhyudaya Pragati, 1312, Shivaji Nagar,
Off J.M. Road, PUNE – 411005
Tel - (020) 25512336/37/39, Fax - (020) 25511379
Email : niralipune@pragationline.com

Printed By :
Repro Knowledgecast Limited,
Thane

☞ DISTRIBUTION CENTRES

PUNE
Nirali Prakashan : 119, Budhwar Peth, Jogeshwari Mandir Lane, Pune 411002, Maharashtra
Tel : (020) 2445 2044, 66022708, Fax : (020) 2445 1538
Email : bookorder@pragationline.com, niralilocal@pragationline.com

Nirali Prakashan : S. No. 28/27, Dhyari, Near Pari Company, Pune 411041
Tel : (020) 24690204 Fax : (020) 24690316
Email : dhyari@pragationline.com, bookorder@pragationline.com

MUMBAI
Nirali Prakashan : 385, S.V.P. Road, Rasdhara Co-op. Hsg. Society Ltd.,
Girgaum, Mumbai 400004, Maharashtra
Tel : (022) 2385 6339 / 2386 9976, Fax : (022) 2386 9976
Email : niralimumbai@pragationline.com

☞ DISTRIBUTION BRANCHES

JALGAON
Nirali Prakashan : 34, V. V. Golani Market, Navi Peth, Jalgaon 425001,
Maharashtra, Tel : (0257) 222 0395, Mob : 94234 91860

KOLHAPUR
Nirali Prakashan : New Mahadvar Road, Kedar Plaza, 1st Floor Opp. IDBI Bank
Kolhapur 416 012, Maharashtra. Mob : 9850046155

NAGPUR
Pratibha Book Distributors : Above Maratha Mandir, Shop No. 3, First Floor,
Rani Jhanshi Square, Sitabuldi, Nagpur 440012, Maharashtra
Tel : (0712) 254 7129

DELHI
Nirali Prakashan : 4593/21, Basement, Aggarwal Lane 15, Ansari Road, Daryaganj
Near Times of India Building, New Delhi 110002
Mob : 08505972553

BENGALURU
Pragati Book House : House No. 1, Sanjeevappa Lane, Avenue Road Cross,
Opp. Rice Church, Bengaluru – 560002.
Tel : (080) 64513344, 64513355,Mob : 9880582331, 9845021552
Email:bharatsavla@yahoo.com

CHENNAI
Pragati Books : 9/1, Montieth Road, Behind Taas Mahal, Egmore,
Chennai 600008 Tamil Nadu, Tel : (044) 6518 3535,
Mob : 94440 01782 / 98450 21552 / 98805 82331,
Email : bharatsavla@yahoo.com

niralipune@pragationline.com | www.pragationline.com

Also find us on   www.facebook.com/niralibooks

Preface ...

It gives me a feeling of immense pleasure and gratitude when placing before the students of BBM and other esteemed readers, the book of *Macro Economic Analysis*. It is based on the revised syllabus set by the Savitribai Phule Pune University, with effect from June 2013.

The field of economics is very dynamic, characterised by continuous changes in its variables which have a deep impact on the business world of the economy. In the business world, with the cut-throat competition, the survival in the market depends on the knowledge of *Macro Economics*.

Economics is a dynamic science, changing to reflect the shifting trends in economic affairs, in the environment, in the world economy, and in society at large. As economics and the world around it evolve, so does this book.

The book presents a clear, accurate and interesting introduction to the macro principles of modern economics.

This book contains the terms and concepts of macro economics. The components of macro economics are well dealt with to understand its importance on forming business strategies.

Macro Economic Analysis deals with Chapters of Classical and Keynesian Theory of Income and Employment and presents tools that help to equip the economy in dealing with economic instabilities during Inflation and Deflation. The Growth and Development of any economy depends on factors like Consumption and Investment Expenditure by firms and government.

Dear Students, you have probably read in the newspaper about the GDP, the consumer price index, the stock market and the unemployment rate, the rising prices, depression in certain sectors of the economy and so on. After you have completed a thorough study of the chapters in this textbook, you will discern precisely what these words mean.

The book also contains Objective Questions and Questions to be solved by students. Various diagrams, figures and flow-charts help to simplify the most complicated of the topics. The language used is simple and flows naturally.

I am thankful to my friends and long time publisher Shri Dineshbhai Furia, Shri Jignesh Furia and the entire staff which includes Prasad Chintakindi, Ilyas Shaikh, Chaitali Takale, and Ravindra Walodare of Nirali Prakashan, Pune without whose unerring support and sustained efforts, this book would not have seen the light of the day. A special thanks to Mrs. Nirja Sharma for her ever-availability to me for solving the queries of the updated syllabus.

I am thankful to Shri Suresh Jotwani, for his unconditional help and encouragement.

I am sure that the book will be a good guidance to the students. Both, my publisher and I will be thankful and will welcome any suggestions for the improvement in any of the contents of the book. We are quite confident that this text book will receive the patronage of all for whom it is intended.

Kiran Jotwani

Syllabus ...

1. **Introduction**
   1.1 Definition and Nature of Macro Economic Analysis
   1.2 Scope, Importance and Limitations of Macro Economic Analysis

2. **Money and Value of Money**
   2.1 Definition of Money
   2.2 Functions of Money
   2.3 Value of Money
      2.3.1 Quantity Theory of Money
      2.3.2 Cash Balance Approach

3. **Theory of Income and Employment**
   3.1 Say's Law of Market
   3.2 Keynesian Theory of Income and Employment

4. **Savings**
   4.1 Consumption Function – Keynes' Psychological Law of Consumption
   4.2 Average and Marginal Propensity to Consume
   4.3 Saving Function - Average and Marginal Propensity to Save.
   4.4 Paradox of Saving

5. **Investments**
   5.1 Investment Function - Autonomous and Induced Investment
   5.2 Investment Multiplier and Foreign Trade Multiplier

6. **Trade Cycle**
   6.1 Nature and Characteristics of Trade Cycle
   6.2 Phases of Trade Cycle
   6.3 Control of Trade Cycle
   6.4 Inflation and Deflation - Meaning, Causes and Control

Contents ...

1. **Introduction** — 1.1 – 1.16

2. **Money and Value of Money** — 2.1 – 2.50

3. **Theory of Income and Employment** — 3.1 – 3.34

4. **Savings** — 4.1 – 4.28

5. **Investments** — 5.1 – 5.36

6. **Trade Cycle** — 6.1 – 6.58

Bibliography — B.1 – B.1

University Question Papers — P.1 – P.2

Chapter 1...

Introduction

Contents ...
1.1 Definitions of Macroeconomics
1.2 Nature of Macroeconomics
1.3 Scope/Importance/Utility of Macroeconomics
1.4 Limitations of Macroeconomics
1.5 Difference between Micro and Macro Economics
- Points to Remember
- Multiple Choice Questions
- Questions for Discussion

Learning Objectives ...
➢ To explain the basic difference between microeconomics and macroeconomics
➢ To help the reader analyze how economic decisions are made about the basic problems, such as how to produce, how much to produce, etc.
➢ To discuss the scope, importance and limitations of macroeconomics analysis
➢ To introduce key economic concepts like 'averages' and 'aggregates'
➢ To discuss the interdependence between microeconomics and macroeconomics

Introduction

Economics is study of allocation of scarce resources among competing ends which have alternative uses. Economics is broadly divided into two parts: Microeconomics and Macroeconomics. Macroeconomics is that branch of economic analysis that studies the behaviour of aggregates, i.e., of all the units combined together.

The term 'macro' was first used in economics by **Ragnar Frisch** in 1933. But as a methodological approach to economic problems, it originated with the Mercantilists in the 16th and 17th centuries. They were concerned with the economic system as a whole.

Malthus, Sismondi and Marx, in the 19th century, dealt with macroeconomic problems. Before Keynes, other modern contributors to the development of macroeconomic analysis were Walras, Wicksell and Fisher. Economists like Marshall, Pigou, Robertson and Hawtrey have developed a theory of money and general prices.

However, the credit of blossoming macroeconomics goes to **John Maynard Keynes**. His famous work, *'General Theory of Income, Output and Employment'* (1936) gave a strong impetus to the growth and development of modern Macroeconomics.

1.1 Definitions of Macroeconomics

In recent years, increasing attention has been given to the study and analysis of the economic system as a whole. This is Macroeconomic approach to economics.

According to **R.G.D. Allen**, 'macroeconomics' refers to *"the study of relations between broad economic aggregates."*

Macroeconomics is the study of aggregates or averages covering the entire economy, such as total employment, national income, national output, total investment, total consumption, total savings, aggregate supply, aggregate demand and general price level, wage level and cost structure. It is aggregative economics which examines the interrelations among the various aggregates, their determination and causes of fluctuations in them.

Prof. Ackley defines Macro Economics as *"it deals with economic affairs in the large, it concerns with the overall dimensions of economic life. It looks at the total size and shape and functioning of the entire economic experience, rather than working of articulation or dimensions of the individual parts. It studies the character of the forest, independently of the trees which compose it."*

Macroeconomics may be, thus, defined as *"that branch of economic analysis which studies the behaviour of not just one particular unit, but of all the units combined together".*

Macroeconomics is a study in *'aggregates'* and hence it is often referred to as *'Aggregative Economics'*. Thus, it is the study of the economic system as a whole. It studies the overall conditions of an economy, such as, total consumption, total production, total savings, total investments, etc.

In the words of **Prof. K. E. Boulding**, *"Macroeconomics deals not with individual quantities as such, but with aggregates of these quantities; not with individual incomes but with the national income; not with individual prices but with the price level; not with individual outputs, but with the national output"*. It, thus, deals not with one firm but all the firms in an economy; not with one industry, but the entire industrial structure of an economy.

Since macroeconomics deals with aggregates, it is known as *'the theory of income and employment or income analysis'*.

> *Macroeconomics deals with great 'averages' and 'aggregates' of the system and not with particular units in it. It is study of macro-quantities and macro-variables.*

To sum up:
  (i) Macroeconomics deals with the functions of the economy as a whole. Macro analysis conceives of equilibrium between demand and supply in the economy as a whole.

(ii) Among other things, macroeconomics seeks to explain how the economy's total output of goods and services, the price level of goods and services and the total employment of resources are demanded.

(iii) Macroeconomics also seeks to investigate into the causes responsible for initiating changes in total output, aggregate employment and the general price level.

The Keynesian economists had developed macroeconomics to a great extent by the 60's. Its field of study is vast and includes as follows:

(i) It deals with the theory of Income, Output and Employment with its two constituents (a) the theory of consumption function; and (b) the theory of investment function.

(ii) The theory of business cycles, i.e., economic fluctuations, is too a part of the theory of income, output and employment.

(iii) Theory of prices – theories of inflation, deflation and stagflation.

(iv) Theory of Economic Growth dealing with the long-run growth of income, output and employment as applied to developed and under-developed countries.

(v) Macro Theory of Distribution that deals with the relative shares of wages and profits in the total national income.

1.2 Nature of Macroeconomics

Macroeconomics studies the aggregates of the entire economy. The nature of macroeconomics can be understood with the help of the following aspects:

1. Determination of National Income and Employment
- Macroeconomics deals with aggregate demand and aggregate supply that determines the equilibrium level of income and employment in the economy.
- The level of aggregate demand determines the level of income and employment.
- Macroeconomics also deals with the problem of unemployment due to lack of aggregate demand.

2. Determination of General Price Level
- Macroeconomics studies the general level of price in an economy.
- It studies the economic fluctuations and business cycles, i.e., it studies the problem of inflation and deflation.

3. Economic Growth and Development
- Macroeconomics deals with economic growth and development.
- It studies various factors that contribute to economic growth and development.

4. Distribution of Factors of Production
- Macroeconomics deals with various factors of production and their relative share in the total production or total national income.

5. Aggregative Approach
- Macroeconomics is 'aggregative' in its methodological approach. Macroeconomics has been developed to describe the typical nature of aggregate economic behaviour.
- It studies the overall 'averages' and 'aggregates' of the system.

6. Economic Variables
- Macroeconomics is concerned with the behaviour of macro-variables and macro-quantities such as aggregate demand, general price level, aggregate supply, total consumption, total expenditure, etc.
- Macroeconomics concentrates on variables such as the aggregate volume to output of an economy, total employment and total investment.

7. Income Theory
- Macroeconomics is referred to as 'Income Theory' in economics. The reason is that when there is a change in aggregate demand or any other aggregate variable, it is linked with the level of income.
- In macro analysis, income and not prices, is the link between demand and supply.

8. Assumptions
- Macroeconomics is a more realistic approach as the theories explained in it are based on fewer assumptions. In this approach, there is no unrealistic assumption of full employment in the economy.
- It studies the determinants of full employment and attempts to know how the fullest possible employment can be attained.

Traditional economic analysis was largely confined to the study of individual aspects of economic behaviour. The results of such analysis were averaged out and *generalized* by the traditional economists to explain the aggregate nature of the system as a whole. However, modern economists realized the folly of extending generalizations of individual behaviour on the aggregate character of the system.

> **The importance of macroeconomics was realized, which is that what is true of the 'part' may not be true for the 'whole'.**

After all, *the problem of aggregates is not merely adding or multiplying the propositions of individual parts to the whole of an economy.*

1.3 Scope/Importance/Utility of Macroeconomics

Macroeconomics is of great theoretical and practical significance. Below we will understand the scope and importance of macroeconomics.

1. **To understand the working of an economy:** The study of macroeconomics is indispensable for understanding the working of the economy. Our main economic problems are related to the behaviour of total income, total output, employment and the general price level in the economy. These variables are statistically measurable, thereby facilitating the possibilities of analyzing the effects on the functioning of the economy. As **Tinbergen** observes, macroeconomic concepts assist in *"making the elimination process understandable and transparent."* For example, the general price level gives us an idea as to whether the economy is facing inflation or recession.

2. **For understanding the behaviour of individual units:** The study of macroeconomics is indispensable even for the purpose of building and developing macroeconomics. For example, the law of DMU could not have been formulated unless the experience of masses of individuals had been collected and taken into consideration. Thus, no microeconomic law can be formulated without a pre-study of aggregate's bearing on it.

3. **In national income:** The study of macroeconomics is very important for evaluating the overall performance of the economy in terms of national income. This led to the construction of the data on national income. With the help of National Income data the level of economic activity can be forecast, i.e., it helps to anticipate the level of fiscal activity and thus help in understanding the distribution of income among different groups of people in the economy.

4. **To deal with challenging problems:** The utility of macroeconomics has greatly increased in recent years as it deals with most of the controversial and challenging issues, namely those of unemployment, inflation, taxation, deficit financing, planning and economic development. No economist can overlook the study of such problems of the modern economic world. For example, *in general unemployment-* general unemployment is caused by deficiency of effective demand. In order to eradicate it, effective demand should be raised by increasing total investment, total productivity, total income and consumption. Thus, macroeconomics has special significance in studying the causes, effects and antidotes of general unemployment.

5. **In economic growth:** The economics of growth is also a study in macroeconomics. It is on the basis of macroeconomics that the resources and capabilities of an economy are evaluated. Plans for the overall increase in national income, productivity, employment are framed and executed so as to raise the level of fiscal development of the economy as a whole.

6. **To formulate policies for business cycles:** Macroeconomics, as an approach to fiscal problems started after the Great Depression, thus its significance is understood in analyzing the grounds of fiscal variations and in providing remedies. Macroeconomics has afforded immense help to the government in formulating and implementing appropriate economic policies. With the knowledge of macroeconomics, the governments are now in a better position to control the business cycles, inflation or deflation. In this way, macroeconomics assists governments to achieve uninterrupted economic growth and full employment with the help of suitable economic policies.

It can be well said that macroeconomic tools lie at the base of all the present day plans of economic policies and at the base of economic development of underdeveloped countries. Macroeconomics has made valuable contributions in the field of social accounting.

7. **In monetary problems:** It is with the help of instruments of macroeconomics that monetary problems can be analyzed and understood properly. Frequent changes in the value of money, inflation or deflation, affect the economy adversely. They can be counteracted by adopting monetary, fiscal and direct control measures for the economy as a whole.

8. **To formulate and execute successfully governmental economic policies:** Now, Governments' intervene actively in economic affairs, whether the framework of society is capitalist, socialist or communist, and in doing so, governments deal not with individuals but with masses of individuals. According to Prof. Boulding, modern governments are concerned more with the aggregates and averages-general price level, general level of production, the general volume of trade-than with individual variables. Hence, it is essential to have accurate and reliable statistics of the 'aggregate variables' as the prerequisite for the formulation of sound government policies. It is here that we can understand how essential the study of macroeconomics is for successful execution of governmental economic policies.

It can be said that macroeconomics is extremely useful from the view point of the fiscal policy. Modern Governments, particularly, the underdeveloped economies are confronted with innumerable national problems. They are the problems of over population, inflation, balance of payments, general under production, etc. The main precision of these governments rests in the regulation and control of over population, general prices, general volume of commerce, general productivity, etc.

9. **To understand accurately the behaviour patterns of aggregate variables:** It is true that it is difficult to discover the behaviour pattern of the aggregates simply by generalising from the character and behaviour of the individual units. With the help of a simple analogy Prof. Boulding has driven home the point aptly, i.e. individual variables and aggregate variables differ. He points out that the forest, though an aggregation of trees,

does not exhibit the characteristics and behaviour of individual trees. It would be misleading attempt if we generalize the behaviour pattern of the forest by studying the behaviour-pattern of individual trees, as there is a clear difference between an individual tree and the forest as a whole.

(i) An individual tree germinates, grows and decays; while a forest goes on forever with the same structure and composition.

(ii) An individual tree may not burn so easily, but forests are often subject to fires.

(iii) An individual tree cannot affect the climate of the surroundings in which it grows, but a forest can and does influence the climate.

In short, the aggregate and its individual components are entirely two different things. If this truth is grasped, then the necessity and justification of macroeconomics becomes self-evident.

Several economists have endeavoured to apply past propositions derived from individual experience to the economy as a whole. Such attempts have led to confusion and muddled thinking. For example, depression conditions in a particular industry may be cured by restriction of output. Some economists argue that during depression conditions in an economy, the cure is to bring about *'general'* restriction of output. This is a fallacious argument. Let us take another example: wage-cut in a particular firm may promote employment, but 'general' wage-cut in the economy may actually result in reducing the volume of employment. *Thus, what is true of a single firm cannot be true of the economy, as a whole.*

Prof. Boulding refers to such paradoxes as 'Macroeconomic Paradoxes'. "Macroeconomic Paradoxes arise when prepositions are true when applied to a single individual but are untrue when applied to the economic system as a whole."

> *It is the existence of macroeconomic paradoxes which necessitate a separate study of macroeconomics.*

The difference between the *individual* and *group* characteristics have to be understood clearly because failure to do so would result in dreadful consequences not only in economics but also in other social sciences. Hence, there is perfect justification in evolving and developing macroeconomics as a branch of economic analysis.

To conclude, it was the publication of *Keynes'* celebrated work 'General Theory' in 1936 that gave a strong momentum to the growth and development of modern macroeconomics. Some of the factors that have contributed to the growing popularity of macroeconomics during the last fifty years are its success in formulating policies during the Great Depression of 1929, and the efforts of several developing countries of Asia and Africa to develop economies in a planned manner.

1.4 Limitations of Macroeconomics

Macroeconomics can be functional and useful in its applications when certain inherent limitations that it suffers from are taken care of.

1. **Excessive Generalizations:** In macroeconomics, the greatest danger is it deals with excessive generalization from *individual experience to the system as a whole*. That is, in macroeconomics analysis the "fallacy of composition" is involved- the aggregate economic behaviour is the *sum total* of the economy of individual activities. But, what is true of an individual component may not be true of an aggregate. For example, there is nothing alarming when an individual withdraws his deposits from a bank, but if everybody tries to withdraw their deposits at the same time, the bank would surely collapse and the banking system will be affected adversely. Thus, care should be taken that too much generalization from individual experience must be ignored. Another example, savings are a private virtue but a public vice. If total savings in the economy increases, they may initiate a depression unless they are invested.

2. **Excessive use of 'aggregates':** The second danger of macroeconomics is the danger of excessive thinking in terms of 'aggregates' which are *heterogeneous* in nature. When we take into account aggregates which are heterogeneous in character, the results can be misleading. As Prof. Bolding points out:

(i) 6 apples + 5 apples = 11 apples (it is a meaningful aggregate).

(ii) 6 apples + 5 oranges = 11 fruits (this too is a fairly meaningful aggregate).

(iii) 6 apples + 5 skyscrapers =? (This is surely a meaningless aggregate).

Thus, it is the (iii) rd type of aggregate that should be avoided. Macroeconomics would lose its utility if we were to resort to meaningless aggregates.

Thus, the main defect in macro analysis is that it regards the aggregates as homogenous without caring about their internal composition and structure.

3. **In Policy-Making:** An indiscriminate and uncritical use of macroeconomics in analyzing the complexities of the real world can frequently be misleading. The study of aggregates may lead us to the conclusions that no change is needed in any government or economic policy. For example, if agricultural prices decline by 50%, while the general price level shows no change. The two types of price changes would neutralize each other. If guided by macro analysis alone, then no modified policy is needed in the economy. But, if considered independently the decline in prices of agricultural goods, it would call for the government to adopt a policy to support the farmers. It implies that measures aimed at controlling general prices cannot be applied with much advantage for controlling prices of individual products. Thus, relying on aggregate results alone may be misleading.

4. Impact on 'individual' differs: An aggregate tendency may not influence all the sectors of the economy in the same manner. For example, a general rise in prices may not affect all the sections of the community in the same manner. Some may be influenced adversely and some favourably. Another example, the national income of a country is the total of all individual income. A rise in national income does not mean that individual income has risen. The increase in national income might be the result of the increase in the incomes of a few rich people in the nation. Thus a rise in the national income of this type has little significance from the point of view of the community.

Thus, the aggregate variables which form the economic system may not be of much significance.

5. Difficulties in measurement- Statistical and Conceptual: The measurement of aggregates presents serious problems despite several improvements in statistical techniques. These problems relate to the aggregation of micro economic variables. If individual units are almost similar, aggregation does not present much difficulty. But if micro economic variables relate to dissimilar individual units, their aggregation into one macroeconomic variable may be incorrect and hazardous. Thus, it is difficult to obtain reliable measures of 'averages' and 'aggregates' which form the subject matter of macroeconomics.

To conclude, macroeconomics enriches our knowledge of the functioning of an economy by studying the behaviour of national income, productivity, investment, savings and consumption. Further, it throws much light in solving the problems of redundancy, inflation, economic instability and economic growth. The concept of *stock* and *flow* are mainly used in the macroeconomics or in the theory of income, productivity and employment. Both the concepts of stock and flow variables are very significant in modern theories of income, interest rate, business cycles, etc.

1.5 Difference between Micro and Macro Economics

Micro and Macro economics, the two approaches to economics, have 'individual' and 'group' characteristics and can be differentiated as follows:

1. Individual vs. Aggregate:

The word 'Micro' is derived from the Greek word *'mikros'* which means small. Microeconomics is the study of economic activities of individuals and small groups (homogenous) of individuals.

The word 'Macro' is derived from the Greek word *'makros'* which means large. Macroeconomics is the study of aggregates and averages. It is the study of the economic system as a whole.

Thus, microeconomics is an 'individualistic approach' to the study of economic theory; whereas macroeconomics is an 'aggregative approach'.

2. Price Theory vs. Income Theory:

'Price mechanism' is the basis of microeconomics. It studies price theory with the help of two economic forces in the market, namely demand and supply. These economic forces help to determine the equilibrium price in the market.

'Income mechanism' is the basis of macroeconomics. It studies national income and its impact on the output and employment in the economy. The national income (or national output) is determined by the economic forces, i.e. aggregate demand (AD) and aggregate supply (AS).

3. Static vs. Dynamic:

Microeconomics is considered as a static analysis and macroeconomics as dynamic analysis.

4. Scope of Study:

Microeconomics has 'price' as its core subject-matter and its field of study extends to:
- Theory of product pricing with its two constituents, namely theory of consumer's behaviour and the theory of production.
- Theory of factor pricing- theories of rent, wages, interest and profit.
- Theory of economic welfare.

The scope of macroeconomics analysis focuses on 'income' theory. It includes:
- Theory of income, output and employment, with its two constituents, viz., theory of consumption function and theory of investment function.
- Theory of trade cycles.
- Theory of prices, i.e., theories of inflation, deflation and stagflation.
- Theory of economic growth.
- Macro theory of distribution.

5. Partial vs. General Equilibrium:

Microeconomics is based on partial equilibrium analysis. It helps to explain the equilibrium conditions of an individual, a firm or an industry. On the other hand, macroeconomics is based on general equilibrium analysis.

6. Exponents:

Prof. Marshall's *magnum opus*, *"Principles of Economics"* (1890) dealt in detail with microeconomics. J. M. Keynes' celebrated work, *"General Theory of Employment, interest and Money"* (1936) is an outstanding work of macroeconomics approach.

7. Objectives:

The main objectives of microeconomics are to maximize utility by consumers (demand side) and maximize profits by firms (on supply side).

The main objectives of macroeconomics are full employment, economic growth, price stability and favourable balance of payments.

8. Slicing Vs. Lumping Method:

Microeconomics is referred to as the study by 'slicing method' because it splits the economy into small, individual units and studies each unit in detail.

Macroeconomics is referred to as the study by 'lumping method' because it studies the economic behaviour in its totality. For study purpose it divides the economy into sectors (lumps).

It can be said that microeconomics is the study of an economy through a worm's eye-view and macroeconomics is the study of an economy through a bird's eye-view.

9. Importance:

The significance of the study of microeconomics is for resource utilization, business decisions and for social welfare. The importance of macroeconomics is for formulation of economic policies for the nation, for analyzing trade cycles, etc.

10. Assumptions:

Microeconomics is based on assumptions concerned with rational behaviour of individuals. The Laws are based on many assumptions that make the study unrealistic. On the other hand, Macroeconomics' theories are more realistic as they are based on fewer assumptions.

11. Difference in Outlook:

Microeconomics deals not only with individual units in the economic system but also deals with some sort of aggregates. However, 'aggregates' dealt in microeconomics are altogether different. For instance, it may study an industry which comprises a large number of firms. But, the 'aggregates' studied in microeconomics are homogenous in nature. On the other hand, 'aggregates' in macroeconomics are heterogeneous in nature.

12. Variables and Quantities:

Microeconomics deals with micro-variables and micro-quantities; e.g., it studies individual demand, individual supply, a particular firm or a particular industry, family income, prices of a particular commodity, etc.

In macroeconomics, the study is of macro-variables and macro-quantities; e.g., aggregate demand, aggregate supply, total output, total consumption, national income, general price level, etc.

To conclude micro and macroeconomics are two clear, rigid and distinct approaches to the study of economics. However, in practice, the distinction is not water-tight, because what is 'individual' in one situation may be 'aggregate' in another situation. For example, study of national income is subject-matter of macroeconomics, but if we are studying international income as a whole, then the study of national income of a country is a study in microeconomics.

Microeconomics and Macroeconomics: Complementary or Competitive to each other?

Microeconomics and Macroeconomics seem like two alternative approaches to economic analysis. Apparently, they seem to be competitive but, in reality, they are complementary to each other. In fact, they are incomplete without each other. We fail to have a complete understanding of the functioning of the economic system unless we integrate the two approaches in a judicious manner. For example, the sales of a firm are determined not just by its own prices, but also by the total purchasing power available to the community that it serves. Thus, the macro factor cannot be ignored even in a microeconomic analysis of the firm.

In the same way, the price of an individual product is determined not only by its own supply and demand, but also by the prices of other products. Hence, it is extremely difficult to separate any economic phenomenon. We study macroeconomics as it deals with aggregate variables, such as national income, total output. We study microeconomics as it deals with the study of decisions of millions of business firms and individuals which result in total output and national income. As such, it will be necessary to examine the principle governing the economic behaviour of individuals, individual firm, etc., in their totality.

As a matter of fact, microeconomics and macroeconomics are 'interdependent'. Just as microeconomics contributes to macroeconomics, macroeconomics, in turn, contributes to microeconomics. The theory of investment is derived from the behaviour of the individual entrepreneur who is governed, on one side, by the marginal efficiency of capital (MEC) and, on the other side, by the rate of interest. Now, this theory of investment applies not only to an individual entrepreneur but also to the economy as a whole. Thus, the theory of 'aggregate' investment function can also be derived from the microeconomic theory of investment. It is because; at this point, the behaviour of the 'aggregate' is no way different from the behaviour pattern of the individual units. In this way, macroeconomics, to some extent, depends upon microeconomics.

Likewise, microeconomics depends on macroeconomics. For example, the rate of interest is the subject-matter of microeconomics, but is influenced by macroeconomic aggregates. Prof. J. M. Keynes states that the rate of interest is determined by liquidity preference of the people and the supply of money in the economy. Both these determinants – liquidity preference and the supply of money- are macroeconomic aggregates.

To conclude, though the two approaches to economics – microeconomics and macroeconomics – differ, yet there is a good deal of interdependence between them. According to **Prof. Samuelson**, *"there is really no opposition between micro and macroeconomics. Both are absolutely vital. You are less than half-educated if you understand one, while being ignorant of the other."* Therefore, the two approaches are not in any way mutually exclusive and, as such, must be properly integrated to secure fruitful results.

Types of Macroeconomics

Macroeconomics is of three types:

1. **Macro-statics:** This is an analysis which is used to explain certain aggregative relations in a *stationary state*. Macro-statics deals with the equilibrium at a *particular* point of time, and throws no light on the process by which the national economy reaches 'final' equilibrium.

   This type of macroeconomics presents a 'still' picture of the economy, as a whole, at a particular point of time and does not study the *path* by which the economy reaches equilibrium.

   Example, $\quad Y = C + I$

   Here, $\quad Y$ = Total income; C = Total consumption; I = Total investment

   The Keynesian equation merely tells us that $Y = C + I$, but does not explain the process by which this equality between Y on one side and C + I on the other side has reached.

2. **Comparative Macro-statics:** The various macro-variables in an economy, such as, consumption, total investment, etc., keep on changing with the lapse of time. In other words, the economy keeps on attaining different levels of equilibriums. Macro-statics involves a comparative study of the different equilibriums attained by an economy.

   This type of macroeconomics does not explain the 'process of adjustment' by which an economy moves from equilibrium to another. Thus, macro-statics presents 'still' pictures of the various equilibriums reached by an economy.

   For example, the *Quantity Theory of Money* tells us that the price level in an economy is influenced by changes in the quantity of money. Supposing the economy is at equilibrium with a certain price level at that particular time. Now, when there is a change (say, increased) in quantity of money, the existing equilibrium is disturbed and a new equilibrium is established at a higher price level.

   Thus, Macro-statics does not study what happens between the disturbance of the old equilibrium and the establishment of a new one.

3. **Macro-dynamics:** This type of macroeconomics has recently been developed by leading economists like Frisch, J. R. Hicks, Robertson, P. A. Samuelson, etc. This is a realistic type of economic analysis, though it is complicated and involves the use of higher mathematics.

   The various processes of adjustments which come into operation as a result of changes in macro-variables are fully highlighted by the method of macro-dynamics.

This type of macroeconomics enables us to see the 'movie' of the entire economy as a progressive whole.

Macro-dynamics presents a full account of all the developments taking place in the economy during the transitional period between the break-up of the old equilibrium and the establishment of a new one.

Points to Remember

- The overall field of study of economics is broadly divided into two parts- Microeconomics and Macroeconomics.
- The term 'Macro' was first coined by Ragner Frisch in 1933.
- Macroeconomics may be defined as that branch of economic analysis which studies the behaviour of not one particular unit, but of all the units combined together.
- Macroeconomics deals with the great 'averages' and 'aggregates' of the system and not with particular units in it.
- Microeconomics and macroeconomics are complementary and competitive to each other.
- The analysis of economic system as a "whole" is macro economics. It is concerned with **aggregates** and **averages** of the entire economy, such as national income, total output, aggregate demand, aggregate supply and the general level of prices.
- In macroeconomics, we study how these aggregates and averages of the economy as a whole are determined and what causes fluctuations in them.
- In macro economics, the theories are based on the basis of empirical knowledge, hence, the assumption of full employment stays invalid. It is very vital that we should investigate how these aggregates of an economy are determined and having known their determinants, how to ensure the maximum level of income and full employment in a country.
- Macro economics deals with how an economy grows. Thus, it analyses the chief determinants of economic development and the various stages and process of economic growth.
- It is generally argued by Classical economists as to why there is a need of separate macroeconomic approach? The justification of a separate macro approach to the study of several economic problems lies in the fact that micro approach is not only inadequate but may lead to altogether misleading conclusions. In economics what is true of a part is not necessarily true of the whole. After all the problem of the aggregate is not merely a matter of adding or of multiplying what happens in respect of the various individual parts of the whole. It may be quite different and for more complicated than a mere

Macro Economic Analysis — Introduction

summation. For example, savings, in times of depression while savings by an individual may be beneficial to him, but savings on the part of the entire population will deepen the depression further as aggregate demand will decline.

- **Scope of Macroeconomics:**
  - Theory of Income, Output and Employment.
  - Theory of Price.
  - Theory of Economic Growth.
  - Macro Theory of Distribution.
- **Popularity/Importance of Macroeconomics:**
  - Helps to understand the working of the economy.
  - Helps to understand the behaviour of individual units.
  - In national income.
  - To deal with challenging problems.
  - To formulate policies for business cycles.
  - In monetary problems.
  - To formulate and successfully execute governmental economic policies.
  - To understand the aggregate variables.
- **Limitations:**
  - There is excessive generalization of the system as a whole.
  - Macroeconomics is an aggregate of heterogeneous macro variables.
  - Presents no reliable measure of 'averages' and 'aggregates'.
  - Study of aggregates, at times, results in faulty economic policies.
  - An aggregate tendency may not influence the whole economy in the same manner.
- **Types of Macroeconomics:**
  - Macro-statics.
  - Comparative Macro-statics.
  - Macro-dynamics.

Multiple Choice Questions

1. Which of the following is a part of the study of macroeconomics?
   - (a) Product pricing
   - (b) General Price level
   - (c) Location of an industry
   - (d) Factor Pricing
2. The Keynesian equation $Y = C + I$ explains a relationship which is of the nature of :
   - (a) Micro-dynamics
   - (b) Micro-statics
   - (c) Macro-statics
   - (d) Comparative macro-statics

3. Which of the following does not contribute a part of macro economics?
   (a) Theory of Income
   (b) Theory of Economic Growth
   (c) Theory of Price
   (d) Theory of Economic Welfare
4. Microeconomics and Macroeconomics are
   (a) Mutually exclusive
   (b) Competitive to each other
   (c) Independent of each other
   (d) Interdependent
5. Which of the following refers to the macroeconomic approach?
   (a) Income from the railways
   (b) Per capita income of the country
   (c) Capital-output ratio in iron and steel industry
   (d) Distribution of coal in the country
6. Macroeconomics deals with
   (a) Averages and Aggregates
   (b) Aggregates and Individuals
   (c) Markets and Individuals
   (8) All of the above

Answers:

1 - (b), 2 - (c), 3 - (d), 4 - (d), 5 - (b), 6 - (a)

Questions for Discussion

1. What is meant by macroeconomics?
2. Discuss the meaning, scope and importance of macroeconomics.
3. Differentiate between macroeconomics and microeconomics.
4. What are the limitations of macroeconomics?
5. Describe the scope of macroeconomics.
6. In what way is macroeconomic approach different from microeconomic approach? What is the significance of this difference for economic theory?
7. What are the different types of macroeconomic analysis?
8. Distinguish between micro and macro economics. What is the relationship between the two- competitive or complementary to each other?

Chapter **2**...

Money and Value of Money

Contents ...
2.1 Definitions of Money
2.2 Functions of Money
2.3 Value of Money
   2.3.1 Quantity Theory of Money (The Cash Transaction Approach)
   2.3.2 The Cash Balance Approach (Cambridge Version)
- Points to Remember
- Multiple Choice Questions
- Questions for Discussion

Learning Objectives ...
➤ To know about the various definitions of money.
➤ The students to know about the significant functions performed by money.
➤ To learn about the relationship between the price level and the value of money.
➤ To be equipped with the understanding relating to the different approaches that explains the relationship between the demand for money and supply of money.
➤ To understand the importance of Classical and Cambridge approaches towards money and value of money.

Introduction

In olden times, need of money was not felt, as man's wants were few. With the multiplication of wants, goods and services were exchanged, thus evolved a barter system of exchange. Today, barter (non-monetised sectors) exists only in backward communities.

Today, life cannot be understood without money. In fact, money is one of the greatest inventions of man.

As barter was an inconvenient method of exchange, people were forced to select some commodity which was *most commonly accepted as a medium of exchange*. Thus, a variety of goods came to be used as money – hides and skins of animals, precious metals, etc. Later, coins were replaced by paper notes for economy and convenience. Next, cheques, promissory notes came to be used in addition to notes. Now, bank deposits (only entries in bank ledgers) serve as the most important type of money.

> *The development of money is from commodity money, metallic money, and paper money to bank money.*

Evolution of Money

The level of monetization is indicative of economic development in the market economies. In India, the use of money was limited before the process of economic development started. The self-sufficient village had very limited scope for transactions against money. But the forces of economic development speeded up the process of monetization.

(1) **Constraints of Barter:** Barter was a characteristic of primitive economic organization. It involved various problems like lack of double coincidence of wants, absence of a common measure of value, difficulty of storing wealth and problems of divisibility. With the progress of economic organization, man adopted division of labour, specialization, large-scale production, and use of machines etc., markets widened. Production in anticipation of demand became the rule. Need of money to serve mainly as a medium of exchange became essential. Man's quest for such a medium gave birth to commodity money.

(2) **Commodity Money:** Various commodities like cattle, ivory, food grains, copper, silver and gold came to be used as money. Over a period of time, man learnt that whatever was to be used as money, must possess certain characteristics. The thing must be easy to test for quality, must be capable of being divided into small parts without loss of value, must be manageable in weight and so on. Gradually, all other commodities except some more precious metals became out-of-use.

By the nineteenth century, commodity money almost exclusively came to mean metallic money. A necessary characteristic of money is its universal acceptability and therefore precious metals ruled the scene for a considerable length of time in human history. Because precious metals were valuable for their own sake, they commanded acceptability. But their scarcity and increasing usefulness in other areas created problems. Moreover, *man learnt by experience that intrinsic value is not a necessary condition for acceptability of money.*

(3) **Paper Money:** The step from barter to commodity money was important because it involved one very important function of money. People accept money not because it can be used directly for consumption (as in case of barter) but because it can be used as a medium of exchange for buying goods they need.

Money is needed not for its own sake but for the things it can buy. Paper money thus emerged as an artificial social convention. *People accept it not because it is valuable in itself but because it is accepted by other people.* We now face a paradox. Money is accepted because it is accepted. Because everyone accepts it as valuable, it is valuable.

(4) **Bank Money:** Modern age is the age of bank money. Bank money is a cheque written on a deposit in a bank. When banks accept deposits and issue cheque-books to the customers, the customers get the right to issue cheques. These cheques are almost money. They can also be called credit-money. Credit requires faith. Credit money is accepted only when the acceptor has faith in the giver.

(5) **Plastic Money:** In course of evolution, plastic cards were introduced by banks, which are also referred to as 'plastic money' in common language. These cards are either *Credit Cards* or *Debit Cards*.

A credit card involves a tripartite arrangement involving the bank, the card-holder and the commercial establishments agreeing to accept the card-based transaction. Debit cards do not involve any credit and therefore no interest is required to be paid. The card-holder can use it upto the limit of the balance in his bank account. It confers great convenience to the user. The amount spent is debited from the account of the cardholder and is transferred to the commercial establishment from whom the cardholder has bought goods/services.

2.1 Definitions of Money

What is money? When you walk into a hotel to buy some meal, you get something of value, something satisfying your stomach. To pay for this service, you might hand the hotelier several worn-out or new pieces of grayish paper decorated with strange symbols, languages and portraits of famous Indian leader. Or you might hand him a single piece of paper with the name of a bank and your signature. Or you might hand him a small plastic sheet to swipe. Whether you pay by cash or cheque or credit/debit card, the hotelier is happy to work hard to satisfy your demanded desires in exchange for these pieces of paper which, in and of themselves, is worthless.

To anyone who has lived in a modern economy, this social custom is not at all odd. Even though paper money has no intrinsic value, the hotelier is confident that in the future some third person will accept it in exchange for something of that value and likewise the third person who will receive it from the hotelier knows that the fourth person will accept the money and so on. To the hotelier and other people in the society, your cash or cheque represents a claim on goods and services in the future.

Thus, what is money? *Money is any object or record that is generally accepted as payment for goods and services and repayment of debts in a given socio-economic context of a country.*

"Money is the pivot around which the economic science clusters".

The main functions of money are distinguished as: a medium of exchange; a unit of account; a store of value; and occasionally in the past, a standard of deferred payment. Any kind of object or secure verifiable record that fulfils these functions can be considered money.

In general, the term 'money' means currency notes, metallic coins held as cash in hand or demand deposits with banks. However, in economics, the term 'money' is used in a much wider sense. There is no unique definition of money and it is true that there is no agreement on the most fundamental of questions: 'What is money'?

Money has been defined differently by different economists. Some definitions are too extensive while others are too narrow in explaining the term 'money'.

1. **Walker:** *'Money is what money does'.* This definition is too wide because, according to this definition, we can include all those things in money which perform the functions of money. Thus, money comprises not only metallic coins and currency notes but also hundies, bills of exchange, cheques, etc.

2. **Robertson:** *'Money is a commodity which is widely accepted in payment for goods or in discharge of other business obligations'.* This definition is too narrow only metallic money (in the strictest sense) would be called 'money', as it has general acceptance, if left to itself.

It can be said that a suitable definition of money should emphasize not only the important functions of money, but also its basic feature, i.e., general acceptability.

3. **Crowther:** *'Money is anything that is generally acceptable as a means of exchange and at the same time acts as a measure and as a store of value.'*

Thus, *'anything is money'*, which is generally acceptable as a medium of exchange and at the same time it must act as a measure and a store of value. Anything implies a 'thing' to be used as money need not be necessarily composed of any precious metal. The only necessary condition is that, it should be universally accepted by people as a medium of exchange.

Crowther's definition appears to be an ideal definition. According to this definition, money performs three different functions: as medium of exchange; as a standard of value and as a store of value. Besides, the commodity chosen as money must be generally acceptable within the community in exchange for goods and services.

Historically, many commodities have performed these functions of money and forms of money have been changing from hides and skins of animals to credit and debit cards. Thus, surfaces an empirical question as to what should be and what should not be considered as money.

Money is the outcome of an emergent market phenomenon establishing commodity money, but nearly all contemporary money systems are based on *fiat money*. Fiat money, like any cheque, is without intrinsic use value. It derives its value by being declared by a government to be legal tender, that is, it must be accepted as a form of payment within the boundaries of the country, for "all debts, public and private". Such laws in practice cause fiat money to acquire the value of any of the goods and services that it may be traded for within the nation that issues it.

The money supply of a country consists of currency (bank notes and coins) and bank money (the balance held in demand deposit accounts and savings accounts). Bank money which consists only of records forms, by far, the largest part of the money supply in developed nations.

A major factor that has made the definition of money complicated is the increasing number of substitutes in the form of assets that have different degrees of convertibility. As a result, the term 'money' has changed from a measurable to immeasurable quantity.

H. G. Johnson has classified the approaches to the definition of money.

1. The Conventional Definition: This is the oldest but most widely accepted approach. This definition emphasizes the basic functions of money, i.e., money as a medium of exchange and as a measure of value. Money, according to this definition is *"money is what money does"*, e.g., grains, metals, cattle, etc., have served as a medium of exchange and as a measure of value. These are called 'commodity money'.

However, this type of money had some problems and hence over a long period of time metallic coins, paper currency and demand deposits evolved. These forms of money perform the basic functions of money. The metallic coins and paper currency are created and issued by the government and are *legal tender*. Hence, they enjoy general acceptance and legal status. These forms of money have perfect liquidity. On the other hand, demand deposits are outcome of the banking system and are *optional*.

2. The Chicago Approach: Milton Friedman's 'interpretation of money' is often referred to as the Chicago Approach. The Chicago school of thought has extended the conventional definition of money to include also the time deposits with commercial banks.

Thus, there are three components to be included in 'money', i.e., currency, demand deposits (by cheque) and time deposits. It is true that the time deposits do not have general acceptance as a medium of exchange, but it is to be included in the supply of money. A time deposit may be for 45 or 90 days, i.e., unavailable for transaction only for a short period or else it would be included in the total supply of money.

3. The Gurley-Shaw Approach: This approach is attributed to John G. Gurley, which goes one step further and consider the *"financial claims against the non-banking financial intermediaries* as money, i.e., currency, demand deposits, commercial bank time-deposits, savings bank deposits, savings and loan association shares, etc., viewed by the public as alternative liquid stores of value.

4. **The Central Bank Approach:** This approach takes a broad view of money supply. The Central Bank controls and regulates the credit flows in accordance with the needs of the economy. The bank needs to formulate a suitable monetary policy to achieve predetermined objectives. Thus, the central bank considers all available means of payment and credit flows as money. As such, money supply comprises of currency and all the assets that can be converted into money (assets that have perfect or near-perfect liquidity).

The Radcliffe committee is referred to as the central bank approach. According to this approach, "money is, in a way, the total credit flow to the borrowers."

The Central Bank uses different measures of money supply, known as M_1, M_2, M_3 and M_4.

2.2 Functions of Money

It is true that from time to time, different commodities have been selected as money, e.g., gold, silver, paper currency, etc. But, which commodity serves best as money depends upon the function that it performs. The various functions of money can be grouped under sub-headings, such as: (I) Primary functions; (II) Secondary functions; and (III) Contingent functions.

(I) Primary Functions

The most original functions of money are its primary functions.

1. **Money serves as a medium of exchange:** Money acts as a medium of exchange as it's generally accepted. On the payment of money, purchase of goods and services can be made, i.e., goods and services are exchanged for money. This is the most important and unique function of money, as money has the quality of *general acceptance*.

    The importance of this function lies in the fact, that it has solved one of the biggest problems of barter system. In ancient times, 'barter system' prevailed, i.e., commodities exchanged for commodities. The main difficulty in that system was the lack of 'double coincidence' of wants. Money solves all these difficulties of the barter system.

    In modern times, the prices of goods and services are expressed in terms of money, the general purchasing power. The money exchange transaction is now in two parts - 'Sale' (money obtained from the sale of goods and services) and 'Purchase' (money used for buying goods and services). In other words, money bifurcates' buying and selling activities separately so it facilitates the exchange transactions.

    Thus, money bestows upon the holder the power to command marketable goods and services at the time he needs them.

Furthermore, money units are of all denominations and easy to make fractional purchases. In this way, the difficulty of indivisibility of certain articles is also eliminated.

2. **Money serves as a standard measure of value:** The second basic function of money is to work as a measuring value of goods and services.

   One of the difficulties faced in the barter system was the lack of a 'common' measure of value in terms of which other values could be expressed. It becomes an important function of money to serve as a common and collective measuring value of goods and services. The prices of all goods and services are expressed in terms of money. With the invention of money, it has become easier and simpler to determine the rate of exchange between the various types of goods and services.

   Thus, money is a common measure of value so it is possible to determine the rate of exchange between various goods and services by the people. Exchange value of commodity can be expressed in terms of money, for example, we can say that 20 meters of cloth cost ₹ 10,000 or $ 250.

   As money serves as a standard measure of value, it also performs as a 'unit of account'. All the records are maintained in terms of the monetary unit, e.g., Rupee, Pound Sterling, Dollar, etc.

   However, it is to be pointed out that money does present a difficulty in its role as a collective measure of values. Any commodity that serves as a measure should be stable in its value. But as we know, its own value is not constant and keeps fluctuating.

   The two functions mentioned above – money as a medium of exchange and money as a measure of value – have a close relationship with each other. Generally, these two functions are performed simultaneously. First, the value of commodity is determined in terms of money and then exchanged at that rate. However, there is a possibility that the two functions do not take place at the same time, e.g., when a housewife exchanges old clothes for utensils or we exchange gold for gold. In these cases, money is used as a measure of value but not as a medium of exchange.

   > *Primary Functions of Money: Money serves as a medium of exchange; Money serves as a standard of measuring value.*

(II) **Secondary Functions**

1. **Money is used as a store of value:** Money acts as a store of value. Money being generally acceptable and its value being more or less stable, it is ideal for use as a store of value. Being non-perishable and also comparatively stable in value, the value of other assets can be stored in the form of money. Property can be sold and its value can be held in money and converted into other assets as and when necessary.

In modern times, money enables a person to keep a portion of his assets in liquid form, i.e., store purchasing power. Under the barter system, savings were discouraged as it was done only in terms of commodities which many a time, were perishable in nature. But this difficulty disappeared with the use of money. Savings are now in the form of money and are more durable. Thus, money serves as a 'store of value' as it can be converted to any other marketable asset such as land, machinery, etc. However, it is understood that money can perform as a store of value only if its own value – in terms of goods and services is fairly stable.

2. **Money is used for deferred payments:** Under the barter system, borrowing and lending was difficult. It was greatly inconvenient as the borrowing and lending were done in terms of goods and services. However, the modern money economy has greatly facilitated the borrowing and lending processes, as both the activities are done in terms of money. Money has proved to be a suitable standard of deferred payments because it is more durable as compared to other commodities. It has general acceptance and is relatively more stable in value. Thus, the loans, which are taken at present, can be repaid in money in the future. The value of the future payments is regulated by money.

   However, when performing as a standard of deferred payments, money suffers from a limitation, i.e., the value of money itself is not stable. Its value keeps on fluctuating and influences different sections of the economy differently.

3. **Money as a means of transfer of value:** Another function which money performs is that it serves as a means of transferring value. Value of any asset can be transferred from one person to another or to any institution or to any place by transferring money. The transfer of money can take place irrespective of places, time and circumstances. Transfer of purchasing power, which is necessary in commerce and other transactions, has become available because of money.

   The field of exchange is extending with growing economic development. Therefore, it was felt necessary to transfer the purchasing power from one place to another. Since money possesses the quality of general acceptability, a person can dispose off his property at one place and buy another property at another place. This function has great importance in the socio-economic life of a community. Idle funds with a person at one place can be used productively by another person at another place.

> *Secondary Functions: Money is used as a store of value; Money is used for deferred payments; Money as a means of transfer of value.*

> *To conclude the primary and secondary functions as: "Money has four functions – a medium, a measure, a standard and a store."*

(III) Contingent Functions

Prof. Kinley explains the contingent functions of money as follows:

1. **Money enhances productivity of capital:** Money is the most *'liquid'* type of capital and it can be put to various uses. Due to this attribute of money, capital can be transferred from less productive to more productive uses. It implies 'liquidity' nature of money helps in the mobility of capital and increases its productivity.

2. **Money forms the basis of credit:** Globally, the importance of credit has increased and as such credit instruments are used on an extensive scale. For example, the use of cheques, bills of exchange, etc., has increased. The basis for various types of credit is money. Without money, credit instruments cannot be circulated. For example, any commercial bank can create credit only on the basis of adequate cash reserves. Further, an individual can issue a cheque only if he has enough funds to that cover that cheque in his deposit account.

   Similarly, ideally the Central Bank of a country cannot issue currency notes, unless there are adequate metallic reserves with it.

3. **Money helps in distribution of social income:** Under barter system, it was difficult to solve the problem of distribution of social income. However, with the invention of money, the share of each factor (in the total production) is determined in terms of money. Production is an effort of collective cooperation of the various factors of production and thus with the invention of money, each factor is paid the reward for its services in money.

4. **Money facilitates equalizing of marginal utilities and marginal productivities:** A consumer equalizes marginal utility from a commodity to its price (MU = price) to maximize his satisfaction. Money has facilitated this equalization as price is value of goods expressed in terms of money.

   Every producer equalizes the marginal productivity of a factor to the reward paid to that factor. Every entrepreneur aims at maximum production at minimum cost and this can be achieved when the various factors of production are equalized to their respective marginal productivities. Money helps to equalize marginal productivities of various factors to the reward paid to those factors.

> *Contingent Functions: Money enhances productivity of capital; Money forms the basis of credit; Money helps in distribution of social income; Money facilitates equalizing of marginal utilities and marginal productivities.*

(IV) Additional Functions

Money also performs certain other functions, such as:

1. **Money assists in maintaining repayment capacity:** Money possesses the quality of general acceptance. Hence, every firm keeps some amount of liquid money to safeguard its repayment capacity. In the same manner, banks, insurance companies and governments have to keep some money in the liquid form, i.e., cash, to maintain their repayment capacity.

2. **Money is a 'general' purchasing power:** It is not necessary that money (i.e. purchasing power) kept for one purpose has to be used for that purpose alone. For instance, if a person saves to buy a flat in future, it is not essential for him to use that saving for purchasing the flat only; he may prefer to spend it on something else. As it is well known, objectives keep changing. Thus, if the objective of the saver changes, he can utilize the money for any other purpose and not for any specific purpose only.

3. **Money imparts liquidity to capital:** Money is the most liquid form of capital. As explained by **Prof. J. M. Keynes**, it is essential to hold capital in its most liquid form for three motives:

   (a) **Transaction motive:** For buying raw materials, to pay wages to the labour force, a businessman has to keep some cash out for his daily operations. Likewise, an individual also keeps money in cash form for its day-to-day transactions.

   (b) **Precautionary motive:** An individual or any businessman keeps some cash to meet contingencies, i.e., for emergency purposes like accident, sickness, arrival of any supplies, etc.

   (c) **Speculative motive:** Several businessmen keep capital in liquid form to carry out speculative motives.

   It is to be remembered that money can perform all the above mentioned functions effectively only when its own value is stable. With an unstable value, money fails to perform its function as it loses 'general acceptance'.

(V) Static vs. Dynamic Functions

According to **Paul Einzig,** the functions of money can be classified as – static and dynamic functions.

Static Functions are those which encourage the working of the economy of a country. For e.g. the functions of money as a medium of exchange, measure of value, store of value and as a standard of deferred payments, are all static functions. If the money cannot perform these functions, the economy of a country cannot work in practice.

Dynamic Functions are those which cause movements in the level of economic activity, *such as money performing as the basis of credit or liquidity.* When money performs its dynamic functions, it actually brings about changes in the level of economic activity in a country.

The static and dynamic functions of money are essential for the healthy functioning of an economy.

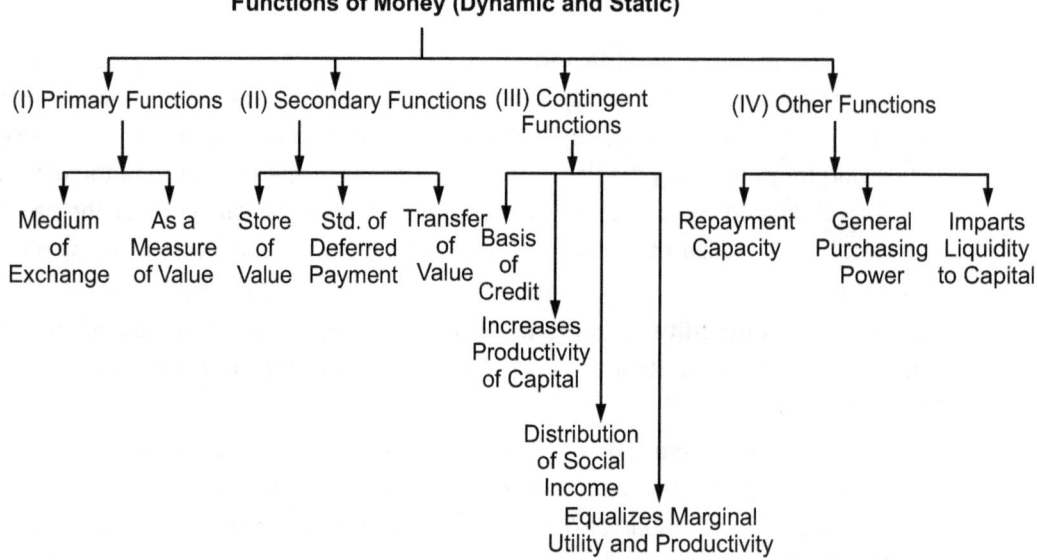

Fig. 2.1: Functions of Money

Money in Developed Economies

The evolution of money through different stages highlights the role that money is called upon to play.

Prof. Samuelson summarizes, *"The essence of money is to serve as the medium of exchange, the medium through which we buy and sell virtually everything. Many things have served as money over the ages, but today is primarily the era of paper and bank money, items which have no intrinsic value."*

So long as an economy is underdeveloped and tradition-bound, its use of money is limited. However, once the local markets become regional, use of money becomes inevitable. Division of labour necessitates payments in cash as every worker produces just a small part of a thing.

With rising levels of living, people get a choice which can best be exercised with the help of money.

As a store of value, money facilitates saving. A modern economy has a very important place for saving and investment.

Monetization or use of money in all sorts of transaction thus has become an important characteristic of modern developed economies.

What money does in a modern economy can be summarized as under?

(1) **Market Mechanism:** The use of money facilitates the functioning of the market mechanism. In the words of **Prof. Halm**, *"The use of money divides the market into buyers and sellers and splits barter into market supply and demand. Supply and demand determine the market prices which are exchange values in units of money. The direction of production is determined according to the existing and expected prices; the prices of means of production - the businessman's expenses - and the prices of the finished goods. The difference between these two sets of prices means profits or losses to the producer. According to expected profits or losses, production is expanded or contracted".*

(2) **Developed Credit Market:** A uniform price in the form of an interest rate can get established only when lending and borrowing are affected through money. This is why developed credit markets which is a precondition for economic development, find a crucial place in monetized economies.

(3) **Freedom of Choice:** Economies functioning at low levels of income provide limited options to the people. Such limited options can be exercised by barter also. It is possible to exchange wheat against cloth and cloth against shoes as long as all these goods are limited in quantity and variety. But a modern developed economy produces thousands of goods with scores of varieties of each. But with such a wide variety available to the people, they would like to have a freedom of choice which is given to them by money. Money, therefore, is said to be a bearer of option. If you have money, you get an option of buying either *a or b or c* or any other commodity of your choice without force or compromise.

(4) **Social Freedom:** The emergence of a homogeneous society based on equality and fraternity is facilitated by the use of money. Monetization has thus served to infuse a greater degree of social freedom in advanced societies. Consider the caste-ridden Indian society. The caste barriers were rigid so long as economic functions of man were thrust on him by birth. Payment of money wages relaxes these rigidities as anybody can pursue any occupation, receive money and spend it the way one likes. This type of social freedom guarantees vertical and horizontal mobility paving the way for establishing a society based on equality.

(5) **Specialization:** Developed economies have specialized economic functions. Because money serves as a standard of value, such a specialization and a minute division of labour are rendered possible.

(6) **Measure of Tastes of Consumers:** Modern developed economies are complex in organization and in the absence of monetization; they could have become very difficult at adjustments. The changes in consumer tastes are like weathercocks, the direction of the wind and producers take hints and adjust their production policies accordingly.

(7) **A Policy Instrument:** Highly monetized economies use money in all their economic activities. This has one great advantage. The government can change the volume of money in circulation. Such changes induce various economic consequences by changing and adjusting the money supply. This is what monetary policy seeks to do. The success of monetary policy thus requires a high level of monetization of the economy.

(8) **Index of Economic Development:** In view of the importance of and the multiplicity of functions performed by money in developed economies, monetization has become an index of economic development. Monetization has brought, to a considerable extent, stability to trade and commerce, production and consumption and to the economy as a whole. In fact, there is extremely rapid innovation and evolution in the kinds of money available, in developed economies.

Demand for Money

Money is demanded by individuals and firms in society. The extent of this demand for money depends upon for what purpose they demand money. Why do people demand money? The answer to this question depends upon the approach towards money.

(A) As a Medium of Exchange: Classical Approach

The traditional approach towards money has been as a *medium of exchange*. The classical economists believed that money is demanded by people for buying goods and services. In this sense, the aggregate demand for money will be determined by the total amount of goods and services exchanged against money and the level of prices. For example, if 100 units of a commodity are taken as the total supply of goods and services exchanged against money, and ₹ 10 per unit is their price, the total demand for money will be ₹ 1,000/-.

(B) As a Store of Value: Keynesian Approach

The demand for money (or *'liquidity preference'* as Keynes called it) can be explained in terms of what Keynes called *'motives'* for holding money. Why is money demanded? Money is demanded because it allows easy and quick transactions (as a medium of exchange), it facilitates unambiguous determination of the price (as a unit of account), and it can store wealth (as a store of value). These three causes which stem from the three functions of money are referred to as three motives for holding money. They are (i) the transactions motive, (ii) the precautionary motive, and the speculative motive. The demand for money is therefore viewed to comprise of these three components.

(1) **Transactions Demand:** People receive their income weekly, monthly and sometimes quarterly or even yearly. But payments are required to be made continuously many times in a day for food, for bus-fare, for amusement and for scores of such other goods and services. In other words, income is received at discrete intervals of time but is paid out more or less continuously. You cannot imagine yourself stepping out of your house without any money in your purse.

The transactions motive for holding money is sometimes classified into two parts: the income motive and the business motive.

   (a) **The Income Motive:** From the point of view of the consumer, it is necessary to hold a part of his income in the form of money. What amount he would like to hold depends upon the size of his income and upon the intervals of time between two income-receipts.

   (b) **The Business Motive:** Just as consumers wish to hold money, the entrepreneurs also wish to hold a certain amount of money in their current accounts or in the form of cash on hand. They have to make payments every day for transport, for postage, for daily wage payments and a number of such business expenses. The money held under this motive depends upon the turnover of the business.

(2) **Precautionary Demand:** In case of transactions demand, money is viewed as a medium of exchange. In case of the precautionary motive, however, money held is expected to perform the function of store of value for facilitating unexpected transactions.

An analogy will make this point clear. Money held under transactions motive is like water in the overhead tank of a building. But for keeping the water level in overhead tank constant, we need to have an underground tank (or a well) containing some reserve of water. For one reason or another, if the municipal authorities do not release the daily supply of water, we shall not be bothered if we have water in reserve in the underground tank. Money held under precautionary motive is like water in reserve in the underground tank. People tend to hold some money balances (i.e. stocks of money). They hold a certain amount of money to provide for the danger of sickness, unemployment, accidents and similar other uncertain perils.

Transactions demand for income stems largely from a lack of synchronization between receipts and expenditures; similarly, precautionary demand arises primarily because of the uncertainty of future receipts and expenditures. Precautionary balances enable people to meet unanticipated increases in expenditures or unanticipated delays in receipts.

(3) **Speculative Demand:** Speculative motive is the third motive for holding money.

For precautionary purposes people hold money as a store of value to be used in difficult times. For speculative purposes also people hold money as a store of value; but the purpose is one of making speculative gains.

People may hold money in demand deposit accounts (i.e. current and savings accounts) to be invested in securities.

There are numerous securities which yield a fixed annual amount of interest which are known as bonds. Government securities and business debentures are examples of bonds. People would like to buy bonds when they are cheap and sell them when their prices are high. In other words, people would like to buy bonds when interest rates are high and sell bonds when interest rates are low. But nobody knows what future interest rates will be. Because of this uncertainty, it is possible for people to make capital gains by guessing correctly when bond prices will rise and fall.

Under the speculative motive, people hold money in order to buy bonds / securities with it when the rate of interest has reached such a high level that they expect it to fall again. They make capital gains by speculating in securities.

Classical theory assumed that a person would hold no money in excess of the amount needed to meet his transactions (including precautionary) requirements. If he does so, he will lose the interest that could be earned by putting that money into a bond. Classical theorists argued that even when the interest rate were very low, it would be better to have some return than none at all.

It was Keynes who pointed out that one who buys a bond is *'speculating'* that the interest rate will not rise during the period of his bond-holding. If he feels it will rise, he would be wise to hold money rather than bonds. This uncertainty regarding future interest rate causes people to hold money for speculative purposes. If people knew with certainty what future interest rates would be, there would be no speculative demand for money.

Income, Rate of Interest and Demand for Money

The foregoing analysis of demand for money makes it clear that the demand for money means the demand for money to hold. When, for instance, we speak of an increased demand for money, we mean that the community wishes to hold a larger amount of money. It is thus necessary to remember that the demand for money or the liquidity preference as it is often called, is always the demand for money to hold.

Now, a very crucial question that arises is what are the factors on which the demand for money depends?

(1) **Transactions demand:** People want to hold some money for transaction purposes. How much, would primarily depend upon the income-size and the price level. Therefore we can say that the transactions demand for money varies directly with

the money income of the community. This is why we say that when money income doubles, average holdings of money for transaction purposes would also double.

If the rate of interest increases, will the people hold the same amount of money? Empirical studies have shown that rate of interest has no significant effect on transactions demand though at very high rates of interest people would try to hold less of cash and more of interest-earning assets. The transactions demand for money, therefore, is rightly considered to be *interest-inelastic.*

If rate of interest is not related to this type of demand, then we can say that transactions demand for money (M_t) is a function of income (Y) or $M_t = f(Y)$.

(2) **Precautionary demand:** Precautionary demand is formally distinguished from transactions demand; but the total amount of money held to meet both demands is viewed primarily as a function of the level of income. In other words, we can assume that the *precautionary demand also to be interest-inelastic.* This assumption simplifies our analysis. If both transactions demand and precautionary demand are functions of income, the two may be combined so that M_t can be understood to include both transaction and precautionary balances. The equation $M_t = f(Y)$ would then suggest that transactions and precautionary demand for money is a *function of income.*

(3) **Speculative demand:** The speculative demand for money is the demand for money as a store of value. People would decide to hold money for making capital gains on the basis of the current rate of interest. If they expect the rate to rise further, they would decide to wait and hold money. If they feel the rate has reached its maximum, they will buy bonds. Thus, *the speculative demand for money depends on the rate of interest.* It is true that people would hold money out of the income they earn. But speculative money-holdings do not change as income changes. They change as the rate of interest changes. In other words, speculative demand for money (M_{sp}) is a function of the rate of interest (r).

We can therefore express the speculative demand for money by the equation: $M_{sp} = f(r)$.

(4) **Total Demand for Money:** Total demand for money would then be found by adding the three components of demand. If M_d is the total demand for money, it can be obtained by combining the two equations $M_t = f(Y)$, which we understand to include precautionary demand, and the equation $M_{sp} = f(r)$. The equation for the total demand for-money will then be: $M_d = f(Y) + f(r)$. We are assuming that the price level is given and constant.

Asset Demand: Portfolio Theory: The function of money as a store of value was emphasized by Keynes. It was this function which led him to conclude that people hold money for speculative purposes also; and this demand is interest-elastic. Transactions demand on the other hand is interest-inelastic.

Two questions can be raised in this regard: (a) Is all non-transactions demand for money just speculative? (b) Is transactions demand perfectly interest-inelastic? Let us examine these two questions, in brief.

(1) **Portfolio Theory:** Modern economists consider *'asset demand'* for money (rather than speculative demand) as an important part of demand for money. It was James Tobin who reformulated the speculative motive into an asset motive. Rational investors spread their wealth among stocks, bonds, houses and money - money being one of the assets. An optimal combination of investments - which is called a *'portfolio'* - will contain some very risky but high-yielding assets, some least risky but low-yield assets and some midway. Take the case of savings bank accounts in India. They are insured upto certain limit and contain no risk. They offer a moderate interest. Savings deposits are withdrawal by cheques, so, they are money. But because they yield interest-income, they are an asset. This demand can be called *asset demand for money*. Thus, money as a store of value is demanded not only for speculative purposes but also as a liquid asset. This is what the portfolio theory says that besides the expected rate of return, risk and willingness to take risk are additional factors here.

(2) **Transactions demand and rate of interest:** As already noted, even the money-stock held for transaction purposes must be sensitive to cost of holding money. The cost of holding money is the interest people would have received. In other words, we are suggesting that the transactions demand for money is not perfectly inelastic in respect of interest-rate. But for making analysis simple it is assumed to be so.

The entire analysis of demand for money can be summarized as follows:

(i) Money is demanded by the people because it performs certain important functions for them.

(ii) Conventionally, money is said to perform the functions of medium of exchange, measure of value, standard of deferred payments, store of value and transfer of value plus a few contingent functions.

(iii) The modern practice is to classify functions of money into three types: medium of exchange, unit of account and store of value. These three encompass all the conventional functions.

(iv) As a medium of exchange, money is demanded for transaction purposes. For future transactions, as a store of value, people demand money for precautionary purposes. Besides, as a store of value, people demand money for speculative purposes and as a liquid asset. Demand for money is always a demand for money to hold; and the money is coins, paper currency and deposits withdrawal by cheques.

(v) Transactions demand for money (including precautionary demand) is a function of income; while speculative demand or demand as an asset, to make it broader - is a function of rate of interest, given the level of income.

2.3 Value of Money

The distance is measured by the meter. But what measures the meter? The answer is distance itself. Similarly the value of goods and services are measured by money. But what measures the money? The answer is goods and services.

What is 'Value of Money?' If we understand correctly, money, in itself, may be quite valueless. For example, the intrinsic value of a 50-rupee note may be zero, as it is only a piece of paper. But, its value arises from its capability to purchase a number of goods and services for the purchaser's use.

Thus, the value of money lies in its 'buying capacity'. In other words, greater the buying capacity, higher will be its value. In **Robertson's** words, *the value of money means, "the amount of things in general which will be given in exchange for a unit of money."*

According to **Crowther**," *the value of money is what it will buy."*

The term "value of money" means the purchasing power of money. It refers to the number of goods and services that can be purchased by a unit of money, i.e., value of money is the 'buying capacity' of money. The larger the quantity of goods and services money can purchase the greater will be the value of money.

Thus, the concept of value of money is a *relative* term, as it expresses the relationship between a given unit of money and the amount of goods and services that can be exchanged for it.

The value of money depends upon the price level of goods and services to be purchased with money. It implies, lower the price level, higher shall be the value of money and higher the price level, lower is the value of money. Thus, there is an inverse relationship between the value of money and the price level. Alternatively, it can be said that the value of money is *reciprocal* of the price level. For example, price of salt is ₹ 10 per kg. Here, a unit of money, i.e., one rupee can buy 100 grams of salt. Thus, in this example value of money is 100 grams of salt. If the price falls to ₹ 8 per kg., the value of money will increase to 125 grams of salt.

The value of money is of two types:

(a) **The internal value of money:** The internal value of money means the purchasing power of money over domestic goods and services.

(b) **The external value of money:** The external value of money means the purchasing power of money over foreign goods and services.

However, to measure the value of money is not easy. Firstly, the question arises: in terms of which *commodity price* should we express the value of money? Naturally, the answer is that since money buys everything that has a price, thus the value of money is to be expressed in terms of all commodities. This will give us practically infinite number of values of money since there are numerous commodities and numerous prices. In other words, this method of expressing the value of money is impracticable.

Sometimes, the value of money is sought to be measured in terms of *"the general price level"*. The general price level is based on the price level of all the commodities taken together.

Thus, $$V_m = \frac{1}{P}$$

Here, V_m = the value of money; P = Price level

The value of money when expressed in terms of the general price level is little understood by an individual, who, at a particular point of time is interested only in a certain amount of goods and services which are useful to him. It implies that the value of money will not be the same to every individual.

To sum up,

- By value of money it means the 'purchasing power' of money over goods and services in a country, for instance, what a rupee can buy in India reflects the value of the rupee.
- 'Value of money' is a relative concept. It expresses the relationship between a unit of money and the goods and services which can be purchased with it.
- The relation between the value of money and price level is an inverse one. If the value of money is represented by letter V and price level by P, then $V = \frac{1}{P}$. Thus, when the price level rise, the value of money falls and vice versa.
- The price level that is taken into account to find value of money is the general level of prices.
- The value of money is of two kinds:
   (a) The *intrinsic value* of money, which refers to the purchasing power of money over domestic goods and services.

(b) The *external value* of money, which refers to the purchasing power of money over foreign gods and services.

> *Value of money' is a relative concept. It expresses the relationship between a unit of money and the goods and services which can be purchased with it.*

2.3.1 Quantity Theory of Money (The Cash Transaction Approach)

Introduction

The Quantity Theory of Money is a very old theory. It was an Italian economist **Davanzatti** (1588) who propounded this theory. Later, the Classical economists explained the value of money in terms of the quantity theory of money. Though the Classical economists like **David Ricardo, J.S.Mill** and **Hume** introduced improvements in this theory but the credit for popularizing this theory in recent years belongs to the well-known American economist **Irving Fisher.**

Statement of the theory

Irving Fisher was an American economist. He provided the transactions approach of the quantity theory of money in his book "The Purchasing Power of Money (1911)". He gave it a qualitative form in terms of his famous *'Equation of Exchange.'* According to Fisher, *"other things remaining unchanged, as the quantity of money in circulation increases, the price level also increases in direct proportion and the value of money decreases and vice versa."*

The Quantity Theory of Money points out the causes which determine the general price level in a country or factors that determine changes in the value of money.

The theory states that the price level (or the value of money) is determined by the supply of money.

> *According to this theory, the value of money varies 'inversely' to the supply of money. On the other hand, the price level varies 'directly' to the quantity of money.*

For instance, if the quantity of money is doubled, the price level is also doubled; however, the value of money will be halved.

In short, the theory stresses a 'mathematical relationship' between the quantity of money and price level on the one hand and, the quantity of money and the value of money on the other. This is referred to as the 'Proportionality Approach to the Quantity Theory of Money'.

However, some Classical economists differ from this strict proportional approach. According to this version, if the quantity of money increases, prices will rise, but by how much is not explained.

There are two versions of the Quantity Theory of Money:
(i) The Transactions Approach;
(ii) The Cash Balance Approach.

(I) Fisher's Version – The Transaction Approach

It was Irving Fisher who presented the transaction version of the Quantity Theory of Money. It was presented in the form of the 'Equation of Exchange' in his famous book 'The Purchasing Power of Money' (1911).

$$MV = PT$$

Fisher's version of the quantity theory of money is based on an essential function of money, i.e., *money acts as a medium of exchange*. Money is not needed for its own sake but to exchange it for goods and services.

The above equation of exchange (MV = PT) has two sides, namely MV and PT.

Here,
- M = The total quantity of money in circulation.
- V = The velocity of circulation of money, i.e., the average number of times each unit of money is spent on the purchase of goods and services.
- P = General Price level, i.e., average price per unit of T.
- T = Total volume of transactions of goods and services against money.

Like other commodities, the price level or the value of money is also determined by the demand and supply of money.

Supply of Money (MV)

The supply of money comprises of the quantity of money in existence (M) multiplied by the velocity of money (V) (i.e., the number of times this money changes hands). Thus, MV means the total volume of money in circulation during a period of time. The supply of money (MV) is equal to the total value of money expenditures in all transactions in the economy during a period of time.

- MV (M and V) gives the aggregate **supply of money** (i.e., total money expenditure) during a given period of time.
- At particular point of time, the supply of money is the total quantity of money in existence at that time (i.e. M).
- The supply of money over a period of time is the total quantity of money (M) multiplied by the velocity of its circulation (V), i.e., **MV**

Demand for Money (PT)

Money is demanded by the people not for hoarding but for transaction purposes. The demand for money (PT) is obtained by multiplying total amount of things (T) by average price level (P). PT is equal to the total market value of all goods and services transacted during a period of time.

Macro Economic Analysis — Money and Value of Money

- PT (P × T) represents the money value of all goods and services bought during a given period of time.
- It represents the total demand for money. Demand for money is for the goods and services that it helps to buy (i.e., for *transaction* purpose).

Thus, Fisher's equation represents equality between the supply of money (MV) and the demand for money (PT). In simple terms, the equation states that the actual total value of all money expenditures (MV) always equals he actual total value of all items transacted (PT).

According to Fisher, at given period of time, the total quantity of money (MV) will be equal to the total value of all goods and services bought and sold (PT).

Therefore,   MV = PT

Or,   supply of Money = Demand for Money.

Or,   Amount of Money × velocity of Circulation = Total spending.

Thus, if an economy has ₹ 3, and that ₹ 3 was spent five times in a month, total spending for the month would be ₹ 15.

The above equation of exchange is referred to as the '*Cash Transaction Equation.*'

It can also be represented as:

$$P = \frac{MV}{T} \quad \ldots (i)$$

Equation (i) shows that the quantity of money determines the price level and the price level, in turn, varies directly with the quantity of money (assuming V and T to remain constant).

In the above equation, only primary money or currency money has been included. However, in modern economy, besides currency notes and coins, it includes banks' demand deposits or credit money too. Thus, Fisher's extended form of Equation of Exchange that includes credit money is-

$$MV + M'V' = PT \text{ (or)}$$

$$P = \frac{MV + M'V'}{T} \quad \ldots (ii)$$

Here,   M' = credit money or demand deposits in the banks.

V' = Velocity of circulation of credit money.

It is clear from the above equation that the price level is determined by the following five definite factors:

- M = quantity of money in circulation;
- V = velocity of circulation of money;
- M' = the volume of bank money;

Macro Economic Analysis — Money and Value of Money

- V' = the velocity of circulation of bank money;
- T = the volume of trade (the quantity of goods and services transacted).

The equation also depicts the relationship that the price level (P) is directly related to M, M', V and V' but is inversely related to T.

Illustration

Fisher's transactions approach to the quantity theory of money can be explained with the help of the following example.

Suppose M = ₹ 5000; M' = ₹ 2500; V = 3; V' = 2; T = 20000 goods.

$$P = \frac{MV + M'V'}{T}$$

$$= \frac{(5000 \times 3) + (2500 \times 2)}{20000}$$

$$= \frac{15000 + 5000}{20000}$$

$$= \frac{20000}{20000}$$

= ₹ 1 per good.

Value of money is (1/p) = 1

If supply of money is halved, i.e. M = ₹ 2500; M' = ₹ 1250.

$$= \frac{(2500 \times 3) + (1250 \times 2)}{20000}$$

$$= \frac{7500 + 2500}{20000}$$

$$= \frac{10000}{20000}$$

= ₹ 0.50 per good. Value of money is 1/p = 2.

Thus, when money supply is halved, i.e., decreases, price level is halved but value of money is doubled.

If supply of money is doubled, M = ₹ 10,000 and M' = ₹ 5,000

$$= \frac{(10000 \times 3) + (5000 \times 2)}{20000}$$

$$= \frac{30000 + 10000}{20000}$$

$$= \frac{40000}{20000} = ₹ 2 \text{ per good}$$

Value of money 1/p = ½.

Thus, when money supply is doubled, i.e. increases, the price level are doubled and the value of money is halved.

In the Equation of Exchange, Fisher establishes the relationship as:
- Price level (or the value of money) is a function of the supply of money, assuming other things to remain the same, i.e., M', V, V' and T
- When these factors remain constant, P will change in direct proportion to M.

Thus, Fisher establishes a direct and proportionate relationship between the changes in the quantity of money (M) and the resultant price level (P).

MV = PT or Supply of Money = Demand for Money, or MV=M'V'=PT (with credit money).

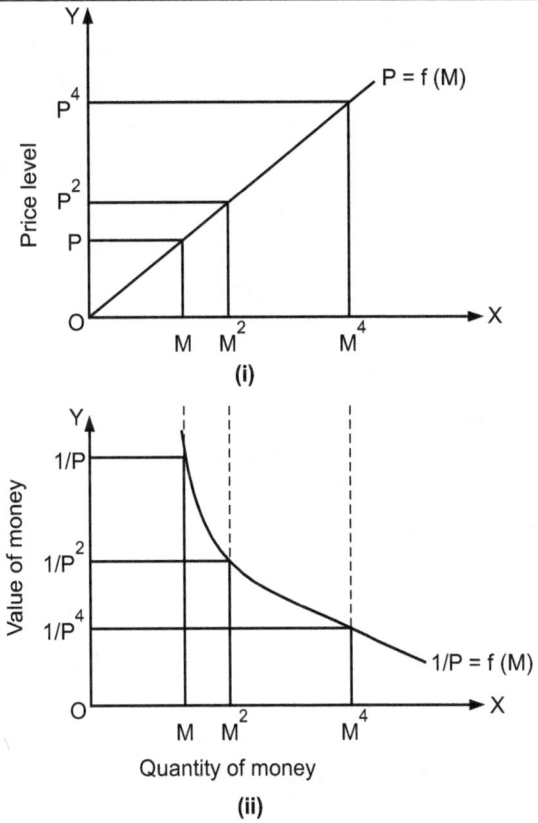

Fig. 2.2: Quantity of Money

Fig. 2 (i) depicts the effect of changes in the quantity of money on the price level. M is Quantity of money and P is the price level.

When M is doubled to M^2, the price level is doubled to P^2. In this way, with further increase in M- M^4, P will also increase in the same proportion- P^4. This relationship is represented by the upward sloping curve {P=f(M)} from the origin at 45^0.

There is a direct and proportionate relationship between the quantity of money and the price level.

In Fig.2 (ii) an *inverse* relationship is depicted between the quantity of money (M) and the value of money (1/P). When the quantity of money is M, the value of money is 1/P. And, when the quantity of money is doubled to M^2, the value of money declines to one-half, of what it was before $(1/P^2)$. When the quantity of money increases four-fold, say, M^4, the value of money is reduced by $1/P^4$. The inverse relationship is shown by the downward sloping curve $\{1/P = f(M)\}$.

There is an inverse relationship between the quantity of money and the value of money.

Assumptions

Irving Fisher used the equation of exchange to develop the classical theory of money. On the basis of the assumptions that, in the long run, under full employment conditions, total output (T) remain unchanged and the transactions velocity of money (V) is stable.

Fisher's equation of exchange is based on the following assumptions:

(i) **P (price level) is an inactive element in the equation:** 'P' is purely a passive element. It exerts no influence on other factors in the equation. It is the 'result' and not the 'cause'. 'P' is determined by other factors; it does not determine them, i.e., the relationship between P and other factors in the equation if one-sided. Thus, rise in 'M' will increase P but a rise in P will not affect M.

(ii) **T (volume of trade) is an independent element in the exchange equation:** The volume of trade (T), according to Fisher, is not affected by any change in any other element in the equation, i.e., M, V, M', V'. On the other hand, T is determined by certain outside factors like climatic conditions, population, technology, etc., in the equation and is an independent factor and remains constant in the short period.

(iii) **V (velocity of circulation of money) is an independent element in the equation:** Like T, V remains constant in the short period. Any change in M or P has no effect on V and this V depends on external factors like banking habits of people, interest rates, and commercial customs of the country. Since these factors remain constant in the short term, V may be taken to be more or less constant during the short period.

(iv) **The ratio of bank money to legal tender money remains the same:** Fisher assumes that the ratio of credit money to legal tender money remains the same. If the ratio does not remain constant, then the quantitative (mathematical) relation between money and prices (as shown in the equation) will not hold good.

(v) **Money is a medium of exchange:** The quantity theory of money assumed that money is used only as a medium of exchange.

(vi) Long period: The cash transaction approach to the quantity theory of money is based on the assumption of long period.

> Fisher considers P as a passive factor in the equation and other elements, i..e., M', V, V' and T as constant. Any change in P is due to changes in M alone (in the supply of money). In this way, Fisher establishes a direct and proportional relationship between the supply of money and the price level. The price level varies directly and the value of money varies inversely with the changes in the supply of money.

Critical Evaluation

Fisher's equation of exchange or cash transaction approach has been subject to severe criticism, as explained below:

(1) The Quantity Theory of Money is based on numerous unrealistic assumptions:
Critics mention that the proportion of V, V', P and M' does not remain the same in the actual working of the economy.

(a) *Fisher assumes that there was no change in the velocity of circulation of legal money (V), when its supply changes,* i.e., M and V are independent of each other. But this assumption is unrealistic because V will automatically change when its supply undergoes a change (i.e. M). For example, when the supply of money (M) is increased, the price level will rise (P). And fearing further rise in price, people will buy more and velocity of circulation of money (V) will rise. Hence, *it is misleading to assume (V) as constant in the equation.*

(b) Fisher assumes a constant and unchangeable relationship between M' and M and that M' changes in accordance with the changes in M. This assumption is contrary to the facts of the situation. In fact, there is no well-defined and unchangeable relationship between M and M'. For example, during prosperity and boom periods, the proportion of M' to M rises as banks create a large amount of credit money to meet the increasing demands for loans and advances from traders and merchants. On the other hand, during depression, the proportion of M' to M declines. In short, the proportion of M' to M is not constant.

(c) Fisher assumes no change in V' as a result of change in M, i.e., the theory assumes M and V' are independent and do not influence each other. This assumption too, is misleading. Because, change in V' is an inevitable consequence of a change in M. Suppose the quantity of M increases, the price level rises and with the rise in price level there will be increasing use of bank money. As a result, the velocity of circulation of bank money or V' will inevitably rise.

(d) **Fisher assumes that 'T' does not change due to change in M:** 'T' represents the demand for money and further that M and T are independent of each other. According to Fisher, when the supply of money (M) is changed, the demand for money does not change. But this assumption is untrue, as 'T' cannot remain constant with any change in M. When M rises, price level (P) rise, profits increase and producers increase the output. This results in the rise of volume of trade (T).

The above assumptions that are implicit in Fisher's equation are unrealistic and misleading. Thus, M, M', V, V' and T are not independent of each other and change in any one of these influences the price level.

(e) **According to Fisher P (or price level) was a passive factor in the equation:** This assumption is not real. 'P' may be active and may influence T. This is natural because rising prices result in rising profits and thus increase the volume of trade. Thus, P is not a passive factor but has an influence on T.

(f) **According to Fisher, change in M is the cause and change in P is the result:** This sequence of cause-effect is not acceptable to the critics. According to the critics, changes in P occur independently and later influence the supply of money (i.e. M). Thus, here, M is determined by P and a change in P is the cause and change in M is the effect. However, Fisher refused to accept this view of the critics. He continued to maintain that it is changes in money supply which cause changes in the price level.

(2) **The theory offers us a long term analysis of money and ignores the short period:** It is well known that there are sometimes violent and far-reaching changes in the value of money in the short period and Fisher's approach does not say anything about the short period.

(3) **There is no direct and proportional relationship between the quantity of money (M) and price level (P):** According to Fisher, there is a direct and proportional effect of change in money supply on the price level. For example, if M is doubled, other things remaining the same, P will be doubled. However, there is no direct and proportional relationship between the quantity of money and the price level. The critics point out that this relationship is more imaginary than real.

(4) **The theory offers no discussion of the velocity of circulation of money:** The theory throws no light on the element V or any other factors that determine it.

(5) **It is difficult to measure 'V':** Prof. Fisher considered the velocity of circulation of money as constant in the short period but changing in the long run. However, economists have no instrument with the help of which they can measure the changes in velocity accurately.

(6) **The theory neglects the velocity of circulation of commodities:** It totally ignores the velocity of circulation of commodities while explaining price changes in the economy. But, like money, there is a velocity of circulation of commodities too.

(7) **The Quantity Theory is based on the wrong assumption of full employment:** Keynes criticizes the theory of transaction approach as it is based on the assumption of full employment. According to Keynes, the quantity theory holds goods only in a state of full employment. And, in real life there is underemployment or unemployment. In such a case, every increase in M will not bring about direct and proportional rise in the price level. Instead of increasing price level, increase in M would increase the output in the economy. Only after the level of full employment, every increase in M will have a direct and proportional effect on P.

(8) **The theory neglects interest rate:** Fisher's Quantity theory of money neglects the role of the rate of interest as one of the causative factors between money and prices. Fisher's equation of exchange is related to an equilibrium situation in which the rate of interest is independent of the quantity of money.

(9) **The theory neglects store of value function of money:** It neglects the store value function of money and considers only the medium of exchange function of money. Thus, the theory is one-sided.

(10) **The Quantity theory is not comprehensive:** According to Keynes, it is improper to include the entire legal money and credit money in the total supply of money. Only a part of the total money supply is used for the purpose of buying goods and services in the economy and a part of this money supply is hoarded by the public and this part is not used for buying goods and services. And, hoarded money has no effect on the sale-purchase transactions in the economy.

(11) **The Theory is mechanical and neglects the human element in the analysis of price changes:** According to Fisher, the price level can be controlled by regulating the various variables like M, M', V and V' and T. But, prices are also affected by the consumers' and producers' decisions about saving and investment. Thus, the price level is determined more by expenditures than by the quantity of money.

(12) **Fisher's Equation of Exchange does not refer to any specific standard value of money:** Fisher's equation deals with the general price level, i.e., prices of both producer and consumer goods. In other words, producer goods are also included in the volume of trade. And, according to Keynes, the value of money cannot be measured precisely if the prices of producer goods are also included in the general price level. Hence, the quantity theory is quite unsatisfactory.

(13) **The theory is redundant:** The theory is redundant and unnecessary. Like any other commodity, the value of money is also determined by the demand for and supply of

money. The general theory of value, explaining the value of commodity, can also be extended to analyze the value of money with its demand and supply tools. Thus, no separate theory is needed.

(14) **The theory offers no explanation of cyclical fluctuations in prices:** According to this theory, the changes in price level (P) are only due to the changes in the quantity of money (M). But, critics mention that changes in the price level are not only due to changes in the supply of money. There can be other causes of changes in the price level. The theory fails to explain those changes in the general price level, which take place due to the operation of the business cycle.

(15) **The Quantity Theory gives no recognition to the importance of timeliness in its discussion:** Critics say the effect of changes in money supply on the price level is not immediate. On the contrary, this effect is slow and gradual. In short, the changes in the price level may not be directly proportional to the changes in the quantity of money.

(16) **It is not proper to call this Theory a 'theory':** According to Prof. Nicholson, the theory expresses only an elementary truth with which everyone is familiar. It is a well-known fact that an increase in the supply of money is followed by a rise in the price level. This is nothing new and hence it is improper to give the dignified status of a theory to this ordinary tendency at work in the economy. Thus, Fisher's equation of exchange is a simple truism and it proves nothing.

(17) **It fails to take into account the changes in the price levels of other nations on the price level of the country:** The quantity theory is based on the assumption that the country in the question stands isolated and has no economic relations with other countries. This assumption is unrealistic when numerous countries today are intimately related with each other through the medium of international trade.

(18) **Fisher's assumption "other things remaining constant" is not tenable:** According to Fisher, things like volume of trade, velocity of circulation of goods, population of the country, output per capita, consumption habits of people does not change in the short period. To assume such dynamic factors as constant qualifies the quantity theory as a static theory of money.

To conclude,
- The Quantity Theory of Money is imaginary and misleading.
- It does not provide for a precise and accurate measurement of the value of money (i.e., purchasing power of money).
- It lacks mathematical exactness as there is no direct and proportional relationship between the quantity of money and the price level.
- The theory is not looked upon as a reliable and useful tool for analysis and policy.

Despite the limitations, the theory occupies an important place in Economics. It throws adequate light on the changes in the supply of money taking place in the economy. The theory proves useful in enabling us to establish control on the general price level. The quantity theory also forms the backbone of the modern banking techniques of open market operations and bank-rate policy.

2.3.2 The Cash Balance Approach (Cambridge Version)

The *cash transaction version* was based on the function of money as a *medium of exchange*. A different approach was presented by the Cambridge economists like Prof. Marshall, Pigou, Cannan, Robertson and J. M. Keynes. This approach is referred to as the *Cash Balance Approach* and is based on the *store of value function of money*.

According to the Cash Balance Approach the value of money depends on the demand for and the supply of money. Thus, the changes in the value of money are caused by changes in either its demand or its supply or both. In short, this theory is an application of the general theory of value to the problem of money, i.e., like value theory, they regarded the determination of value of money in terms of supply and demand for money. According to Robertson, "Money is only one of the many economic things. Its value, therefore, is primarily determined by exactly the same two factors that determine the value of any other thing, namely, the conditions of demand for it and the quantity of it available."

The Cash Balance approach considers the demand for and supply of money at a particular point of time, rather than over a period of time as transaction theory does it.

Supply of Money

The supply of money at a particular period of time comprises all the cash and bank deposits subject to withdrawal by cheques.

Demand for Money

According to Fisher's 'Equation of Exchange', demand for money is equal to the money-value of business transactions in the economy, i.e., $M = P \times T$ (money is demanded by people to buy goods and services in the market).

According to Cambridge economists *demand for money* refers to that total quantity of money which is held by private individuals, commercial firms and government to meet their day-to-day transactions and precautionary needs i.e., demand for money is demand for cash balances which the community wishes to hold.

Thus, the cash balance approach considers the demand for money not as a medium of exchange but as a store of value. This difference was expressed by Robertson as money "on the wings" and money "sitting". Money "sitting" reflects the demand for money in the Cambridge equations (Cash Balance).

Cash transaction approach-money as medium of exchange, i.e., "money on the wings".
Cash balance approach-money as a store of value, i.e., "money sitting".

According to the Cambridge economists, the demand for money arises out of the **liquidity preference** of the people. The greatest liquidity pertains to the cash held by the individual in his own hands, because he can make use of it according to his requirements. In economic terms, this desire of the individual is referred to as his "liquidity preference". Thus, higher the liquidity preference of the people, greater the demand for money, i.e., they hold higher cash balances. In short, the liquidity preference exerts an influence on the demand for money.

To conclude, according to the cash balance approach, the value of money depends upon the demand for and supply of money.

With **'given' demand**, the value of money varies inversely and price level directly with the quantity of money (supply of money).

With **'given' supply of money**, the value of money varies directly and the price level inversely, with the demand for money.

An increase in the demand for money means smaller demand for goods and services, as the people can have more cash-balances and cut down their expenditure on the goods and services. As a result, the price level will fall but value of money will rise.

'Cambridge Equations' (or cash balance approach), explain the relationship between the supply of and demand for the money.

Some of the important equations are explained as under:

(1) Marshall's Equation: Dr. Marshall's cash balance equation is expressed as:

$$M = KPY$$

Here, M = Total supply of money (i.e. total amount of currency + demand deposits in banks).

P = Price level.

Y = Total real income (purchasing power).

K = that fraction of the real income which the public desires to hold in the form of money.

In this equation, the value of money (i.e. purchasing power of money) can be obtained by dividing the total quantity of goods which the public desires to hold out of the total income (KY) by the total supply of money (i.e. M).

Therefore,
$$P = \frac{KY}{M}$$

Here, P = Purchasing power of money

According to the Marshall's equation, the value of money is influenced not only by changes in M, but also by changes in K. In fact, K exerts more important influence on P than on M. For example, a change in K (the desire of the public to hold money) may influence P even when the supply of money remains the same.

(2) Pigou's Equation: A new equation was put forward by Prof. Pigou in the cash balance approach.

$$P = \frac{KR}{M}$$

Here, P = Value of money (or purchasing power of money). Unlike in the transaction approach, here P is not the price level, it is the value of money.

R = The aggregate real income expressed in terms of a particular commodity enjoyed by the community at any given point of time.

K = That part of R (i.e., that part of aggregate real income) which is held by the public in the form of cash balances.

M = Total money stock or total cash held by a community.

Money held by the community not merely in terms of cash but also in the form of bank deposits, subject to withdrawal by cheques. Thus, to include bank deposits, the extended form of equation is:

$$P = \frac{KR}{M}[C + h(1 - c)]$$

Here, C = The proportion of money which the public keeps in the form of legal tenders.

h = The proportion of cash reserves to deposits held by the banks.

(1-c) = that proportion of total money which is held by the people in the form of bank deposits.

According to Pigou's equation, P (i.e., the value of money) varies directly with K or R, and inversely with M.

The price level varies inversely with K or R and directly with M. If P is interpreted as price level as in the transaction equation then Pigou's equation is expressed as:

$$P = M/KR$$

According to Pigou, the value of money depends upon the demand of the people to hold money, i.e., K was more significant than M for bringing about changes in the value of money.

Significance of Pigou's Equation

1. It is useful as it explains the reason as to why people wish to hold a greater proportion and at other times a smaller proportion of their income in the form of money.

2. During inflation, people tend to keep a smaller proportion of their income in the form of money (i.e., K declines). The reason is that during a period of rising prices, the value of money continues to fall. Thus, people prefer to spend the money today, as tomorrow its value would be still lesser.
3. During a period of falling prices, K is high as people wish to hold a greater proportion of income as money.

Limitations

Keynes has criticized the equation on following grounds:
1. Pigou sought to measure K and R in terms of a single commodity, i.e., wheat, which was inadequate and misleading.
2. The two most important functions of money are:
   - Money serves as a medium of exchange, and
   - Money serves as a store of value.

But Pigou, in his equation, has overlooked the former function of money (money as a medium of exchange) and stressed on the latter function (i.e., money as a store of value). This equation has concentrated only on the quantity of money as the determinant of purchasing power of money, hence it is inadequate explanation.

(1) Robertson's Equation: Another Cambridge equation similar to Pigou is the one presented by Robertson.

Robertson's equation is: $P = \dfrac{M}{KT}$

P = Price level.
M = Money supply.
T = Annual volume of trade (i.e., total amount of goods and services to be bought during one year).
K = That proportion of T which people desire to hold in the form of cash.

According to the above equation:
- P changes directly with M;
- P changes inversely as K or T.

Similarity between Fisher's and Robertson's Equation

Fisher's transaction equation is, $P = \dfrac{MV}{T}$

Robertson's cash balance equation is,

$$P = \dfrac{M}{KT}$$

In both the equations, P, M and T are almost same though V is a reciprocal of K, i.e.,

$$V = \frac{1}{K}$$

But the main difference is that Fisher's equation considers money as a medium of exchange and Robertson's equation considers money as a store of value.

(2) Keynes' Equation: Keynes' equation is referred to as 'The real Balance Quantity Equation' in his famous book, 'A Tract on Monetary Reforms'.

The equation is: $n = pk$ or $p = \frac{n}{k}$

Here,
n = Total supply of money in circulation;
p = General level of prices of consumption goods;
k = those consumption units for which the purchasing power is kept by the public in the form of cash. According to Keynes, 'K' is the real balance.

Keynes points out that doubling of the quantity of money in circulation will cause a doubling of the price level, provided K remains the same.

To include bank deposits in money supply, the extended version of Keynes is

$$n = p(k + k') \quad \text{or} \quad p = n/(k + rk')$$

Here,
r = ratio of banks' cash reserves to their deposits.
k' = the number of consumption units the people decide to hold in the form of bank deposits.

In this equation, Keynes observes that assuming k, k' and r to be constant, a change in n will cause a direct and proportionate change in p. According to Keynes, in the short run, all the factors – k, k' and r are constant. It is only in the long run that these factors change.

Merits of Keynes' Equation

1. The demand for money in a country, according to this equation, does not depend upon the total quantity of goods and services that are produced within the country, but is influenced by the propensity of the community to hold cash.
2. The price level is determined by that proportion of the people's income which they decide to keep with themselves in cash to buy goods and services for consumption.

Critical Evaluation of Keynes' Equation

1. In Keynes' equation, 'P' indicates the price level of consumption goods only. This is incomplete, as it does not include investment goods.

2. There is no accurate measurement of k and k' in the above equation. It is difficult to say, with any definiteness, as to what proportion of their income is kept by the people in cash and what proportion is maintained in the form of bank deposits to meet their consumption requirements.
3. The velocity of circulation of money finds no place in Keynes' equation.
4. 'p' in the above equation relates to the prices of current consumption goods only, but for investment and speculative purposes also.
5. The equation fails to state the effect of a change in bank rate on k'.
6. Keynes assumed that people hold money to secure consumption goods. This is not true. People demand money for various businesses and for personal purposes too.

Critical Evaluation of the Cash-Balance Approach

The various Cambridge Equations discussed under the Cash Balance Approach suffer from following shortcomings:

1. **Unrealistic Assumption:** The cash balance theory is based on an unrealistic assumption, i.e., the demand for money has uniform unitary elasticity. It is untrue because in a dynamic society, elasticity of demand for money cannot be unitary. Thus, this theory presents an inadequate explanation in a progressive set-up.

2. **It fails to explain the speculative motive:** The theory fails to explain all the determinants of demand for money. It neglects the discussion of the speculative motive for holding money. A sizeable part of the demand for money arises on account of the speculative motive. In fact, it is the speculative motive that causes violent changes in the demand for money in the economy.

3. **It refers to consumption goods only:** A serious limitation that is observed in Pigou's and Keynes' Cambridge equations are that they seek to explain the value of money (or purchasing power) in terms of consumption goods only. It is illogical as in the actual market there are not only consumption goods but also investment goods. Thus by restricting the equation to only consumption goods, the cash balance theory has narrowed down the concept of the value of money.

4. **The theory neglects other factors:** Even as regards to k, a narrow view has been projected in the equations. The amount of cash (K) to be held by the people is said to be determined wholly by their real income (R). This is a narrow view of the concept k, as k is also influenced by factors other than the real income. For example, business habits of the people, price level, and the monetary and political conditions prevailing in the country influence K.

5. **P is the cause and effect of K:** According to the cash balance theory, the price level or the purchasing power of money is determined by K (cash held by the people). For example, the larger the cash holdings (or K) the higher shall be its value (or lower

the price level). In other words, K exerts an influence on P. It is pointed out by critics that K not only influences P, but is also influenced by P. For example, when prices are rising, the proportion of their income which the people wish to hold in cash (i.e., K) declines. Here, we observe that P has influenced K.

6. **K and T are not constant:** Like the cash transaction approach, the Cambridge equations also assumed K and T as given and constant. In a dynamic set up, neither K nor T can be assumed as constant. Thus, this theory too suffers from the same limitations as observed in Fisher's equation.

7. **It is difficult to measure T:** In Fisher's equation, it was difficult to measure T. T represents all the goods and services produced in the country. Since all goods and services cannot be reduced to a homogenous unit, it is difficult to measure T. The same difficulty arises in the case of R in the Cambridge equations. R represents real income of the community. It refers to all those goods and services which are produced within the country. Since all these goods and services are expressed in different units – kilogram, meter, etc. – it is difficult to have an accurate measurement of the real income of the country. Thus, the Cambridge equations suffer from the same defect as found in Fisher's equation.

8. **It neglects the rate of interest:** The cash balance approach is not a comprehensive theory. For example, rate of interest is an important determinant of prices. But, this factor finds no place in the Cambridge equation. In fact, it is a grave lacuna in the cash balance theory.

9. **The theory lacks quantitative exactness:** It is not easy to visualize in terms of the Cambridge equations, the extent to which prices and output will change due to a given change in the supply of money. Thus, the theory lacks quantitative exactness.

10. **It overlooks certain determinants of P:** The cash balance theory, while analyzing the changes in the price level, overlooks important factors such as income, savings and investment which, according to the present day economists, have an important bearing on the price level (or value of money) to changes in the demand for money alone.

11. **It ignores secondary bank deposits:** The cash balance theory neglects those bank deposits which come into existence as a result of lending operations of the commercial banks. The commercial banks have two types of deposits. The first kind of deposits is those which are made by the people out of their current income due to saving. The second kind of deposits is those which are the outcome of the lending operations of the banks. While lending to needy borrowers, the lenders deposit either the entire loan money or a part of it in the bank, to be drawn as per requirements. Thus, a bank automatically creates deposits when it makes advances

to the borrowers. It is the second type of bank deposits which have been ignored in this approach.

12. **Simple truism:** Like fisher's transaction equation MV = PT, the Cambridge equation M = KPY, is also a simple truism.

Inspite of the shortcomings discussed above, the theory has its importance. It has emphasized the importance of the **demand for money** as the main determinant of the value of money. It is well known that changes in the demand for money exert a predominant influence on the value of money. Thus, the theory has made a valuable contribution in clarifying the problem of the value of money.

Similarities and Differences between the Cambridge and Fisher's Equations

Similarities:

(i) **Similar conclusions:** Fisher's and the Cambridge equations lead to the same conclusion that there is a direct and proportionate relationship between the quantity of money and the price level and that there is an inverse and proportionate relationship between the quantity of money and the value of money.

(ii) **Similarity in Equations:** Both the approaches present almost similar equations. The Cash balance equation of Robertson $P = \frac{M}{KT}$ closely resembles Fisher's equation $P = \frac{MV}{T}$. The symbols in the two equations convey almost the same implications, though an apparent difference is seen in V and K. But, even K and V tend to be reciprocals of each other. In Fisher's equation, $V = \frac{TP}{M}$ and in Robertson's equation, $K = \frac{M}{PT}$. Thus, K is the reciprocal of V, i.e., $K = \frac{1}{V}$ and $V = \frac{1}{K}$. It means that there is no fundamental difference between the two equations. K and V represent different aspects of the same phenomenon. V stands for the velocity of circulation of money, greater the spending, greater is V. K represents the demand for money as a store of value. An increase in K (i.e., money demanded as a store of value) means decrease in V (velocity of circulation of money) and vice versa. The two factors V and K are determined by the same factors. By substituting 1/K for V in Fisher's equation (MV = PT), we arrive at M = KPT, which is same as the Cambridge equation. Similarly if we substitute 1/V for K in the Cambridge equation (M = KPT), we obtain MV = PT which is Fisher's equation.

(iii) **Same elements in equations:** MV + M'V' of Fisher's equation, M of Robertson's equation and of Pigou's equation and n of Keynes' equation refer to the same thing, i.e., total quantity of money, with a slight difference.

- In Fisher's equation, credit money is represented by M' and in Cambridge equation, bank money is not represented separately as total supply of money including credit money as well.
- V' stands for velocity of circulation of money (Fisher's equation) and there is no mention of velocity of circulation of money or bank money in the Cambridge equation.

(iv) Both the equations represent two different views of the *same* phenomenon. The Cambridge equation stresses money as a stock and treats money as "money sitting", while Fisher's equation emphasizes money as a flow and treats money as "money on wings". Yet both the versions emphasize the medium of exchange function of money.

Differences:

(i) The P element in both the equations mean differently. For example, in Fisher's equation P refers to the general price level (prices of goods). However, in Cambridge equation P relates only to the price of consumer goods.

(ii) The two approaches of the quantity theory of money use different functions of money, i.e., different reasons for which money is demanded. For example, Fisher's equation stresses the 'medium of exchange' function of money while the Cambridge equation stresses the 'store of value' function of money.

(iii) The Cambridge version presents money as a stock concept. According to it, the money supply represents a given stock at any particular point of time. Fisher's version presents it as a flow concept as money supply is a flow over a particular period of time.

(iv) Fisher's equation shows the importance of velocity of circulation of money (V). While the Cambridge equation shows that part of the community's income which is held in the form of cash balance, i.e., it stresses on the 'store of value' function of money.

(v) Fisher explains the value of money over a period of time, while the Cambridge economists explain the value of money at a particular point of time.

(vi) The two approaches have dealt with the nature of money in different ways. Fisher's approach emphasizes the spending of money on goods and services (i.e., on V) and the Cambridge approach emphasizes the holding of money by the people (i.e., on K).

Which Approach of the Quantity Theory of Money is Superior?

The Cambridge Version of the Quantity Theory of Money is superior to the Fisher's version for the following reasons:

(1) **Cambridge version is more realistic:** Fisher's approach is mechanical as it treats price level as the only function of the quantity of money in circulation. Thus, it gives no importance or place to human motives as determining factors on price level. By emphasizing on K, the Cambridge version brings in human motives.

(2) **Fisher's version is incomplete:** Fisher's equation is incomplete as it considers quantity theory of money in circulation to the determinant of the value of money (or the price level), i.e., it is a one-sided version. On the other hand, the Cambridge version considers both demand for and supply of money as real determinants of the value of money. Thus, the Cambridge version is more comprehensive in nature.

(3) **Cambridge version is based on subjective factors:** The Cambridge version is more realistic as it emphasizes subjective factors as the main determinant of the demand for money. Fisher's version considers purely objective factors while discussing the demand for money.

(4) **Cambridge approach has a broader view:** The Cambridge version is comprehensive as it considers the income level and changes in it as an important determinant of the price level. Fisher's approach neglected income level as an influencing factor on price level. According to it the price level is determined by the quantity of money and the total number of transactions in the economy.

(5) **Cash balance more significant than cash transaction:** According to some economists the two equations while explaining the value of money, the Cambridge equation $P = \dfrac{M}{KT}$, is more valuable than the Fisher's equation $P = \dfrac{MV}{T}$. The reason is that it is easier to know the cash balances of an individual than to gain information about his expenditure on various types of transactions.

(6) **Cambridge equation analyses cyclical fluctuations:** The symbol K of the Cambridge equations proves to be a better tool in the analysis of cyclical fluctuations than V in Fisher's equation. Violent and far-reaching changes in K can be the main cause of cyclical fluctuations in the economy. For example, the 'flight from currency' (which means sudden decline in K) was one of the causes of runaway inflation in post-war Germany in 1923.

(7) **Determinants differ:** In Fisher's equation we observe that the change in the price level is caused by a change in the quantity of money in circulation. In Cambridge equation, the price level may change even without a change in the quantity of money, if K undergoes a change. Even if the quantity of money remains the same

but K changes, then the price level cannot remain the same. Thus, according to the Cambridge version, K is a more important determinant of the price level than M as emphasized by Fisher's equation.

(8) **Foundation for Keynesian theory of Interest:** The Cambridge version of the Quantity theory has provided the foundation for the building-up of the Keynesian liquidity preference theory of interest. This theory of Keynes is an important constituent of the modern theory of income, output and employment.

To conclude, it is on these grounds that the Cambridge version enjoys superiority over Fisher's version.

General Review of the Two Approaches of the Quantity Theory of Money

With the critical evaluation of the two versions of the Quantity Theory of Money it is clear that both the approaches suffer from certain inadequacies while explaining the value of money and the changes in it.

(i) The rate of interest is an important determinant of the price level in a country and the quantity equations give no importance to the rate of interest. This is a serious drawback in both the versions.

(ii) Both the versions seem to confuse 'cause' with the 'effect'. According to both the versions it is the changes in the price level which cause changes in the economic activities of the country. It is said that the trade cycle is caused by changes in the price level. However, the reality is that changes in the price level are the result and not the cause of the changes in economic activities.

(iii) The two versions do not provide us with solutions to deal with the short-term fluctuations in the price level. As pointed earlier, the quantity theory deals with the long-run changes in prices and fails when it comes to dealing with cyclical fluctuations in prices.

(iv) Both the versions of the quantity theory are incomprehensible as they fail to include all the determinants of the price level. Both the equations include only the immediate determinants like M, V, T, K and R. These determinants are important but the quantity equations throw no light on several institutional, psychological, technical and economic factors which exert a significant influence on the value of money.

(v) The quantity equations fail to explain the 'causal' process by which the price level (or the value of money) is determined. Both the versions present us with the final result, i.e., changes in the quantity of money affect the price level. Thus, both the equations present us with the final equilibrium without throwing any light on the process by which that equilibrium comes to be established.

(vi) Both the versions suggest that by regulating the supply of money, we can attain stability in the price level. But this may not be possible under all circumstances. For example, during the Great Depression of 1929, several governments attempted to raise prices through large increase in the supply of money but their efforts showed no success. Thus, it is clear that there is no direct and immediate functional relationship between quantity of money and the prices.

(vii) Critics mention that it is the income and not the quantity of money which is the determinant of the value of money. The sequence goes as follows: when income increases, it increases spending, resulting in greater velocity of the circulation of money, hence there is greater demand for goods and services and consequently higher the price level. Thus, it is the income rather than the quantity of money which is determinant of the value of money.

Keynes' Restatement of the Quantity Theory of Money

This is also known as Keynes' Theory of Money and Prices. The two approaches to the quantity theory of money – Fisher's and Cambridge- failed to clearly explain how *a change in the supply of money influences the price level.* Thus, it did not throw light on the causal process by which a change in the quantity of money brings about a change in the price level. Keynes attempted to explain this causal process in his *General Theory* by a reformulation of the quantity theory of money.

- The classicists held the view that increases in the supply of money *directly* increased the price level.
- Keynes held the view that the price level increased in response to an increase in money supply, not directly but *through the rate of interest*, income, output and employment.
- According to Keynes, the first impact of an increase in money supply lowers down the rate of interest. It is because more money is available to satisfy the liquidity preference of the community for the speculative motive. A lowered rate of interest tends to promote investment. Increased investments lead to increased incomes. And, with the process and *roundabout method* output and employment increases. This influences the prices, i.e., the prices of raw materials and other accessories and even increases the wages.
- In Keynes' view, increased money supply does not *directly* raise the price level. Thus, the influence of rate of interest on prices in response to the changes in the supply of money has been ignored by both the versions.
- Keynes discarded the assumption of the existence of full employment and had in fact started with a more realistic assumption, namely, that of unemployment.

- Suppose that there is a good deal of unemployment in the economy and the money supply is increased. The rate of interest will fall in response to the increased money supply and with unemployed resources, a lowered rate of interest would lead to an increase in investment and output. All additional increase in the supply of money will serve to mobilize the unemployed resources and increase the output till the point of *full employment* is reached. In such a situation wherein the expansion of money supply leads to increase in output will not increase the price level.
- *After the point of full employment is reached*, the output is static and now with the expansion of money supply will lead to increase in the price level.
- *Thus, true inflation may be said to begin when the elasticity of the supply of output in response to changes in the supply of money falls to zero. According to Keynes, true inflation begins only when the point of full employment has been reached.*
- At this point, any expansion of money supply would be immediately followed by an equivalent rise in the price level, assuming that V remains constant and Fisher's version becomes valid.
- But, when the price level is rising so rapidly (value of money falling), people would not like to keep money in their possession, i.e., they would like to part with money and 'V' goes up. After the point of full employment, M continues to increase and goes on increasing the 'V', leading to a situation referred to as *hyper inflation*.
- Even the Keynesian concept of liquidity preference can be used to explain the phenomenon of hyper inflation.
- Liquidity preference is another name for velocity of circulation. When liquidity preference (LP) reduces, the velocity 'V' rises. When the value of money falls (due to price level rise), LP goes down and hence people would not like to hold an asset whose value is progressively declining. The LP for the speculative motive also sharply declines. In this way, after the point of full employment, as money continues to expand, LP continues to decline, and lead to hyper inflation.
- Keynes' view that so long as the point of full employment has not reached; all increase in money supply would increase the output and not the price level.
  However, this Keynesian view is based on the assumptions that there is perfect elasticity of the supply of productive factors when there is less than full employment and production is not subject to diminishing returns or increasing costs.
  However, both the assumptions are unrealistic in practice. The supply of productive factors cannot be perfectly elastic in response to the increasing output, nor is production subject to diminishing returns. Thus, as the output rises, costs rise and thus increase the price level in response to the increase in money supply, even before the point of full employment. But such a rise in the price level cannot be called true inflation.

- Following causes can be enumerated for the pre-full employment inflation:

(1) **Money wages increase:** With increasing output, increases the demand for more and more workers. It leads to scarcity of labour force and trade unions, with their bargaining power are able to secure increased wages. This increased burden of higher wages on employers is passed on to the consumers in the form of higher prices.

(2) **Shortages in equipments and raw materials:** These shortages are due to the reason that all the resources of an economy do not reach the stage of full employment at the same time, i.e., some at an earlier stage and such resources' scarcity is faced. The resources that are scarce will register high price and increase the production cost and in turn raise the price of the finished product.

(3) **In the short run increasing costs operate:** As the volume of output increases, the cost per unit (average cost) goes up. The law of diminishing returns operate because: (a) new machinery and equipments cannot be increased immediately when the demand for output increases and hence the existing machines and equipments are put to stress by overworking through employment of more workers. (b) as the output increases, more labour may have to be engaged who may not be very competent in their work as the old experienced workers. Thus, the costs increases and returns diminish in the short run.

Conclusion: Keynes' Contribution to Quantity Theory of Money

1. **Keynes' version superior to Fisher's version:** Keynes' version enables us to look at inflation in its right perspective. According to Keynes only that expansion of money supply results in inflation that takes place after the point of full employment. Hence, Keynes' approach to quantity theory of money enables us to distinguish between inflationary and non-inflationary expansion of money supply. The danger of inflation becomes real if money expansion proceeds beyond the stage of full employment.

2. **True inflation:** According to Keynes' so long as there is unemployment, *employment* will change in the same proportion as the quantity of money, and when there is full employment, *prices* will change in the same proportion as the quantity of money. Any price rise before the point of full employment is not true inflation. True inflation comes into being only if money supply expansion continues even beyond the point of full employment.

3. **More realistic assumption:** Keynes' reformulated quantity theory of money was not based on unreal assumption of full employment. In fact, Keynes believed that full employment was an exception and it was existence of unemployment that allowed the increase in money supply to be absorbed in increased output and lead to no increase the price level.

4. **Indirect relation between prices and quantity of money:** The classical version established a direct relation between the prices and the quantity of money. Keynes pointed out that there is an indirect relation between prices and quantity of money. The changes in the quantity of money influenced the rate of interest, which in turn affected investment, output and prices. Thus, Keynes explained the real causal process that existed between the quantity of money and prices.

5. **Theory of money integrated with the theory of income, output:** It is Keynes who for the first time integrated the theory of money with the theory of value and theory of output. The classical economists had rigidly separated the monetary theory from the general economic theory. For Keynes the causal process was quite different. Money supply expansion in the context of unemployment, led first to an increase in the output. As the output continues to expand, certain new factors come into existence that leads to rise in costs. The costs rise due to inelastic supply of certain factors of production. This brings in the theory of value with costs, elasticity of supply and demand etc.

Despite the great merits, Keynes' reformulated quantity theory has its own drawbacks that result from unrealistic assumptions.

1. The theory assumes that the productive resources- land, labour, capital- are *perfectly elastic* in supply before the economy attains full employment. This is unrealistic because in an underdeveloped country these shortages appear much before the point of full employment is attained.

2. The theory assumes that the supply of productive factors is *perfectly inelastic* beyond the point of full employment. This assumption is far from being real.

3. The theory assumes that before the point of full employment, the effective demand increases in proportion to the increase in the quantity of money, failing which the output will not increase. This assumption, too, is totally unrealistic.

4. The causal process explained by Keynes between the quantity of money and price level is through rate of interest. In reality investment, output, income, employment, costs and prices will depend upon two other determinants, such as, marginal efficiency of capital (MEC) and the propensity to consume. For example, if MEC is low then even a lower rate of interest will not be able to induce any increase in investment, output, income and employment. Thus, until these two elements remain constant, the whole chain of causation may not work at all.

Despite these shortcomings, Keynes' theory of money and prices is superior to the traditional quantity theory.

Milton Friedman's Approach

Keynes gave a lot of importance to the relationship between the demand for money and the rate of interest. This is consistent with his liquidity preference theory of interest.

The result was that the relationship between the price-level and the demand for money was completely over-looked by the people.

In fact, the influence of the Keynesian analysis was so overwhelming that people have practically forgotten the quantity theory of money.

But in 1956, **Prof. Milton Friedman restated the quantity theory of money** and published an article on it. Once again, the quantity theory of money attracted the attention of several economists.

According to Friedman, the quantity theory of money is not a theory stating anything about price-level or production. *It is a theory about the demand for money.*

- This means that the meaning conveyed by the equation $M = \frac{PT}{V'}$ is acceptable to Friedman.
- This equation tries to state that the **demand for money** changes in the same direction and proportion to the change in the price-level.
- Similarly, the real income, i.e. T, is also a factor determining the demand for money. This is also acceptable to Friedman.
- But, the old belief that a change in income brings about a change in the demand for money in the *same direction and proportion*, is not acceptable to Friedman.
- Friedman thinks that an increase in income brings about an over-proportionate increase in the demand for money.
- Thus, the demand for money is like the demand for education and entertainment in Dr. Engel's law. Friedman thinks that money is a form of asset. But, while mentioning the determinants of the demand for money, he mentions one more determinants in addition to income and the price level. He calls this 'cost of holding money'. This cost is of two types:

(i) The loss incurred by that portion of interest which he might have earned if he had loaned out the same amount instead of keeping it with him and in the form of cash.

(ii) The second type of cost is equal to the rate of interest in the price level (because as the price-level increases, the value of money, kept in the form of cash, goes on decreasing).

Thus, according to Friedman, four factors determine the demand for money. They are:

(i) The price level;
(ii) The level of real income and output,;

(iii) The real interest, and

(iv) The rate of increase in the price level.

- The **supply of money** is completely independent.
- If the supply of money changes, the following are the chain of events which will follow :
- Let us assume that the economy is monetarily in equilibrium i.e. the supply of money and the demand for money *is equal* to each other.
- In such a state, let us assume that the central bank of the country purchases securities in the open market. This will increase the total supply of money. Similarly, the liquidity of banks will increase, and they will make an attempt to loan the additional funds obtained from the central bank.
- Individuals who have sold their securities to the central bank will try to invest their money in shares, bonds, debentures, etc. This will increase the demand for these assets and their prices will rise.
- The alternative assets to shares, debentures, etc. are buildings, landed properties, stocks of consumer goods etc. People may invest their money in these assets, which may increase their prices too.
- This will prompt producers to increase production, and gradually, this process may spread to other commodities. The increase in the supply of money will increase production and prices.
- The demand for money always moves in the same direction as prices. This will increase the demand for money. The above process continues *till the demand for money becomes equal to the supply of money.*
- Thus, if the supply of money increases, the money income (real income x price) will also increase. If the supply of money decreases, money income will also decrease.
- This approach of Prof. Friedman is based on the following two statements:

1. The direction of a change in the rate of interest and the supply of money is one and the same.
2. A change in the rate of interest has a greater influence on the demand for various assets, goods and services, than on demand for money.

Critical Evaluation of Milton Friedman's Approach

- Keynes has criticized the quantity theory of money. He was of the opinion that the demand for money was dependent on the price-level, real income and the rate of interest.
- Friedman and Keynes differed in their opinion. (a) The first difference is that Friedman thinks that the demand for money is a stable function of money income and rate of

interest expected in terms of money, but Keynes does not think so. (b) Secondly, Keynes thinks that the demand for money is extremely interest elastic, but Friedman thinks it is not so interest elastic.

- Keynes explanation of the effects of changes in the supply of money is different from Friedman's explanation.
- Lastly, the manner in which they have explained the changes in the supply of money which influence the rate of interest, are different. According to Keynes, if the supply of money increases, the rate of interest will fall. But considering to Friedman, an increase in the supply of money may reduce the rate of interest initially, but the increase in production and prices, which may follow immediately, will cause an increase in the rate of interest.

The following are the main objections raised against Friedman's approach by critics:

(1) In money, Friedman includes time deposits in banks. The critics object to this and say that if time deposits are excluded from definition of money, then the relationship between the total income and the demand for money will not be as taken by Friedman.

(2) The statement that the demand for money is less elastic with the rate of interest is also dependent on the above definition of money. If we exclude time deposits in money, and define money as, "money consists only of legal tender money and current deposits", then the demand for money will be interest elastic, as stated by Keynes. This means that the demand for money will have a greater influence on the changes in the rate of interest.

(3) Lastly, the critics have taken objection to the statement that an increase in the total supply of money increases the rate of interest. They say that equilibrium may be brought about even when the rate of interest is low. An increase in the rate of interest is not necessary to establish equilibrium.

Points to Remember

- Money is one of the greatest inventions of man.
- Till date, there is no agreement on the most fundamental of questions, as to "what is money?"
- According to Walker- "Money is what money does".
- According to Crowther – "Money is anything that is generally acceptable as a means of exchange and that at the same time acts as a measure and as a store of value".
- Different approaches have been presented to define money:
  - ➤ The Conventional Definition;
  - ➤ The Chicago Approach;

- ➢ The Gurley-Shaw Approach;
- ➢ The Central Bank Approach.
- **Functions of money can be classified under different headings, namely:**
  - ➢ **Primary functions:** (i) Money as a medium of exchange; (ii) Money as a standard measure of value.
  - ➢ **Secondary functions:** (i) Money as a store of value; (ii) Money used for deferred payments; (iii) Money as a means for transfer of value.
  - ➢ **Contingent functions:** (i) Money enhances productivity of capital; (ii) Money forms the basis of credit; (iii) Money helps in distribution of social income; (iv) Money equalizes MU and MP.
  - ➢ **Additional/ Other functions:** (i) Money assists in repayment capacity; (ii) Money is general purchasing power; (iii) Money imparts liquidity to capital.
- **Value of money:** The value of money is a relative concept. It lies in its 'buying capacity'.
- Quantity Theory of Money has two versions:
  - ➢ (a) The Cash Transaction Approach.
  - ➢ (b) The Cash Balance Approach.
- The Cash Transaction Approach is the Fisher's version. He presented the 'Equation of Exchange' as $MV = PT$ or $P = MV/T$.
- With bank money the expanded equation of exchange is –
  $MV + M'V' = PT$ or $P = MV + M'V'/T$.
- Fisher's version is based on the function of money as a *medium of exchange*.
- Fisher's equation is based on several assumptions that had to face scathing criticism despite the fact that the theory occupies an important place in economics.
- The Cash Balance Approach is represented by various Cambridge economists.
- The Cash Balance Approach is based on the function of money- money as a *store of value*.
- Cambridge economists like Prof. Marshall, Pigou, Cannan, Robertson and J.M.Keynes have presented this version.
- **Marshall's equation:** $M = KPY$ or $P = KY/M$
- **Pigou's equation:** $P = KR/M$ or $P = M/KR$
- To include bank deposits, the equation is $P = KR/M \{C + h(1-C)\}$
- **Robertson's equation:** $P = M/KT$
- **Keynes' equation:** $n = pk$ or $p = n/k$
- **Expanded equation:** $n = p(K + rK')$ or $p = n/(K + rK')$
- There are certain similarities and differences between the two approaches of the Quantity Theory of Money.
- Both the versions, observed in general review, depict certain limitations such as:
  - ➢ Rate of interest as determinant on the price level is neglected.

- The cause-effect relationship is not clear in the two versions.
- Both the approaches emphasize the long-run analysis and ignore the short-run analysis.
- Both the versions of the Quantity Theory are incomprehensive, i.e., they do not include all determinants of the price level.
- 'Final equilibrium' has been depicted in the two versions without explaining the process of it.
- It is income and not the quantity of money that determines the value of money, as explained in both the versions.

Multiple Choice Questions

1. The relationship between value of money and general price level is:
   (a) Direct
   (b) Indirect
   (c) Proportional
   (d) Inverse

2. Other things remaining the same, the quantity of money in Fisher's approach has:
   (a) Direct proportional relationship with price level
   (b) No relation with the value of money
   (c) Direct proportional relationship with value of money
   (d) Inverse proportional relationship with price level

3. Keynes' contribution to the Quantity Theory of money lies in:
   (a) Emphasis on immediate causes of changes in the price level
   (b) Integrates the 'Theory of money with the theory of value and the theory of output'
   (c) Considers Money supply as an important determinant of price level
   (d) Provides long-term analysis

4. The volume of K in Cambridge equation depends on:
   (a) Money supply
   (b) Interest rate
   (c) Real national income
   (d) Velocity of circulation

5. One of the following is not an assumption for Quantity Theory of Money
   (a) Constant velocity of circulation
   (b) The price-level is not an assumption for Quantity Theory exchange
   (c) Volume of transaction does not remain constant
   (d) Constant ratio between legal tender money and credit money

6. In the equation P = MV + M'V' /T which element is not assumed to be constant?
   (a) P
   (b) T
   (c) M
   (d) V

7. Which of the following statements is true for Cambridge approach when compared to Fisher's approach?
   (a) Dependence on interest rates for cash balance
   (b) More importance of money supply
   (c) Long-term analysis
   (d) More importance of demand for money.

Answers:

   1 - (d), 2 - (a), 3 - (b), 4 - (c), 5 - (c), 6 - (c), 7 - (d)

Questions for Discussion

1. Explain, with comments, the various definitions of money.
2. Discuss in detail the functions of money.
3. Write short notes on:
   (a) Primary functions of money; (b) Contingent functions of money.
4. What do you mean by 'value of money'? Discuss its relationship with the price level.
5. Write in brief how changes in the value of money are measured? What are the difficulties in measuring them?
6. Critically examine Fisher's Equation of Exchange.
7. How far is the cash balance approach superior to the cash transactions approach?
8. Compare and contrast the cash transactions and cash balance approaches to the value of money.
9. Bring out the distinction between 'V' in Fisher's equation and 'K' in Cambridge equation.
10. Under the Cash-Balance approach, how does Keynes' equation differ from other equations?
11. Critically examine the Cambridge approach to the Quantity Theory of Money.

Chapter 3...

Theory of Income and Employment

Contents ...
3.1 Say's Law of Market
    3.1.1 Propositions/Implications of Say's Law
    3.1.2 Critical Evaluation of Say's Law
3.2 Keynesian Theory of Income and Employment
- Points to Remember
- Multiple Choice Questions
- Questions for Discussion

Learning Objectives ...
➢ To study the theory of income and employment as given by Classical economists
➢ To understand the argument as presented by J. B. Say "Supply creates its own demand"
➢ To learn about the Keynesian theory of Income and Employment
➢ To understand the factors that influence income and employment in an economy
➢ To study about the most significant concept of Keynes – Multiplier
➢ To understand the propagation of income through Multiplier

Introduction

The determination of output, income and employment in an economy has a crucial place in macro economics. It has occupied the attention of a number of economists. The two major versions of the theory are: **(i) The Classical Theory (which has Say's Law of Market as its core) and (ii) Keynes' Theory.**

Contents of Classicism

The body of economic thought related to a galaxy of economists as Adam smith, J. S. Mill, Alfred Marshall and Pigou is often regarded as the Classical Theory. By Classical economics, Keynes means the traditional principles of economic theory which have been handed down from generations since the time of Ricardo. The various economists who have evolved and refined these principles are often referred to as Classical economists. When Keynes speaks of 'classical theory', he means 'the followers of Ricardo, those who adopted and perfected the theory of Ricardian economics'.

The Classical Theory of Employment

The Classical Theory of Employment assumes that there is always full employment of labour. In fact, full employment is considered to be the normal situation and if at any time any lapses are found from full employment, it is considered as an abnormal situation. Thus, even if there is not actual full employment at any time, the classical theory asserts that there is always a tendency in the economy towards full employment.

The assumptions of the Classical theory of employment are as follows:

(a) There is an existence of full employment even without inflation.
(b) There is a free market price system.
(c) Wages and prices are flexible.
(d) Existence of perfect competition in labour and product markets.
(e) Labour is homogenous.
(f) There is a laissez-faire capitalist economy. It is a 'closed' economy (no foreign sector).
(g) There is close coordination between money wages and real wages.
(h) Since "Supply creates its own demand", there can never by any deficiency in demand, therefore no over-production.
(i) Total output of the economy is divided between consumption and investment expenditure.
(j) Technology and capital stock are constant in the short-run.

It is the free play of economic forces that brings about the fuller utilization of economic resources including labour. Any interference with the free play of market forces shall fail to bring about full employment.

> **Thus, the Classical economists advocate that the Government should keep its 'hands off' the economic field if there is to be full employment of labour and other resources.**

The basic assumption of the Classical Theory that there is always full employment of resources is justified in classical economics by Say's Law of Market. In fact, this law is the core of Classical economic theory.

3.1 Say's Law of Market

J. B. Say (1767 – 1822), a French economist, propounded this law in his book entitled *'Traité d'économie Politique'* which later became a very popular treatise on political economy in France.

Say's Law of Markets is the core of the Classical theory of employment. In the 19th century, French economist J. B. Say enunciated the proposition that *"supply creates its own demand."* Therefore, general over-production and the problem of unemployment in the economy are logical impossibilities.

Say disbelieved those writers and businessmen who thought that over-production and unemployment were common occurrences. He rejected this view by his proposition, *"Supply creates its own demand."*

In Say's own words, *"It is production which creates market for goods."*

He explains that the main source of demand is the flow of factor incomes generated from the main source itself.

When any new productive process is initiated and certain output results, the demand for that output is simultaneously generated on account of the payment of remuneration to the factors of production.

Thus, every output that is brought into existence, injects an equivalent amount of purchasing power in circulation, which ultimately leads to its sale, so that *there is no surplus output or over-production.*

The above explanation of Say's Law presents the following important facts about the law:

1. **Production creates market (demand) for goods:** The process of the manufacture of a motor car also brings into being an equivalent amount of purchasing power in the form of wages, profits, etc., which would ultimately lead to its purchase. Hence, there can be no overproduction of any commodity at any time. This is the essence of Say's Law.

2. **Barter System as its basis:** In its original form the law is applicable to a barter economy where goods are ultimately sold for goods. Hence, whatever is produced is ultimately consumed in the economy. In other words, people produce goods for their own use to sustain their consumption levels. According to **Prof. Hansen**, Say's Law is *"a description of a free-exchange economy"*. It throws light on the truth that the main source of demand is the flow of factor income generated from the process of production itself. Thus, *the existence of money does not alter the basic law.*

3. **General Overproduction impossible:** Say is prepared to admit that the supply of a particular commodity may exceed its demand temporarily due to incorrect calculations of a particular entrepreneur. But, general overproduction is impossible. If general overproduction is not possible, there is no possibility of general unemployment.

The Classical economists, following Say's Law, assume that there does not exist unemployment, i.e. they assume the existence of full employment at any time.

It is to be understood that the *'full employment'* assumed by the classicists is consistent with the existence of voluntary unemployment.

The classicists are prepared to admit the existence of a certain amount of 'frictional unemployment' in their 'full employment society'. But, what they are not prepared to admit is the existence of 'involuntary' unemployment.

When it is pointed out to the classical economists that, in an actual society, involuntary unemployment does exist and millions remain unemployed although they are willing to work, the classicists answer that such unemployment is due to *'interferences'* with the free working of the economic system. Such interferences can be collective bargaining by trade unions to raise the wages, or government intervention when it assures the minimum wages, of the payment of doles to the unemployed, i.e., unemployment insurance.

4. **Labour Market:** *Prof. Pigou*, the greatest modern representative of classicism, argues that the removal of interferences and the existence of free competition would force the wages down until it is profitable for employers to engage everyone who wants to work. Thus, the classicists believe that involuntary unemployment is due to the rigidity of the wage structure. If the wages are lowered sufficiently at a time of unemployment, all involuntary unemployment would disappear. Hence, the classicists suggest that a cure for unemployment is to ensure the free working of the economic system and removal of all sorts of 'interferences' whether by the central or by the state government. *Thus, free and unrestricted working of an economic system would ensure non-existence of overproduction or unemployment.*

5. **Saving – Investment equality:** The owners of the factors receive income in the form of rent, wages and interest that is not all spent on consumption but some proportion of it is saved, which is automatically invested for further production. Hence, investment in production is saving which helps to create demand for goods in the market. Thus, saving-investment equality is maintained to avoid general overproduction.

6. **Rate of Interest as an equalizing factor:** Say's Law of Market regards rate of interest as the equilibrating factor between saving and investment. Any disequilibrium between the two- saving and investment- the equality is maintained through the mechanism of the rate of interest. For example, if at any given time investment exceeds savings, the rate of interest will rise. This will encourage savings and discourage investment, thus bringing equality between savings and investment. On the other hand, when savings is more than investment, the rate of interest falls, investment increases and savings decline till the two are equal at the new interest rate.

3.1.1 Propositions/Implications of Say's Law

The important implications of Say's Law that present the true picture of the market law are:

1. **Supply creates its own demand:** The first implication of the law is that there is automatic adjustment of every element with the working of the economy, i.e., if supply is there, it creates its own demand. For example, if the supply increases, demand will also increase and there will be adjustment between the two economic forces. The government should not interfere with the working of the economic system.

2. **General overproduction impossible:** The second implication is that general overproduction is impossible. As J. S. Mill observed, "whatever the amount of the annual produce, it can never exceed the amount of the annual demand." Thus, as production increases, the incomes of the concerned factors also increase. As a result, new demand is created and increased stock is sold off in the market.
3. **General unemployment is not possible:** The third implication of this law is that since general overproduction is not possible there shall be no general unemployment. And even if there is some unemployment, then it shall be purely of temporary nature and it will automatically disappear in the due course of time.
4. **Proper utilization of resources:** The fourth implication of Say's Law is that the employment of the unemployed resources will pay its own way. When unemployed resources are employed, they help to produce goods and services in the economy. As such national income increases and it becomes possible to pay the newly employed factors out of it. Thus, the economy suffers no loss by employing the unemployed resources for production. In fact, it gains, as they pay for themselves when employed.
5. **Automatic Mechanism:** The fifth implication of Say's Law states that the economic system is automatic and works itself without any external stimulus. Thus, there is a built-up flexibility in the economic system. Even if some obstacles crop up, the system gets over them in due course of time. The government should not interfere with the working of the economic system. In fact, the government should keep its hands off and leave the prices, wages and interest free to adjust itself to the changing situation.
6. **Saving as a social virtue:** All factor income is spent in buying goods which they help to produce. Whatever is saved is automatically invested for further production. In other words, saving is a social virtue.
7. **Perfect Competition:** J. B. Say's Law of Market is based on the assumption of perfect competition in the labour and product markets.
8. **Role of money as neutral:** The law is based on the proposition of a barter system where goods are exchanged for goods. But, it is assumed that the role of money is neutral. Money does not affect the production process.

Determination of the Level of Output and Employment (Classical Version)

The Classical Theory of Income and Employment, based on the short-run, can be explained through three stages:

(a) When there is no saving and investment;
(b) With saving and investment;
(c) Introduction of money and prices.

(a) When there is no saving and investment, the entire income will be spent on consumer goods produced. Thus, quantity demanded will be equal to the supply of output produced.

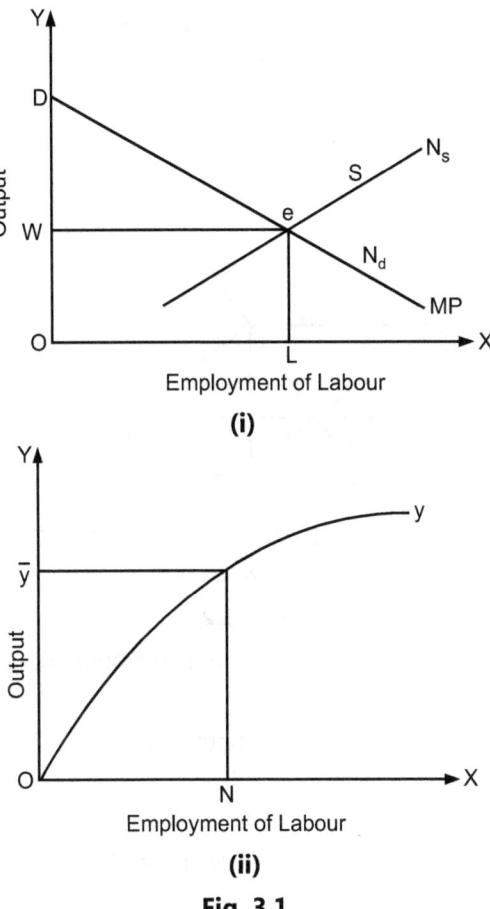

Fig. 3.1

In **Fig. 3.1 (ii)** wages earned by ON quantity of labour employed and profits earned by producers will be spent on OY output. Thus, the expenditure on output and value of the output produced will be equal.

There is full employment of labour and hence there is no possibility of involuntary unemployment. The real wage will change quickly to bring about equality between demand for and supply of labour.

Now, even if a part of income is not spent (i.e. it is saved), there will be no deficiency of aggregate demand. This is because that all savings, according to classical economists, will be invested by the producers. What is not spent on consumer goods will be saved and investment expenditure made by entrepreneurs equals the amount of savings.

This equality between savings and investment is brought about by changes in the *rate of interest*. Interest, in turn, is determined by the supply of savings on one hand and demand for investment on the other (N_s and N_d). This equality between savings and investment brought about by change in interest rate would then guarantee that the aggregate demand for output would be equal to aggregate supply. In this way, full employment of labour would prevail.

(b) With Saving and investment:

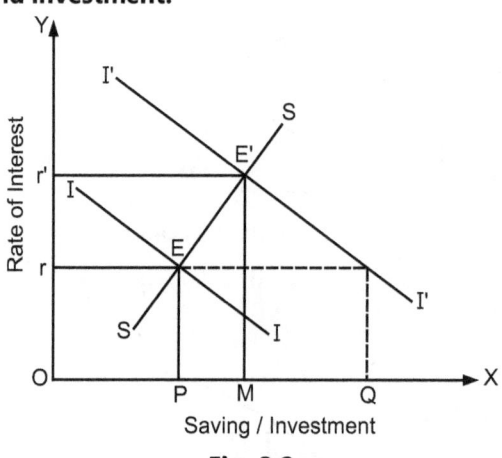

Fig. 3.2

In **Fig. 3.2**, SS is the Savings curve, I I is the investment curve. SS and I I are equal at point E and Or is the rate of interest.

When investment increases, the I I curve shifts to the right I'I'. At Or rate of interest the investment OQ is greater than OP saving.

Saving remaining the same, an increase in investment will result into a rise in interest rate. At Or' rate of interest SS curve intersects I'I' at E'. As a result, both savings and investment are equal at OM.

(c) With introduction of money and prices: The classical economists believe that, in a monetary economy, full employment will prevail. In terms of quantity theory of money (Fisher's equation) MV = PT, it is assumed that the aggregate output (volume of transactions) remains constant at full employment level. The quantity of money determines the price level of output and it also determines the money wage consistent with a given real wage.

Real wage is the ratio of money wages and the price level, i.e.

Real Wage (WR) = W/P

Here, W = money wage; P = price level.

The wage price combination influences real wages which are consistent with the full employment level.

Pigou's Version

Pigou believed that under free competition the tendency of the economic system is to automatically provide full employment in the labour market.

In Pigou's words, "with perfect and free competition……there will always be at work a strong tendency for wage rates to be so related to the demand that everybody is employed."

The entire proposition can be put in the equation as given below:

N = qy / W

Here, N = number of workers; q = fraction of income earned as wages; y = national income; W = wage rate.

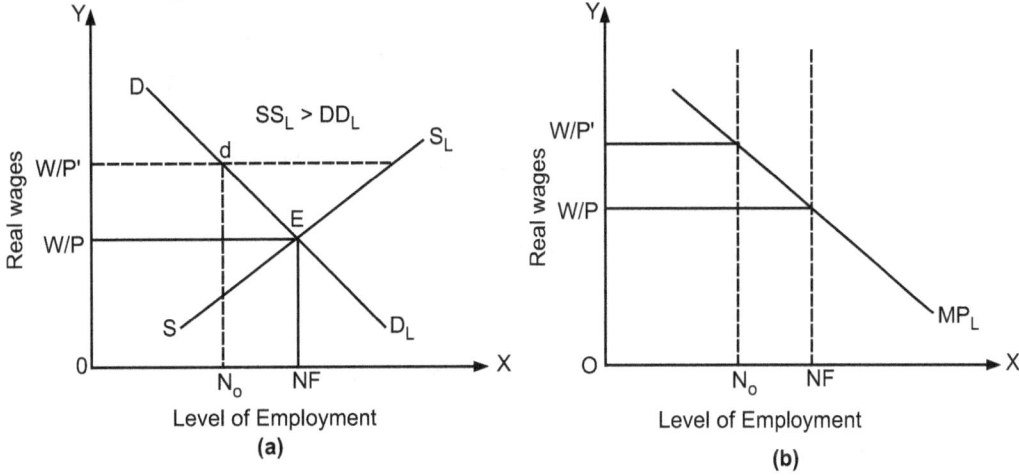

Fig. 3.3

In **Fig. 3.3** (a) we see that if real wages W/P' is at a higher level, supply of labour exceeds demand for labour by ds, resulting in unemployment to the extent of NoNF. If wage is reduced to W/P, unemployment disappears and full employment level is attained.

In **Fig. 3.3** (b), MP_L is the marginal product of labour which slopes downwards as more labour is employed. Since every worker gets wages equal to his marginal product, as such, the full employment level NF is reached when the wage rate falls from W/P' to W/P. Thus, *the key to full employment is a reduction in money wages.*

To conclude,
- In the Classical model of employment, changes in money wages and real wages are directly related and are proportional.
- The relationship is based on the assumption that prices are proportional to the quantity of money.
- In a perfectly competitive economy, a reduction in money wages reduces the cost of production and prices and increases the demand for goods.

> - With wage cut, more labour will be employed to increase the production as total output is an increasing function of the number of workers.
> - As employment increases, total output is an increasing function of the number of workers.
> - As employment increases, total output increases till full employment is reached.
> - Due to the operation of Say's Law, the full employment level of output will create demand to that level. Thus, under normal perfect competitive conditions, full employment will be maintained without inflation.

3.1.2 Critical Evaluation of Say's Law

Say's Law has been severely criticized from two angles:

1. The supply of goods does not create its own demand (i.e., from the production point of view).
2. The supply of labour does not automatically adjust itself to its demand (i.e., from the employment point of view).

In detail we shall discuss the critical evaluation below:

1. **According to J. B. Say, "every supply creates its own demand."** It implies that every production is accompanied by the necessary purchasing power that ensures its disposal. Thus, general overproduction is impossible. This law is based on an assumption that people spend their entire income to buy goods and services and save nothing, and whatever is produced is ultimately sold off in the market.
   - Critics point out that this assumption is way away from reality because the fact is that people do not spend their entire income and some part of the income is saved for future use.
   - To the extent of the savings done, *reduction* will take place in the present demand for the goods and production will remain unsold to that extent.
   - Thus, 'savings' constitute a sort of *'leakage'*. The withdrawal of purchasing power from the income stream, due to savings, results in deficiency of aggregate demand. *This leads to overproduction in the economy.*

However, the classical economists were not disturbed by the criticism. According to them, if the community saved, that saving would soon be converted into investment and the investment would have the same effect on the economy as expenditure on goods.

They further argued that an increase of savings would reduce the rate of interest and in turn step up investment (with a fall in the rate of interest).

Thus, the entire savings would be converted into investment expenditure and there would be no deficiency of aggregate demand and Say's Law would hold good.

In **Prof. McConnell's** words, "As the classical economists saw it, the economy was analogous to a gigantic bath tub wherein the watermark measured the level of output and employment. Any leakage down the drain of savings would be returned to the tub through the tap of investment. This had to be the case because the interest rate connected the drain pipe and the tap."

Critics mention that this argument of the classicists depends upon a misconception regarding the role of interest rate as neither saving nor investment is much influenced by the rate of interest.

It is well-known fact that the main determinant and influencing factor of investment is not the rate of interest but the *expectations of profit.* If the business prospects are conducive, investment is encouraged *even if the rate of interest that the businessman has to pay is high.* On the other hand, a fall in the rate of interest will not automatically push up the volume of investment. Hence, there is every possibility of a deficiency of demand arising in the economy as a result of saving.

To conclude, every supply may not create its own demand. The critics of classicism principles demonstrated the falsified conclusions of Say's Law during the Great Depression (1929-1932) when overproduction became a universal phenomenon in all the capitalist countries of the world.

2. **J. B. Say argued that since overproduction was impossible, general unemployment was also impossible:** *Say clearly pointed out that the supply of labour would automatically adjust itself to its demand and thus involuntary unemployment was impossible.*

   Everyone who was desirous of getting a job at the current wage rate would be able to secure it and hence there would be no unemployment. Even if there was some percent of unemployment, it would disappear as wages would fall and demand for labour would rise.

This thesis was unacceptable to the critics of classicists. They pointed out that unemployment is found in almost all the capitalist nations and at times it is of intense nature and of long duration. Even a reduction in the wage level does not cure the situation. On the other hand, it may worsen the situation, as with reduction in wages, purchasing power reduces and leads to deficiency in aggregate demand, overproduction and more unemployment.

3. **Money is not neutral:** *Say's Law of Market is based on a barter system and ignores the role of money in the system.* According to Say, money does not affect the economic activities of the market.

   On the other hand, Keynes has given due importance to money. He regards money as a medium of exchange. Money is held for income and business motives.

Individuals hold money for unforeseen contingencies while businessmen keep cash in reserve for future activities.

4. **State Intervention:** *Say's Law is based on the existence of laissez-faire policy.*
Keynes has highlighted the need for state intervention in case of general overproduction and mass unemployment for adjusting supply and demand within the economy through fiscal and monetary measures.

5. **Self-adjustment not possible:** According to Say's Law, full employment is maintained by an automatic and self-adjusting mechanism in the long-run.

Keynes believes that "in long run, we are all dead." Further, he stated that it is not the automatic adjustment process which removes unemployment but it is an increase in the rate of investment which cures unemployment.

Criticism of Classical Theory of Employment

Keynes turned away from Classical belief and severely criticized these principles.

1. **Rate of interest as equality factor:** Keynes did not agree with the classical view that savings and investment were equal at the full employment level and in case of any disequilibrium; the equality could be achieved by the mechanism of rate of interest.

   According to Keynes, level of savings depends upon the level of income and not on the rate of interest. Similarly, investment is determined not only by the rate of interest but by marginal efficiency of capital (MEC). Keynes argues that even a low rate of interest cannot increase investment if MEC (business expectations) are low.

2. **Laissez-faire policy:** Keynes did not agree with the classical view that the laissez-faire policy was essential for an automatic and self-adjusting process of full employment equilibrium.

   Keynes argues that a capitalist system was not automatic and self-adjusting due to its non-equalitarian (inequality) structure of the economy. Hence, under such conditions, it is not laissez-faire but state intervention that is essential for adjusting supply and demand within the economy through its monetary (by banking system) and fiscal measures (by the government).

3. **Economic system as self-adjusting:** The classical idea that the economic system was self-adjusting was derived directly from Say's Law of Market, which states that supply always creates its own demand, and there could be neither overproduction nor underproduction.

   Keynes refused to accept Say's formula. Due to the non-egalitarian structure of society, there are two main classes – the rich and the poor and the wealth is unequally distributed between them. The rich have too much of wealth but do not consume it. On the other hand, the poor have too little wealth and cannot meet all their requirements.

Thus, national consumption cannot keep pace with national production and it results in deficient aggregate demand, i.e., in overproduction and unemployment.

It is an erroneous analysis on part of classical economists who assert that there can never be overproduction and general unemployment.

The economic system is never self-adjusting; in fact state intervention is necessary to bring about adjustment between supply and demand.

4. **Wage- flexibility:** Keynes strongly opposed Pigou's plea for wage-flexibility as a means of promoting employment at the time of depression.

   Keynes was in favour of wage – rigidity to promote and expand employment. For example, in a particular industry (say textile industry), assume that the employers resort to wage cuts to lower their costs. Reduction in wages will lower their costs; prices will have to be reduced. The demand will increase; employment has to be increased to produce this increased output. Thus, wage cut increases employment. So far so good and the classical analysis is perfectly valid up to this point.

   But, if conclusions of particular industry wage cut is extended to *general wage-cut*, i.e., in all industries, the costs in all industries would fall, but that would not increase effective demand because the purchasing power in the hands of the workers would be curtailed and aggregate effective demand would decrease and reduce the volume of employment. Thus, a general wage-cut would actually lessen the volume of employment.

5. **Reduction in money wages:** Keynes opposed money wage cuts on the ground that they were economically undesirable, leading to a general decline in the effective aggregate demand.

   If general unemployment was due to money wages that were too high, the solution would not be to cut money wages but to cut worker's *real wages* by raising prices of wage goods through monetary inflation.

   Keynes voted for reduction in real wages due to two main reasons – (i) the workers were less agitated over the cut in real wages than in money wages; (ii) cut in money wages could be opposed by workers and could be resisted by strike action, but cut in real wages could not be the subject matter of a strike against the employer.

   Due to all these reasons, Keynes consistently opposed any cut in money wages.

6. **Unrealistic approach:** Keynes attacked classicism for its unrealistic approach to the problem faced by the capitalist world.

   Pigou objected to the present day state interference with the free working of the economic system. He argued that it were these "interferences" which hindered the free working of the economic system and caused unemployment in the economy. And, if the government *kept its hands off*, if "interferences" were done away with, the economic system would begin to function smoothly and automatically, thus ensuring full employment of labour and other resources.

Keynes discarded this logic as a faulty argument because even if we wish, we cannot do away with these "interferences" as these government interferences are part and parcel of the modern capitalist system.

Thus, the complete classical approach is unrealistic, out-of-date, and obsolete and is difficult to be accepted in the changed conditions of today or even tomorrow.

Keynes' Departure from Classicism

Keynes made several radical departures from the principles of Classicism, as discussed below:-

1. **Short-term equilibrium:** Keynes attached great importance to the short-term equilibrium and opposed the classical insistence upon long-term equilibrium. This was a radical departure and made economics a more realistic science.

2. **Spending as a virtue:** Classicists insisted on saving and thrift as it led to capital formation. Keynes advocated spending and thriftlessness during depression. For Keynes, spending was a virtue and saving was an unmitigated evil. Keynes launched a vigorous attack on thriftiness and saving both in his 'Treatise' and in his 'general Theory' as it led to curtailment of effective aggregate demand and to unemployment.

3. **Universal in application – a 'General Theory':** Keynes' theory was a 'General Theory' and not a special theory. That is, it was applicable to all situations – full employment, less than full employment, inflation, deflation, etc. On the other hand, classical theory was applicable only to the full employment situation.

4. **Liquidity preference:** Classical economists believed that interest was the reward for waiting, time-preference and the rate of interest was determined by the intersection of saving and investment. Keynes departed from this belief to argue that rate of interest was determined by the interaction of liquidity preference and supply of money.

5. **Functional Budget:** The classical economists favoured a balanced budget. Keynes believed that the budgeting should be adjusted to the requirements of the economy, i.e., if the level of output and employment was low, the government should adopt a deficit budget.

6. **Macro approach:** Keynes departed from classicism by giving a 'macro' flavour to the economic theory as the old traditional classical analysis was cast in purely 'micro' terms. Keynes' work contained the first systematic treatment of national income or aggregative income. Keynes went further to integrate national income with his theory of employment, interest and money. This is a more realistic approach.

7. **Underemployment equilibrium:** The classical assumption is of existence of full employment. Keynes argued that in actual society, there could never be full employment, but something less than full employment.
8. **Wage-cut and employment:** Keynes made another radical departure from the classical track on the question of relationship between wage-cut and employment. Keynesian economics brought about a transformation in this context. Classicists argued that wage-cut had a favourable effect on the volume of employment. But, today, due to Keynes' theory, economic theorists are now not so easily convinced of the favourable effects of wage-cutting on employment.
9. **Dynamic elements:** Keynes diverged from the Classicists by including dynamic elements in his theory, particularly in the form of expectations which plays an important role in the determination of Marginal Efficiency of Capital (M.E.C). Thus, Keynes gave a dynamic flavour to the 'general Theory'.
10. **Economic of government:** In Robinson's words, "Keynes' most significant contribution was his success in relating academic economics to the economics of government." In short, he tried to make his theory serve as a guide to the government in the execution of economic policies. For example, Keynes' remedies of cheap money and public works programme for a depressed economy are well-known. Keynes was primarily a 'depression economist'. Keynes' work has not only theoretical importance but also practical implications.

3.2 Keynesian Theory of Income and Employment

Introduction

The core principle of Keynes' theory of employment is effective demand.

In a capitalist economy, the level of employment depends on effective demand. Keynes' attributes unemployment *"to a lack of effective demand, to a deficiency of expenditure on consumption and investment."*

Determination of Employment

Keynes measures the total output of an economy in terms of employment. Thus, greater the output, the greater will be the employment and vice versa.

On the other hand, the total output (i.e. national output) depends upon effective demand.

Effective demand comprises of: (a) Consumption demand and (b) Investment demand.

Consumption demand is demand for consumption goods and Investment demand is demand for capital goods.

Effective demand determines output and output determines employment, then it can be said that it is *effective demand that determines the volume of employment.*

It is clear that if unemployment is present, it is due to lack of sufficient effective demand. *To cure unemployment, the remedy is to increase effective demand.*

A common feature experienced in a capitalistic economy is the presence of unemployment, except in war time. It is thus clear that a deficiency of aggregate effective demand is a normal feature of capitalism.

Now, the question arises as to why total effective demand is deficient in a capitalistic economy? The reason is that as the national income increases, total consumption does not increase in the *same proportion* as the rise in total income. Thus, a gap arises between the total income and total consumption and it is to be filled by an increase in investment.

Therefore, to promote employment, effective demand should be increased by increasing investment.

Economic activity fluctuates from year to year. In some years normal growth does not occur. Firms find themselves unable to sell all of the goods and services they have to offer, so they cut back on production, workers are laid off, unemployment rises, and factories are left idle. With the economy producing fewer goods and services, real GDP and other measures of income fall. Such a period of falling incomes and rising unemployment is called a recession (if it is relatively mild) and depression (if it is more severe).

What causes short-run fluctuations in economic activity? Although there remains some debate among economists about how to analyze short-run fluctuations most economists use the model of *aggregate demand and aggregate supply.*

Aggregate Demand and Aggregate Supply

The concept of effective demand will now be analyzed.

Effective demand is determined by two factors, namely "Aggregate Demand Function" (ADF) and "Aggregate Supply Function" (ASF).

How do different forces interact to determine overall economic activity?

Fig. 3.4 shows the relationship among the relationship among the different variable inside the macro economy.

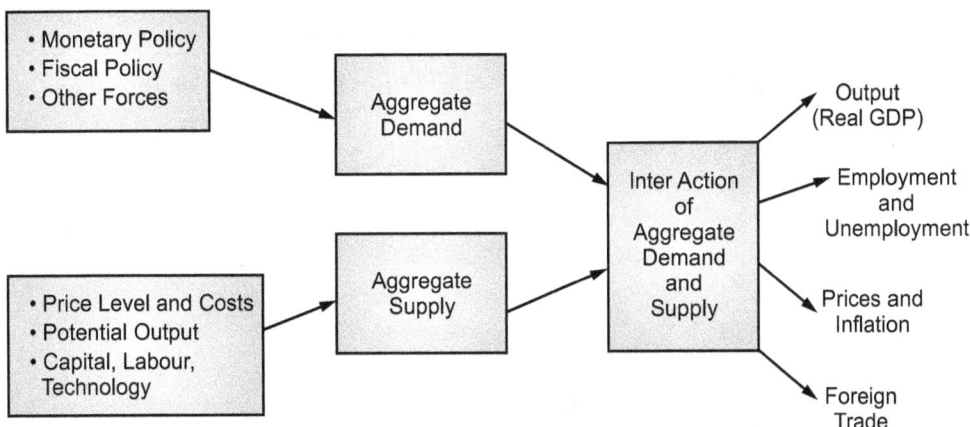

Fig. 3.4: Flow-chart Showing Relationship among Different Variables Inside Macro Economy

The flow-chart separates variables into two groups- (i) those influencing aggregate supply; (ii) and those influencing aggregate demand. These two groups help us to understand what determines the levels of output, prices and employment.

Aggregate Demand (AD):

Aggregate Demand (AD) refers to the total amount that different sectors in the economy willingly spend in a given period.

AD is the sum of spending by consumers (C), businesses (I) and governments (G) and it depends on (i) the level of prices, (ii) monetary policy, (iii) fiscal policy and (iv) other factors.

Thus, the total purchases are affected by the prices at which goods are offered, by exogenous forces like wars and weather and by government policies.

Aggregate Demand Function (ADF) "is a schedule of the various amounts of money which entrepreneurs in the economy expect from the **sale** of their output at varying levels of employment."

ADF refers to the **receipts** of the entrepreneurs in an economy.

ADF can be defined as, "The maximum expected sales proceeds from different levels of output." It is the maximum that consumers are willing to pay for different levels of output. In other words, it represents the total revenue (expected) from the sale of various levels of output.

However, the capacity of the individuals to pay would depend on the level of income, as the level of income in an economy itself depends on the level of output and employment.

In short, ADF is a *positive* function of the level of output and employment, i.e., as output increases, the aggregate demand price also increases.

We can depict this above mentioned relationship in the given aggregate demand schedule (Table 3. 1).

Macro Economic Analysis — Theory of Income & Employment

Table 3.1 : Aggregate Demand Schedule

Levels of Output/Employment (in units)	Maximum Expected Sales Proceeds (in ₹)
10	350
20	500
30	650
40	800
Full employment level {50	950
{50	1100

In the above schedule (Table 3. 1), we observe that as output (i.e. employment) goes on increasing, the expected sales proceeds (i.e. expected receipts to entrepreneurs) go on increasing. After the level of full employment is reached, the demand price (or expected sales proceeds) goes on increasing but output (employment) remains the same. In our illustration, we can assume 50 units as the full employment level.

In **Fig. 3.5**, we observe that ADF curve slopes upwards from left to right with an indication of a positive function between ADF and level of output/income/employment.

In **Fig. 3.5** it is point (A) where the ADF curve begins, shows OA as autonomous consumption, i.e. even at zero level income, some consumption does take place.

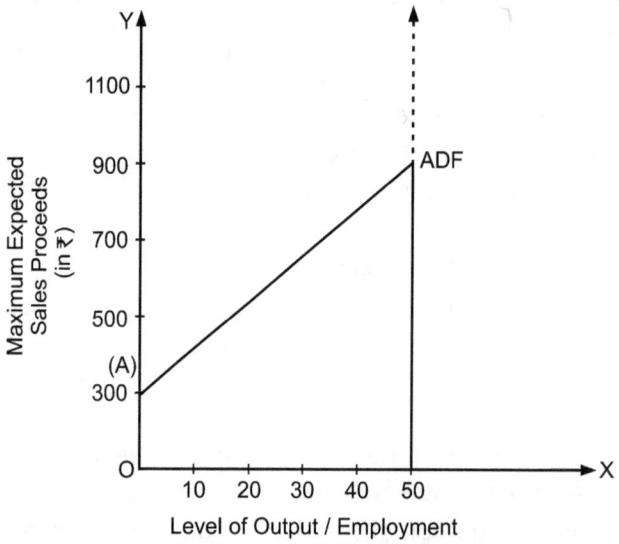

Fig. 3.5 : Level of Output/Employment

In **Fig. 3.5**, we observe that initially, as the levels of output/employment increases, the minimum expected receipts (or total costs) also go on increasing till the level of full employment is reached. After this point, output/employment remains the same, but the total costs go on increasing. Hence, ASF slopes upwards from left to right and later becomes vertical.

Aggregate Supply (AS):

Aggregate supply refers to the total quantity of goods and services that the country's entrepreneurs are willingly to produce and sell in a given period.

Aggregate Supply (AS) depends on (i) the price level that entrepreneurs can charge; (ii) on economy's capacity or potential output; (iii) potential output depends on availability of productive inputs (labour and capital) and managerial and technical efficiency with which those inputs are combined.

Aggregate Supply Function (ASF) is a "schedule of the various amounts of money which the entrepreneurs in an economy must receive from the sale of output at varying levels of employment."

Thus, ASF represents the **costs.** In general, entrepreneurs would like to sell everything they can produce at high prices.

No rational producer would accept a price lower than his cost of production. What is true to an individual producer is true to all entrepreneurs or producers in an economy.

ASF is a "schedule of minimum amount of receipts required to induce varying quantities of output/employment in the economy."

ASF depicts the relationship between varying levels of output (employment) and the total costs of producing these levels of output. Thus, ASF can be considered as the supply price of various levels of output.

Table 3.2 : Aggregate Supply Schedule

Levels of Output/Employment (in units)	Maximum Expected Receipts (in ₹)
0	0
10	200
20	400
30	600
40	800
Full employment level {50	1000
{50	1200

Table 3.2 shows that initially, as the output increases, the total costs or minimum expected sales receipts also increase. This continues till the level of full employment is reached by the economy. After this point, output (or employment) will remain the same, but costs continue to increase.

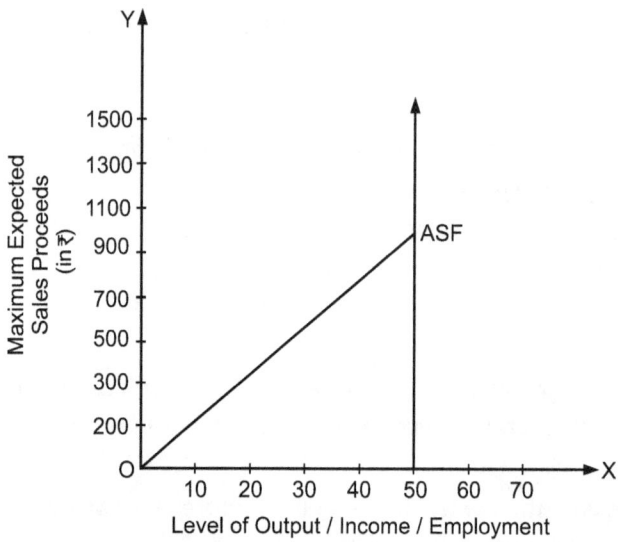

Fig. 3.6 : Level of Output/Income/Employment

Fig. 3.6 represents the table 3.2 given above. Thus, ASF depicts the relationship between varying levels of output (employment) and the total costs of producing these levels of output. At each level of output it shows the supply price of the producer.

Diagrammatic Representation (ADF and ASF together determine national output/employment).

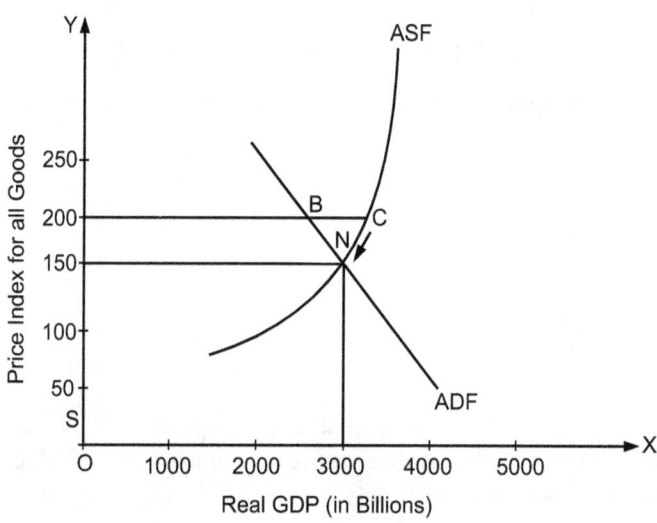

Fig. 3.7 : National output/Employment/Price determined by ADF and ASF

National output and overall price level are determined by the twin blades of scissors of aggregate supply and aggregate demand.

Using both blades of the scissors of aggregate supply and demand, we achieve equilibrium as seen in Fig. 3.7.

National output and price level settle at that level where buyers willingly buy what businesses willingly sell. The resulting output and price level determine employment, unemployment and international trade.

It is natural that the costs must in no case be more than the receipts, i.e. ASF should not be greater than ADF.

If at any particular level of employment, the entrepreneur finds that *receipts are less than their costs* (i.e. ADF < ASF), they will stop production and refuse to offer employment to that particular number of workers.

So long as the costs remain less than the receipts, the employment in an economy will go on increasing till both of them are equal (ASF = ADF).

In Fig. 3.7, we observe:
- On X-axis is the total output (real GDP) of the economy.
- On Y-axis is the overall price level (measured by Consumer Price Index).

The downward-sloping curve is ADF curve. It represents that consumers, businesses, foreigners and governments would buy at different aggregate price levels (with other factors influencing AD remain the same).

The upward-sloping ASF curve represents the quantity of goods and services that entrepreneurs are willing to produce and sell at each price level (with other determinants influencing ASF remain the same).

National output and the overall price level are determined at the intersection of the ADF and ASF (point N). This equilibrium occurs at an overall price level where firms willingly produce and sell what consumers and other buyers willingly buy.

> As in Marshall's analysis, price is determined by the market forces of demand and supply. In the same way, in Keynesian analysis, effective demand is determined by the forces of aggregate demand and aggregate supply. However, the resemblance is superficial as they explain very different phenomena. The macroeconomic AD and AS curves are different from the DD and SS curves of microeconomics.

The complete proposition can be restated as follows:
(i) Employment depends upon Effective Demand (E.D.).
(ii) E.D., in turn, is governed by Aggregate Demand Function (ADF/receipts) and Aggregate Supply Function (ASF/Costs).

(iii) Effective Demand is a point where the two, ADF and ASF, are exactly balanced to each other, i.e. E.D. ASF = ADF.

(iv) If ASF > ADF, then unemployment takes place. If ASF > ADF then (costs < receipts), employment/output increases.

Effective Demand = ASF = ADF

Keynes found that, in a purely capitalist system, the level of E.D. was deficient to support full employment and therefore, advocated government intervention to solve the problem of unemployment. Thus, Keynes' theory is often referred to as the *Demand Deficiency Theory*.

Illustration of Equilibrium: (at less than full employment).

The equilibrium level of output, income and employment in Keynes' theory is determined at a point of "effective demand", where

$$ADF = ASF = E.D.$$

Since no rational producer will produce at a level of output where costs exceed revenue nor will he stop producing when revenue exceeds the costs, the equilibrium is only when cost equals revenue. This is Effective Demand (ASF = ADF) which determines equilibrium level of employment and output in Keynes' theory.

Further, this equilibrium in Keynes' analysis can occur before the level of full employment (i.e. at less than full employment).

Table 3.3: Equilibrium Level of Output/Employment

Levels of Output/Employment (Units)	Minimum Expected Receipts (ASF) (in ₹)	Maximum Sales Proceeds (ADF) (in ₹)	Comparative Equilibrium Levels	Impact on Output/Employment
10	200	350	ASF < ADF	Increase in output/employment.
20	400	500	ASF < ADF	Increase in output/employment
30	600	800	ASF < ADF	Increase in output/employment
40	800	800	ASF = ADF	Equilibrium level
Level of full Employment. 50	1000	950	ASF > ADF	Decline in output/employment.
50	1200	1100	ASF > ADF	

In Table 3.3, the equilibrium level of output and employment is where ASF = ADF and it is attained at less than full employment level. According to Keynes this is due to 'deficient demand' in aggregate demand (consumption demand + investment demand) which leads to unemployment in an economy.

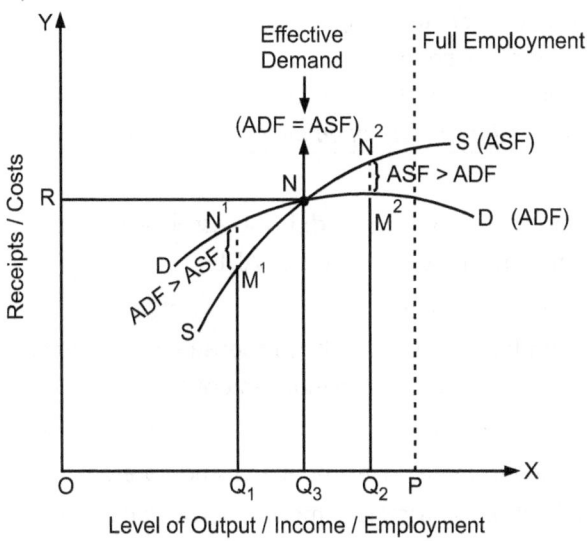

Fig. 3.8 Equilibrium at less than full employment

In **Fig.3.8**, we observe that the curve DD represents ADF (aggregate receipts which the entrepreneurs expect at varying levels of employment). The curve SS represents ASF (aggregate costs which the entrepreneurs must cover at varying levels of employment).

The two curves ASF and ADF intersect each other at N. This is the point of effective demand. At this point N, ADF and ASF are exactly balanced. OR = receipts = costs and OP is the equilibrium level of output and employment. At any other point, the two curves cannot be in equilibrium.

For example, at point N', the ASF = M^1Q^1 but ADF = N^1Q^1 (i.e. ADF > ASF). N^1M^1 is the excess and the entrepreneur will employ more workers as they stand to gain. At N^2, the ASF = N^2Q^2 but ADF (receipts) = M^2Q^2 (i.e. costs > receipts), hence OQ_2 number of men cannot be employed. Thus, only OQ number of men can be employed as, at the point Q, ADF is exactly equal to each other.

A word of caution: At N, the point of intersection, the economy will be in equilibrium, but at this point, the economy does not have full employment. The equality between ADF and ASF can and often does, take place at a point of less than full employment.

ADF and ASF can be equal at the level of full employment provided that the investment demand is high enough to fill the gap between the consumption and income that corresponds to full employment. According to Keynes, the typical investment demand is generally 'deficient' to fill the gap and hence *ADF and ASF will intersect at a point of less than full employment.*

> Of the two forces – ADF and ASF- Keynes, in his General Theory, pays little or no attention to ASF. In fact, he assumes ASF to be given. Since Keynesian economics is short-term economics dealing with a short-period – ASF, necessarily will be assumed to be 'given'. Thus, Keynes paid exclusive attention to ADF. His 'General Theory' is only an analysis of the ADF. That is why some writers call his theory of employment a theory of "aggregate demand".

Significance of ADF

Assuming ASF to be given, as Keynes did, the essence of 'General Theory' is effective demand for employment, which is determined by ADF.

ADF is determined by two factors:

(i) The consumption function (C), i.e. the propensity to consume.
(ii) The investment function (I), i.e. the inducement to invest.

According to some writers, employment depends upon 4 factors: consumption (C), private investment (I), government investment (G) and foreign investment (E). However, Keynes' model of employment is a simple model of two factors: consumption demand (C) and investment demand (I).

Therefore, AD = **C + I**

Where, AD = Aggregate Demand; C = Consumption Demand; I = Investment Demand.

Hence, if employment is to be increased, expenditure both on consumption goods and on investment goods should be increased.

Keynesian economics is the economics of spending

During deflation, the remedy is to increase total spending by the economy on 'C' and 'I' goods to increase employment. And, it is reverse during inflation, when the remedy is to cut down total spending by the community on consumption goods. Thus, it can be said that Keynes' economics is applicable to both the situation – inflation and deflation.

Keynes' remedy to unemployment is government intervention

According to Keynes' if a private, capitalist economy is left to itself, the consumption and investment expenditures are not high enough to achieve full employment. Therefore, Keynes advocated introduction of government expenditure to overcome the shortages in aggregate demand to attain full employment.

Hence,   **AD = C + I + G**

Government intervention could take the form of government expenditure, taxes, subsidies and deficit financing.

When government intervenes in the economy and undertakes expenditure, it increases the aggregate demand which helps the economy achieve full employment.

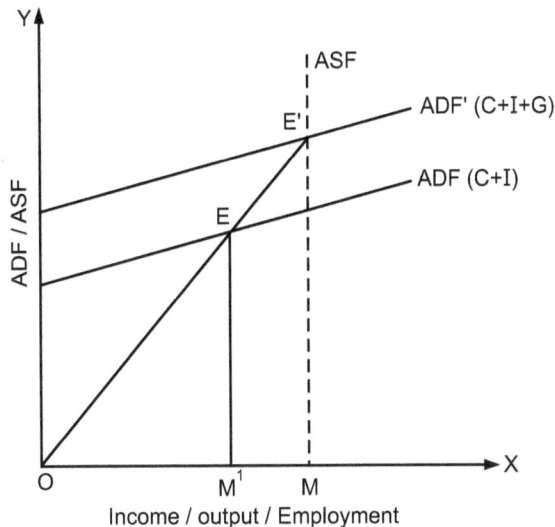

Fig. 3.9 : Level of Income/Output/Employment

Fig. 3.9 shows that when AD = C + I (absence of government expenditure); equilibrium is at point E (as ADF = ASF) and the employment level is determined at point M (which is less than full employment level M^1).

When Government expenditure G is introduced, the new aggregate demand ADF' = C + I + G. The new equilibrium is at E', where ADF' = ASF and the level of employment is M', which is full employment level.

To sum up, the deficiency in the aggregate demand is filled by government expenditure to achieve full employment. Keynes strongly advocated government intervention to solve the problem of unemployment and stabilize the economy.

The following paragraphs will throw some light on the two factors of aggregate demand, i.e. consumption function and investment function.

1. **The Consumption Function(C):** Keynes refers consumption as consumption function or the propensity to consume.
   - The consumption function is an important determinant of effective demand or employment.
   - The consumption expresses the relation between income and consumption expenditure.
   - The Psychological law of consumption, as explained by Keynes, depicts that as *income increases, consumption also increases, but in a lesser proportion.*

- According to Keynes, consumption demand is considered to be relatively stable in short-run. It cannot be changed (increase or decrease) as the consumption demand is fixed by the long-established customs and habits of the community.
- Thus, if employment is to be increased, then the second determinant of employment, i.e., the inducement to invest is to be dealt with.

2. **The Investment Function (I):** The inducement to invest is determined by more complex factors and it is the second component of effective demand.
    - Investment in the Keynesian sense refers to an addition to real capital assets, such as construction of new factories, buildings, roads, plants, etc.
    - Thus, investment according to Keynes is only real investment and not financial investment.
    - If an economy has to attain full employment, investment expenditure should increase at a rate high enough to sustain a high level of investment demand to fill the continuously increasing gap in aggregate demand caused by deficiency in consumption demand.

The investment demand is dependent on two factors:
(1) Marginal efficiency of capital (MEC); and
(2) The rate of interest.
- The rate of interest is considered to be relatively stable in the short run.
- Hence, it is the fluctuations in the MEC which finally determine the level of investment.
- MEC has been defined *as the highest rate of return over cost accruing from an additional (or marginal) unit of a capital asset.* MEC is the expected rate of profit from business.

One condition that is essential to and also indispensable for *fresh investment* is that,
- The marginal efficiency of a new capital asset should be considerably in excess of the market rate of interest.

The MEC is determined by: (i) the supply price of capital assets and (ii) the prospective yield from capital assets. The MEC is unstable because expectations regarding the prospective yield from capital assets are subject to the psychological factors.

The rate of interest is determined by the: (i) demand for money (liquidity preference) and (ii) the supply of money. Liquidity preference is determined by three motives – (a) transactions motive; (b) precautionary motive and (c) speculative motive.

Finally, *government investment expenditure is autonomous* in the sense that it does not depend on independent economic variables such as MEC and the rate of interest.

Hence, Keynes advocated government intervention to bring about full employment in a capitalist economy.

Private investment, which is induced investment (investment dependent on rate of interest and MEC) by itself, cannot generate aggregate demand to sustain full employment equilibrium and thus, *government intervention is advocated.*

(Keynesian theory is depicted in the flow-chart below)

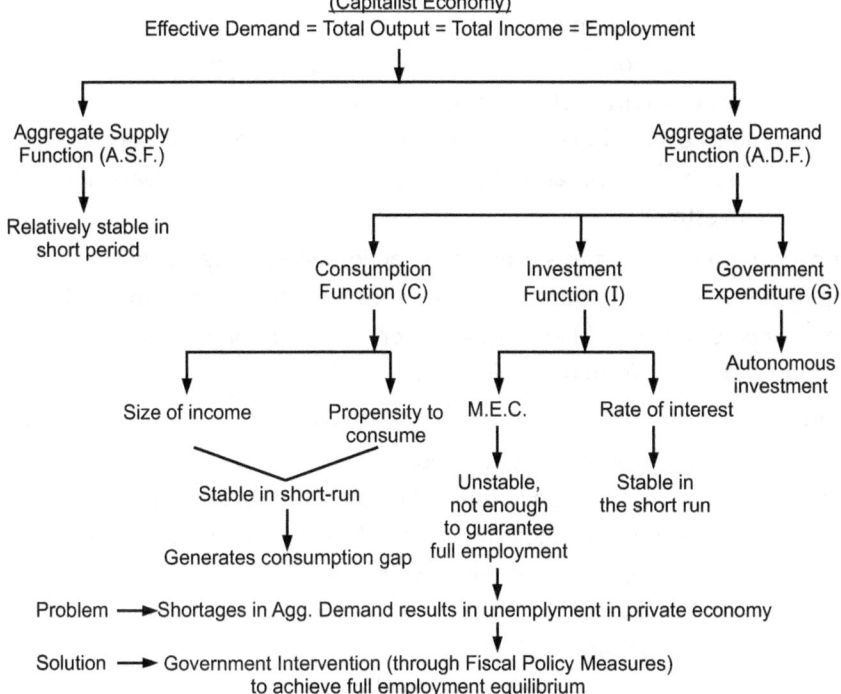

Fig. 3.10 : Flow-Chart Keynesian Model of Employment and Output

Summary of Keynes' Theory of Employment

The flow-chart explains as follows:

(i) Effective demand = Total Output = Total Income = Employment. All these four quantities are equal to each other. Effective demand results in output; output generates income and also provides employment.

(ii) Effective demand is governed by two factors – ASF and ADF. Keynes assumed ASF to be 'given' in the short term and thus concentrated completely on ADF.

(iii) ADF is governed by the consumption demand, investment demand and government expenditure. In his two-sector model, Keynes ignored government expenditure.

(iv) The consumption expenditure i determined by: (a) size of income and (b) community's propensity to consume. Keynes' theory is a short-term theory; hence the expenditure on consumption is stable as it does not change in the short period.

(v) Investment expenditure is governed by (a) MEC and (b) the rate of interest. Investment expenditure is highly unstable.

(vi) MEC is determined by: (a) the supply prices of capital assets (b) the prospective yield from capital assets. MEC is 'unstable', as expectations regarding the prospective yield from capital assets is subject to the psychological factors.

(vii) Rate of interest is determined by: (a) community's liquidity preference, (b) the supply of money. The liquidity preference is determined by 3 motives – transactions motive, precautionary motive and speculative motive.

(viii) Government expenditure is autonomous as it does not depend on economic variables such as MEC and the rate of interest, while private investment is an induced investment.

The above summary serves to spotlight the action which may be taken to curb deflation and unemployment. The Keynesian theory furnishes a practical programme of action to fight deflation and unemployment. That is, government intervention would remedy the situation in the economy and cure it from unemployment.

Assumptions of the Keynesian Theory of Employment

(i) Keynes' theory is a short-run equilibrium analysis, in the capitalist economy.

(ii) There is perfect competition in the labour and product markets.

(iii) In the short-run, the technology and stock of capital are assumed to be constant and hence output level is determined by the level of employment.

(iv) Keynes assumes increasing costs in the industry, i.e., increased output can be produced as increasing marginal cost.

(v) Keynes' model of employment is a closed economy model as it keeps the 'External' sector out of its analysis.

(vi) Government intervention is only to stabilize the economy.

Evaluation of Keynesian Theory of Employment

Keynes' contribution can be understood as under:-

(1) Equilibrium at less than full employment: This is one of the Keynes' most significant contributions to economics. Keynes criticized the earlier classical assertion that there was always a tendency towards full employment of labour and other resources in a laissez-faire economy. Keynes challenged this statement and declared that laissez-faire economy was not capable of maintaining full employment conditions.

In fact, Keynes points to the possibility of underemployment equilibrium not only in the short-run but also in the long-run. This tendency of economic system – in the long run – to have equilibrium at underemployment is termed by Keynes as "secular stagnation". This is indeed a great achievement of the economic theory.

(2) **The Consumption Function:** Another great contribution to economic analysis by Keynes is the understanding of the 'Consumption Function' (or the propensity to consume). Empirical evidence from different sources supports Keynes' psychological law of a stable consumption function. In recent years, a large number of empirical studies, undertaken in the U.K. and USA, go to prove Keynes' concept of a stable consumption function.

(3) **Dynamism in Economic Theory:** Keynes, for the first time, introduced the dynamic element in economic theory. He pointed out the importance of future expectations in taking investment decisions. Thus, a dynamic flavour was seen in Keynes' analysis when he introduced future expectations in investment function.

(4) **The Investment Multiplier:** The multiplier (K) can be considered as Keynes' path-breaking contribution to economic analysis. Today, the multiplier is an integral part of the modern theory of employment. The investment multiplier expressed as a relationship between an initial increment in investment and the final increment in the aggregate income. Subsequent writers have now extended the use of multiplier – for instance, Khan's Employment Multiplier.

(5) **The 'General' Nature of Keynes' Theory:** The classical theory was a 'special' theory that applied only to full employment situation, whereas Keynes' theory is equally applicable to all sorts of situations – underemployment, full employment or over employment conditions. Indeed, we can full witness the 'general' character of the Keynesian theory.

(6) **The Liquidity Preference Theory of Interest:** This theory of interest is a great contribution of Keynes to economic theory. Keynes regards interest to be a 'monetary' phenomenon. He further analyzed the 'liquidity preference' of the people (desire to have liquidity) into three motives, namely – the transaction motive, the precautionary motive and the speculative motive.

(7) **Keynes Adopts Macro Approach:** Keynes has successfully adopted the 'macro' approach in economics. The pre-Keynesian economics was based on the 'micro' approach. As against this, Keynes analyzed the economy as a whole and explained how the variables – aggregate demand, total income, total output, consumption, aggregate investment, total employment and general price levels are determined. Thus, Keynes based his theory of output and employment on macro-approach. In this way, Keynes succeeded in giving an altogether new turn to economic theory.

(8) **Investment – A significant determinant:** Keynes considered investment as a very significant determinant of employment. Further, he pointed out that "investment" is only "real investment", i.e. addition to real capital assets as well as the accumulation

of wealth by the society. As pointed out earlier, of the two determinants of employment, i.e. consumption and investment, it is investment that is a variable factor. By regulating the rate of investment, government can ensure full employment or economic stability.

Practical Significance of Keynesian Theory of Employment

The above discussion of Keynes' contribution to the economic theory clearly brings out the great practical importance of his theory of employment.

(i) Keynes discarded the old, discredited policy of laissez-faire. He proved with the help of his theory that in certain situations, state interference in economic matters was in the interest of the public and the economy. He proved that there were no automatic adjustments in the private economy that would lead to full employment and as such the state had to intervene actively to step up the effective demand in the economy.

(ii) Today, there is hardly any government which does not strive towards the objective of full employment. All types of economies – planned or unplanned – have come to accept full employment as the final goal of their economic policies. Thus, the present day popularity of full employment policy is attributed to Keynes, who believed that full employment is not a normal phenomenon but it has to be achieved by state intervention.

(iii) According to Keynes, the budgetary policy of the government should be decided in the light of the economic situation present in the country. In other words, Keynes proved with the help of his theory that a "balanced budget" was not always the best policy that the government must adopt. Keynes points out that in certain situations the policy of "deficit budgeting" was the most appropriate policy for stepping up the volume of income, output and employment in the economy.

(iv) Keynes gave an important place to fiscal policy in his programme of full employment. For instance, he laid great stress on public works programme to combat depression and mass unemployment. Modern governments have accepted public works as an important part of their unemployment fighting programme and undoubtedly the credit for this is to Keynes.

Weaknesses of Keynes' Structure

In any fair and balanced evaluation, achievement must be balanced by the weaknesses in Keynesian work.

1. **Keynes' theory ignores the long-period:** Keynesian economics emphasizes the short-period. Keynes himself once remarked, "In the long-run we are all dead." Prof. F. A. Hayek, an eminent anti-Keynesian remark that concentration on short-run effects is a serious intellectual error.

2. Keynes' theory is **purely macro-economic analysis** and neglects micro-economic issues.
3. Keynesian economic structure **does not apply to communism** as it is fundamentally a capitalist theory.
4. Keynes' **liquidity preference theory of interest is not original**. It is said that years before Keynes put forward the doctrine – interest is purely a monetary phenomenon – was already very old and Ludwig Von Mises had dismissed it as early as 1912.
5. **Keynes' theory is not general**, i.e., it is not applicable anywhere and everywhere. Its application is limited to industrially developed countries like USA and UK where capitalist society prevails.
6. **Keynes completely ignored the Accelerator:** The accelerator and multiplier are almost parallel concepts. The multiplier shows the effect of investment on consumption and the accelerator shows the effect of changes in consumption on investment. Some critics regard Keynes' failure to deal with the principle of acceleration in his General Theory as a serious omission.
7. **Keynes concentrates on inducement to invest:** To increase employment, Keynes depended almost exclusively on one factor, namely the inducement to investment. The consumption function has little significance to Keynes as it is more or less stable in the short period. Hence, for expanding employment, Keynes depends heavily on inducement to invest as a determinant of employment. Some economists, including Pigou, found fault with this belief of complete dependence on inducement to investment.
8. **Keynes furnishes no comprehensive treatment of unemployment:** Critics point out that unemployment was not merely cyclical; there were other varieties of unemployment too, such as technological or even frictional unemployment. Prof. Paul Sweezy points out that Keynes failed to tackle technological unemployment. According to Dr. Klein, a complete economic theory should tell us how to get both full and fair employment.
9. **Keynesian economics is based on assumption of perfect competition:** Like the classical economists, Keynes theory is based on unrealistic assumption of perfect competition. This assumption has been almost wholly discarded in modern economic analysis and that makes Keynesian theory obsolete and outdated.
10. Keynes' concept of consumption function is severely criticized. Prof. Henry Hazlitt, a leading critic of Keynes, considers consumption function only a truism. Prof. Hazlitt criticizes Keynes' consumption function on the ground that **it is a case purely in quantitative terms** "whereas every civilized human being conceives his actual consumption just as much in qualitative terms."

Criticism of Keynesian Policy of Full Employment

The following criticism has been levelled against the full employment policy of Keynes:

(i) It is pointed out by critics that the capitalist economy is automatic and self-regulating and there is no need for interfering with the free working of economic forces. If left free, it would result in the best utilization of resources. This is a classical argument and has been successfully laid down by Keynes.

(ii) Keynes' prescription of deficit financing as a source to finance the public works programme to fight unemployment is dangerous as it would lead to national bankruptcy. They argue that just as an individual should not live beyond his means, in the same way the state too should confine itself strictly to its own resources.

(iii) Keynesian programme cannot cure partial economic equilibrium, i.e. depression in a particular industry, trade or region. Keynes' theory deals with the economy as a whole and is not applicable to individual sectors.

(iv) Keynes' prescription of cheap money policy may fail to stimulate business activity during depression as marginal efficiency of capital (MEC) may be lower. At such times, there is a general loss of business confidence and however low are the interest rates, it does not help in reviving the economic activity. In USA, the cheap money policy failed miserably during the period (1930-1940) to achieve the goal of eliminating mass unemployment. Thus, as Ludwig Von Mises says, "the Keynesian miracle has failed to materialize; the stones have not turned into bread."

(v) Critics point out that all the Keynesian remedies such as cheap money policy, monetary inflation were known and practiced by the mercantilists of the 17th century. That is, Keynes advocated nothing original or new.

(vi) Some critics question the very necessity of a full employment programme. Say's Law of Market already provides full employment in a capitalist economy. A general insufficiency of demand is not possible and so there can be no mass unemployment. This is truly a classical argument.

Points to Remember

- Two major versions of the theory of Output/Employment.
- (a) The Classical Theory (Say's Law of Market).
- (b) Keynes' Theory.
- **Say's Law of market** – "supply create its own demand."
- General overproduction, mass unemployment are impossibilities in the economy.

- Voluntary unemployment and frictional unemployment co-exist with full employment.
- Laissez-faire economy essential as the economy is automatic and self-adjusting.
- Proper utilization of resources without government interference.
- Saving is a social virtue.
- Keynes departed from classicism after levelling various criticisms against it.
- Keynes' theory of employment shows dependence on effective demand.
- To promote employment, effective demand should be increased by increasing investment.
- Effective demand = total output = total income = employment.
- Both the versions are criticized in their respective approaches.
- It is argued that the Keynesian theory is simply classical economics, "further developed or embroidered."

Multiple Choice Questions

1. One of the following statements is correct-
   (a) Classical economists gave no significance to rate of interest in influencing savings and investments.
   (b) Say's Law is based on the assumption that the people spend only a part of their income on the purchase of goods.
   (c) Classical economists believed that equality between saving and investment at full employment was brought about by the rate of interest.

2. All, except one is not an assumption of Classicists:
   (a) Perfect Competition
   (b) Deficiency in demand is impossible
   (c) Flexibility of prices and wages
   (d) Full employment only as a result of inflation

3. Keynes' theory of employment is economics of depression because:
   (a) It is general theory
   (b) Employment depends upon effective demand
   (c) Supply function is stable in the short-run
   (d) It is comparative static analysis

4. Keynes' theory of employment applies to:
   (a) Full employment equilibrium
   (b) Stability of Investment function
   (c) Long-term analysis
   (d) Stability of ASF in the short-run

5. Which is not an implication of Say's Law?
   (a) Supply creates its own demand
   (b) Absence of general over-production
   (c) Automatic adjustment of economic elements
   (d) Presence of involuntary unemployment

6. Say's Law does not hold good under condition of:
   (a) Money economy
   (b) Barter economy
   (c) Equality of saving and investment
   (d) Inflexible wages and prices

7. One of the following statements is incorrect:
   (a) Keynes held that the level of saving depended upon the level of income
   (b) Keynes believed that long-term equilibrium was more important than short-term equilibrium
   (c) Keynes did not accept the classical view that economic system was self-adjusting
   (d) Keynes did not accept Pigou's plea for wage flexibility as a means of promoting employment

8. One of the following statements does not support Keynesian theory of employment:
   (a) Employment depends upon effective demand
   (b) ASF is assumed to be given in the short-run
   (c) ASF exceeding ADF expands employment
   (d) Effective Demand depends upon ADF and ASF.

Answers:

1 - (c), 2 - (d), 3 - (c), 4 - (d), 5 - (d), 6 - (d), 7 - (b), 8 - (c)

Questions for Discussion

1. Explain how J. B. Say denies the possibility of general overproduction or general unemployment?
2. Explain the Classical Theory of Employment. On what grounds has it been challenged by Keynes?
3. "Flexibility in wage rate is a necessary condition to full employment." Comment.
4. State and explain Say's Law of Market. On what grounds did Keynes refute it?
5. Indicate the implications of Say's Law of Market.
6. What is meant by effective demand?
7. Discuss the General Theory of Employment, propounded by Keynes.
8. Describe the Keynesian model of income and employment.
9. Discuss the achievements and limitations of Keynesian economics.
10. What is the practical importance of the Keynesian Theory of Employment?
11. What are the basic assumptions of the Classical theory of employment?

Chapter 4...

Savings

Contents ...
4.1 Consumption Function: Keynes' Psychological Law of Consumption
4.2 Average and Marginal Propensity to Consume (APC and MPC)
4.3 Saving Function: Average and Marginal Propensity to Save
4.4 Paradox of Saving
- Points to Remember
- Multiple Choice Questions
- Questions for Discussion

Learning Objectives ...
➢ To learn about the consumption and saving functions.
➢ To know about the most celebrated Psychological law of consumption.
➢ To study the two attributes to saving function- average and marginal propensity to save.
➢ To understand the paradox of savings.
➢ To discuss the factors influencing consumption and saving function.

Introduction

Generally, demand for goods depends upon the price. Likewise, consumption of a commodity depends upon the level of income. In other words, there is a close relationship between consumption and income, for example, a rise in income leads to rise in consumption. The consumption-income relationship is represented by the Consumption Function. It is one of the important tools of Keynes' economics.

4.1 Consumption Function: Keynes' Psychological Law of Consumption

The propensity to consume or the consumption function expresses a relationship between two quantities – income and consumption.

Actually, the consumption function is also called the schedule of the propensity to consume. In other words, *the consumption function is a schedule of the various amounts of consumption expenditure corresponding to the different levels of income.*

Table 4.1 : Consumption Schedule (in ₹ Crores).

Income (Y)	Consumption (C)
0	20
60	70
120	120
180	170
240	220
300	270
360	320

Table 4.1 may be considered to be the schedule of the propensity to consume at different levels of aggregate income.

Thus, the consumption function (or propensity to consume) shows how the consumption expenditure changes with the variation in income. If consumption is represented by C and income by Y, then the propensity to consume is $C = f(Y)$. It implies that consumption is a function of income.

The consumption function or the propensity to consume indicates a 'functional' relationship between the two aggregates, namely, total consumption expenditure and national income.

There is a fine distinction between consumption and propensity to consume. Consumption refers to the total expenditure on consumption that is being incurred out of the total income of an economy. For example, if a country with a total income of ₹ 100 crores spends out of it ₹ 75 crores on consumption, then ₹ 75 crores represents its consumption.

The consumption function or the propensity to consume indicates a 'functional' relationship between the two aggregates, namely, total consumption expenditure and national income.

There is a fine distinction between consumption and the propensity to consume. Consumption refers to the total expenditure on consumption that is being incurred out of the total income of an economy. For example, if a country with a total income of ₹ 100 crores spends out of it ₹ 75 crores on consumption, then ₹ 75 crores represents its consumption. When we plot a Consumption Schedule indicating the change in consumption as a result of change in income, such a schedule is referred to as the *propensity to consume* (or the consumption function).

In short, consumption means the amount spent on consumption at a given level of income while the consumption function refers to complete tabular statement (Schedule) showing consumption expenditure at various levels of income.

In Table 4.1 consumption is an increasing function of income because consumption expenditure increases with an increase in income. It can be observed that when income is zero, people spend out of their past savings on consumption to satisfy their basic wants. When the income of the economy is ₹ 60 crores, the consumption expenditure is ₹ 70 crores (₹ 10 crores is dis-savings).

When consumption is equal to income at ₹ 120 crores and the equality point is known as the 'break-even point' or call it as point of 'zero savings'.

After the break-even point, income increment is ₹ 60 crores and consumption increment is by ₹ 50 crores. This implies a *stable* consumption function during the short-run, as assumed by Keynes.

Table 4.1 depicts the basic proposition of Keynes' Psychological law of consumption, i.e., when income increases, consumption also increases but not in the same proportion in which the income increases.

The relationship between that of income and consumption on one hand and that of income and savings on the other can be depicted with the help of a Fig. 4.1.

OX-axis measures income (Y), OY-axis measures consumption (C).

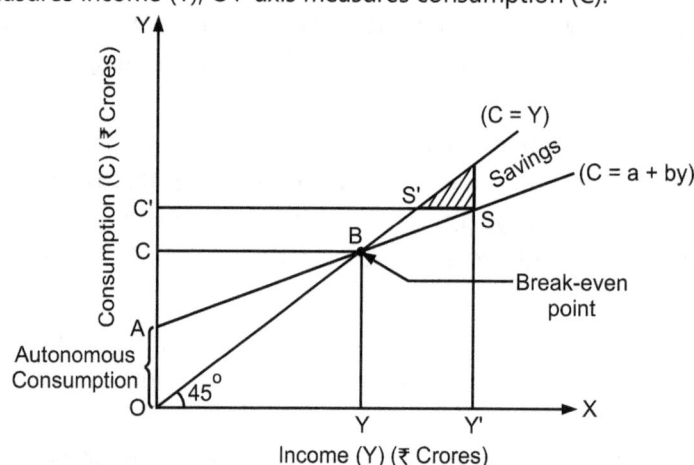

Fig. 4.1 : Graphical Representation of a Point f 'Zero Savings'

In **Fig. 4.1**, the unity line (45^0) points out that any point on this line will depict income and consumption equality.

The 'C' curve is a linear consumption function based on the assumption that consumption changes by the same amount (₹ 50 crores). Its upward slope (or positive slope) from left to right indicates that consumption function is an *increasing function of income*.

'B' is the break-even point where C=Y (or it is zero savings point), i.e. OY=OC.

When income rises to OY', consumption also increases OC'. It can be observed that consumption has increased in a lesser proportion to the increase in income, CC' < YY'. The part of the income not used for consumption is shown by the vertical distance between the 45^0 line and C curve, i.e., SS'.

Thus, the consumption function measures not only the amount spent (i.e. consumption) but also the part of income which is not used (i.e. savings). As we know that propensity to save is actually the propensity of not consuming. Hence, it can be said that the saving curve can be derived from the income-consumption curve as the part of income which is not spent is saved. The distance between consumption (C) and Income (Y) represent savings.

Keynes' Psychological Law of Consumption

Introduction

Keynes' Psychological Law of Consumption is also referred to as the 'Fundamental Law of Consumption'. Keynes propounded the fundamental psychological law of consumption which forms the basis of the consumption function. In Keynes' words, *"the fundamental psychological law upon which we are entitled to depend with great confidence both from our prior knowledge of human nature and from the detailed facts of experience, is that men are disposed (inclined) as a rule and on an average, to increase their consumption as their income increases but not by as much as the increase in their income."*

The law mainly implies that there is a tendency on the part of the people to spend on consumption less than the increase in income.

Propositions of the Law:

The law is generally considered to be consisting of three related propositions:

(i) **When the aggregate income increases, aggregate consumption expenditure also increases but by somewhat smaller proportion:** The reason for this tendency is that as the income increases, consumer's wants get more and more satisfied. As a result, there is no longer a necessity to spend the additional increase in income on consumption.

Thus, with the increase in income, expenditure on consumption will definitely increase; but not in the same proportion in which the income increases. It implies that when aggregate income increases, aggregate consumption expenditure increases in a lesser proportion.

(ii) **An increase in income will be divided in some proportion between savings and spending:** This proportion is the outcome of the first proposition. It is evident that when the entire increase in income is not spent on consumption, a part of that increased income is saved.

It is a simple logic that when the income of a person increases, the whole of the increased income is not spend on consumption. He uses a part of the increased income for the better satisfaction of his earlier wants and part of it is devoted to the satisfaction of new wants. The balance of the increased income is saved.

Savings are to tide over hard times and savings can also be utilized to add to his income through investment. In this manner consumption and savings move together at the same time. It is quite possible that initially a person may not save but as his income increases he does save some part of his increased income.

(iii) **Increase in income always leads to more consumption and savings than before:** It is not possible for a person to spend less when his income increases, unless he happens to be a miser. Under normal conditions a person will increase his consumption expenditure when his income increases as he would prefer to enjoy greater amenities and comforts of life.

As a result his spending and savings both rise, when his income increases.

The core of Keynes' Psychological Law of Consumption is the first proposition, i.e., when the aggregate income increases, total consumption expenditure also increases but in a lesser proportion.

This proposition emphasizes on the fact people fail to spend on consumption items in the full amount of an increment in income. The law depicts a general indication of the actual macro-behaviour of consumers in short period.

The three propositions of the law can be explained with the help of the following schedule.

Table 4.2 : (in ₹ Crores)

Income (Y)	Consumption (C)	Savings (S)
0	20	-20
50	60	-10
120	120	0
186	170	10
240	220	20
300	270	30
360	320	40

First Proposition:

Increase in income is greater than increase in consumption

At zero level of income, only the consumption of basic necessities takes place. This is known as *autonomous consumption*.

When income increases to ₹ 50 crores, consumption is ₹ 60 crores. However, with every increase in income from ₹ 180 crores to ₹ 360 crores, consumption expenditure also increases from ₹ 170 crores to ₹ 320 crores respectively, but in a lesser proportion.

Second Proposition:

Income is divided into C and S, i.e. Y = C + S

It is observed that as income (Y) goes on increasing consumption (C) increases in a constant proportion (₹ 60 crores in (Y) and ₹ 50 crores in (C), i.e., consumption increases *less* than the increase in income and savings are *positive*. Thus, the total income gets divided into C and S (Y=C+S).

Third Proposition:

C and S both rise with rise in income

In **Table 4.2** we observe that with an increase in income neither consumption nor savings have fallen. As the income increases from ₹ 120 to 180, 240, 300, 360 crores of rupees; consumption also increases from ₹ 120 to 170, 220, 270, 320 crores of rupees respectively.

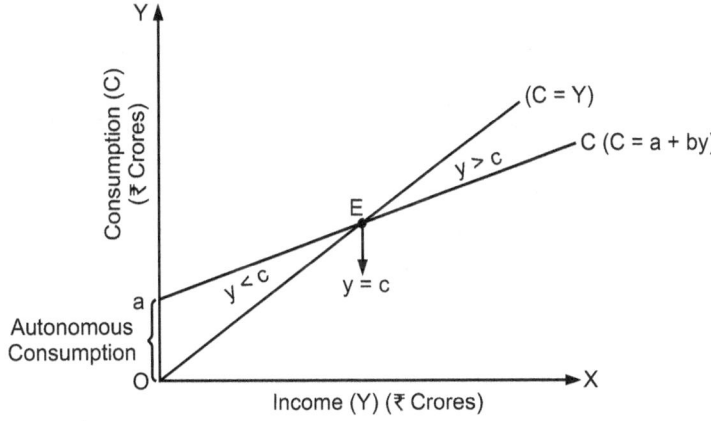

Fig. 4.2 : Keynes' Psychological Law of Consumption

(i) In **Fig. 4.2** the 45^0 line C=Y is the unity line, i.e. any point lying on this line will depict that income is equal to consumption. For example, ₹ 120 crores is Y and ₹ 120 crores is C, shown by point E.

(ii) The consumption function C = a + by is positive sloping function that shows that as income increases consumption increases but at a lesser proportion.

(iii) Point 'a' depicts *autonomous consumption* (independent of the level of income). It shows that even at zero income some minimum consumption is necessary or consumption cannot be zero.

(iv) Beyond point E, Y is greater than C (Y>C). This implies that there are positive savings.

Assumptions

The operation of the Keynes' law of consumption depends upon certain assumptions and they can be referred to as *limitations* of the law.

1. **It assumes a constant psychological and institutional complex:** Keynes assumes that the existing psychological and institutional complex does not undergo any change and that the consumption depends on income alone. The psychological and institutional factors like distribution of income, price-level, tastes and habits, fashions, etc., of the people remain the same. Based on this assumption the law can be considered as a reality in the short-period as these factors generally remain unchanged. But in the long-run these factors undergo a change and hence propensity to consume can no longer remain constant. In other words, the law has little validity in long-period.

2. **It assumes the existence of normal conditions in the economy:** The law assumes that there are no abnormal conditions present in the economy such as war, political disturbances, run-away inflation etc.

   Under normal conditions not only this law but even the most fundamental laws of economics undergo changes. Thus, this law holds good only when normal conditions are present in an economy.

3. **It assumes the existence of a laissez-faire capitalist economy:** The law is based on the assumption that the country is rich, prosperous and follows a policy of laissez-faire. The law will have little validity in a poor community. Because in a poor nation there arises no question of making a choice between consumption and savings. In such a nation the people have many unsatisfied wants which they would like to satisfy whenever there is any increase in their income. And, sometimes the whole of the increase in income may be spent on consumption; thereby impairing Keynes' Psychological Law of Consumption.

   However, Keynes' law if sully applicable to the low-consumption and high saving economies like USA and UK.

Implications of Keynes' Law of Consumption (or Importance of Keynes' Law)

Keynes' Psychological Law of Consumption has some important implications:

1. **Invalidates Say's Law of Markets:** J. B. Say's law states that *"supply creates its own demand"*. As such there cannot be *general overproduction* or *general unemployment*. Keynes' psychological law invalidates Say's Law because the consumption function is stable in the short-run and as such a gap between the increase in income and the increase in consumption expenditure is observed. It implies that all that is produced (income) is not taken off the market (spending), as the income increases. In other words, *supply fails to create its own demand*. In fact, supply exceeds demand and results in general over- production and glut of commodities in the market and consequently results in mass unemployment.

2. **Importance of Investment:** Keynes' Law highlights the importance of the consumption function. The consumption expenditure mostly depends upon the income of the individual, provided the other factors are stable. The law explains that due to the stability of the consumption function, there is a gap between the increase in income and the increase in consumption expenditure. This gap has to be filled by investment and if the investment is not correspondingly increased, there is bound to be depression and unemployment in the economy. Hence, Keynes' psychological law of consumption stresses on the importance of investment in any programme of full employment.

3. **Government Interference:** The law states that the consumption expenditure does not increase in the same proportion to the increase in income. The lag in consumption expenditure inevitably results in over-production and mass unemployment in the economy. In such circumstances, a laissez-faire policy does not work and the intervention by the Government is essential to set the matters right.

4. **Declining tendency of the Marginal Efficiency of Capital (M.E.C):** As the increase in consumption expenditure is lesser than the increase in income hence M.E.C is adversely affected. Due to inadequate demand the M.E.C declines and the profitability of industry receives a set-back. Investment falls and economic progress of the nation is retarded.

5. **Explanation of the Turning Points of the Business Cycles:** The law also explains the 'turning points' of the business cycle. It explains the 'downturn' from a boom. This is because though the community's income increases, the consumption expenditure does not increase in the same proportion. Likewise, it explains 'upturn' from depression, which occurs because although people's income decreases, the consumption expenditure cannot be reduced in the same proportion.

6. **Danger of Over-savings:** The law states that the increase in consumption expenditure does not keep pace with the increase in income. Thus arises the danger of an *over-saving gap* in the economy. Keynes' remarks that the rich and prosperous communities are more exposed to the danger of this over-saving gap than the poor and backward economies.

7. **Unique Nature of Income Generation:** This law also explains the unique nature of income generation in an economy. When the supply of money is increased in an economy the income does not increase in the same proportion. The reason is that the people do not increase their consumption expenditure in the same proportion in which the income increases.

Keynes' Consumption Function (Propensity to Consume) is based on the Psychological Law of Consumption

4.2 Average and Marginal Propensity to Consume (APC and MPC)

The Consumption function has two technical attributes:
(1) The Average Propensity to Consume (APC);
(2) The Marginal Propensity to Consume (MPC).

Average Propensity to Consume (APC): The concept of average propensity to consume indicates *"the ratio of aggregate consumption expenditure to aggregate income"*. Thus, APC is the ratio of C to Y. It is expressed in symbol terms as $\frac{C}{Y}$.

For instance, if the aggregate income of a community is ₹ 1000 crores and the consumption expenditure is ₹ 900 crores, then the average propensity to consume is or $\frac{9}{10}$ or 90%. This implies that the community spends 90% of its income on consumption.

A.P.C can be illustrated diagrammatically as follows: (Fig. 4.3)

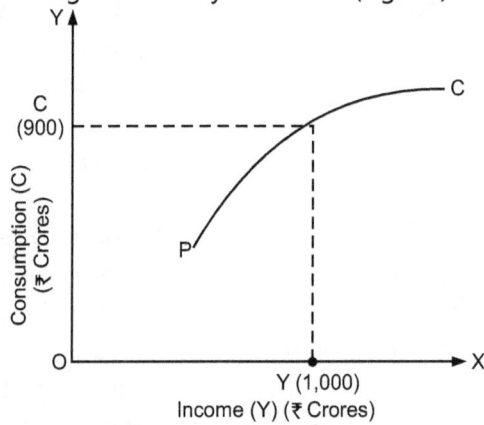

Fig. 4.3 : Average Propensity to Consume

- OX-axis represents Income (Y) and OY-axis represents Consumption (C).
- The curve PC represents the propensity to consume.
- OY = ₹ 1000 corers; OC = ₹ 900 crores.
- At the aggregate income of ₹ 1000 crores, the consumption expenditure is ₹ 900 crores.
- A.P.C = $\frac{900}{1000}$ or $\frac{9}{10}$ or 90%.

Thus, the value of APC for any level of income can be found by dividing consumption expenditure by the aggregate income. No empirical attempt has so far been made to find out the *average propensity to consume* in India.

In U.S.A., the APC in ordinary times has been estimated at 88% of the national income, and in a poor nation like India the APC may be considered to be much higher than 88% though there is no scientific attempt made to estimate it.

Marginal Propensity to Consume (MPC): Marginal Propensity to Consume (M.P.C) differs from the Average Propensity to Consume (A.P.C). M.P.C indicates how an additional increase of income will be divided between spending and savings.

Marginal Propensity to Consume is *"the ratio of change in consumption to the change in income or the rate of change in the average propensity as income changes"*.

The marginal propensity to consume can be found by dividing an increase (or decrease) in consumption by an increase (or decrease) in income.

Symbolically, it is stated as $\frac{\Delta C}{\Delta Y}$.

Here, Δ indicates the change in income or consumption.

Illustration: If the aggregate income increases by ₹ 10 crores and the consumption expenditure by ₹ 7 crores, then the marginal propensity to consume will be –

$$\text{M.P.C.} = \frac{\Delta C}{\Delta Y} \text{ or } \frac{9}{10} \text{ or } 90\%$$

Diagrammatic Illustration

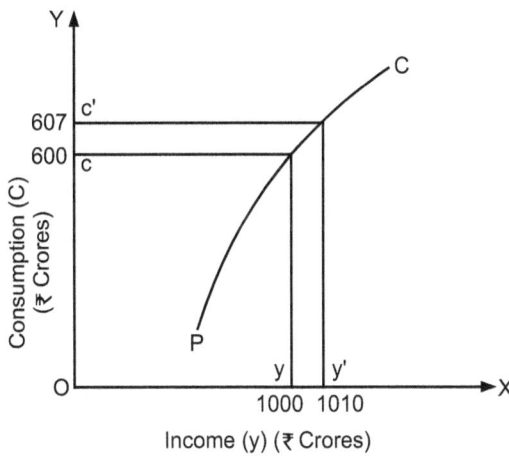

Fig. 4.4 : Marginal Propensity to Consume

- OX-axis measures Income (Y), OY-axis measures Consumption (C).
- PC curve represents the propensity to consume.
- In **Fig. 4.4** we observe that while the income increases by ₹ 10 crores, the consumption expenditure increases by ₹ 7 crores.
- Thus, an increase of ₹ 10 crores in income (Y) is followed by an increase of ₹ 7 crores in consumption expenditure (C).
- The M.P.C. = $\frac{6}{10}$ or 0.6 or 90%.

The distinction between A.P.C and M.P.C can be illustrated in **Table 4.3**.

Table 4.3 : Depicts APC and MPC at different levels of income

Income (Y)	Consumption (C)	A.P.C. (C/Y)	M.P.C. (ΔC/ΔY)
1	2	3	4
120	120	$\frac{120}{120} = 1$ (100%)	---
180	170	$\frac{170}{180} = 0.92$ (92%)	$\frac{50}{60} = 0.83$ (83%)
240	220	$\frac{220}{240} = 0.91$ (91%)	$\frac{50}{60} = 0.83$ (83%)
300	270	$\frac{270}{300} = 0.90$ (90%)	$\frac{50}{60} = 0.83$ (83%)
360	320	$\frac{320}{360} = 0.88$ (88%)	$\frac{50}{60} = 0.83$ (83%)

Significance of M.P.C.

The concept of M.P.C is of vital importance in the theory of employment.

(i) It enlightens us on the possible division of additional income between consumption and savings.

(ii) It tells us how the extra income will be divided between consumption and investment, because in the Keynesian system, Savings=Investment.

(iii) Marginal propensity to save can be derived if marginal propensity to consume is known. The formula is (1- marginal propensity to consume) or MPS = $\left(1 - \frac{\Delta C}{\Delta Y}\right)$.

For example, if MPC is 0.6 then MPS is 0.4. Thus, MPC + MPS = 1

Thus, if one quantity, i.e., either MPC or MPS is known then the other quantity can easily be derived. This is because that the income of a community is divided between consumption and savings. Hence, if consumption is a known quantity then savings can easily be derived by deducting consumption from income.

It is essential to remember that marginal propensity to consume must always be positive and less than 1. It is less than 1 as increase in consumption always falls short of the increase in income, i.e., all that is earned is never spent 100%, some part is diverted towards savings.

Relationship between A.P.C. and M.P.C.

(i) As the income rises, M.P.C falls. A.P.C also declines but M.P.C falls to a greater extent than A.P.C. Thus, with an increase in income both the propensities decline, although the decline in one case (M.P.C) is greater than in the other one (A.P.C).

(ii) M.P.C is higher in case of the poor than in the case of rich people. The reason is that greater the income of any person, more of his basic human wants have already been satisfied and thus greater is the tendency for him to save to provide for the future. Thus, M.P.S of the rich class shall be more than that of the poor class.

If, at any time, aggregate consumption has to be increased, then the purchasing power should be transferred from the rich class (having low M.P.C) to the poor class (having high M.P.C). On the other hand, if aggregate consumption is to be reduced, the purchasing power must be taken away from the poor class by taxing their consumption.

In case of nations it applies the same, i.e., the M.P.C is higher in a poor nation and lower in a rich nation. It is for the same reason as mentioned above. In a rich nation, most of the basic wants of the people have already been satisfied and thus all the additional increase of income is saved resulting in high M.P.S and low M.P.C. Conversely, in a poor country as most of the basic human wants of the people remain unsatisfied additional increments of income go to increase consumption resulting in higher M.P.C but lower M.P.S.

To conclude, M.P.C is higher in underdeveloped and backward countries, e.g., Asia, Africa, etc., and lower in advanced and developed countries, e.g., U.S.A., U.K., etc.

Factors Influencing the Consumption Function (Propensity to Consume)

Let us recapitulate the difference between the consumption and propensity to consume. *Consumption expenditure* is part of income that is spent on consumption. This amount is subject to change because the expenditure on consumption increases with increase in income. Propensity to consume is schedule (tabular form) of consumption expenditure which indicates the different amounts spent on consumption by a person at different levels of income.

On basis of the consumption function we can draw a consumption curve. A consumer may change his consumption expenditure (increase or decrease) but he remains on the *same* consumption curve in the short-run, i.e., the shape, slope and position of the curve does not change. Hence, we can say that *during the short-run the amount of consumption expenditure changes but the consumption function remains the same.*

Factors which govern the propensity to consume to high or low are as follows:

(A) Objective Factors:
  (1) **Money Income:** An important factor influencing a community's propensity to consume is money income. As the income rises, the consumption also increases and vice versa.
  (2) **Changes in Consumer's Tastes and Fashions:** Changes in consumer's tastes and fashions may influence the propensity to consume. It is true that such changes may not be substantial enough to affect the consumption function in the short-run.

(3) **Availability of Consumer Credit:** The availability of consumer credit gives extra purchasing power in the hands of an individual to buy consumer goods over and above those which he could buy with his regular income. Facilities like 'purchase on installment' have encouraged increasing the consumption function. Such facilities are now not only in developed nations but has been extended even in developing countries.

(4) **Price and Wage Levels:** A rise in price level reduces the purchasing power and reduces the propensity to consume and vice versa. Likewise, other conditions remaining the same, a rise in the wage level will increase the propensity to consume and vice versa. Thus, changes in price and wage levels determine the propensity to consume.

(5) **Change in the Expectations of Consumers:** The consumption function is affected not only by present changes but also by the expectations of future changes. For example, outbreak of war considerably affects the propensity to consume by creating fear about future shortages. People anticipating these shortages increase their purchase and even resort to hoarding of essential goods. As a result the consumption function shifts upwards.

(6) **Distribution of Income and Wealth:** Propensity to consume is also determined by the way the community's wealth is distributed among its various sections. For example, greater the inequality in the distribution of wealth, lower shall be the propensity to consume. Conversely, greater the equality of wealth distribution in the economy, higher will be the consumption function.

In order to have an equal distribution of wealth, Keynes does not agree to any drastic social reforms and to mitigate inequalities in distribution of wealth he does suggest progressive taxation. Progressive taxation may increase the propensity to consume but it has to a certain extent the disadvantage of discouraging private investment.

(7) **Indebtedness:** The level of consumer's credit also determines the willingness of consumers to consume out of current income. If the consumers are in debt and a certain proportion of their current income is committed to installment payments on previous purchases, they may be obliged to economize their current consumption to reduce their earlier indebtedness.

(8) **Change in Fiscal Policy:** Changes in fiscal policy have their impact on the propensity to consume. Heavy indirect taxation always impinges on the consumption function and is likely to depress it. It is well-known that the propensity to consume was drastically cut down as a result of heavy indirect taxation, rationing and price control during the Second World War. All these changes completely disturb the normal relationship between consumption and income.

(9) **Attitude to Thrift/Savings:** The propensity to consume is also affected by people's attitude towards thrift. If the masses believe that savings is a social virtue then the propensity to consume shall be adversely affected. On the other hand, if people's attitude towards thrift works on the Keynesian pattern then the consumption function will be higher and the propensity to save will be lower. Government policies can also have an impact on the people's attitude towards thrift. For example, during the Second World War, the Government of India waged intensive propaganda campaigns to encourage the people to save by bringing war bonds. These campaigns were quite successful in boosting the saving schedule and the fact that many consumer durables were not available in large quantities, it helped in lowering the consumption function.

(10) **Corporate Policies:** The business policies of corporations in relation to depreciation and reserves influence the propensity to consume. For example, conservative policy with regard to depreciation and reserves will reduce the income available for distribution among the shareholders and thereby reduce their consumption expenditure. Likewise a cautious dividend policy will depress the propensity to consume, by taking away from the shareholders, controlled incomes which they otherwise would have spent on consumption.

(11) **Windfall Gains or Losses:** Unexpected changes in the stock market leading to gains or losses tend to shift the consumption function upwards or downwards. For example, the windfall gains due to the stock market boom in the American economy after 1925 led to rise in the consumption spending of the stockholders in proportion to the increased income and consequently the consumption function shifted upwards. In the same way, unexpected losses in the stock market lead to the downward shifting of the consumption curve.

(12) **Social Insurance:** When insurance premium is paid it means a reduction in purchasing power for the people and to that extent it acts as a drag on the consumption function.

(13) **Rate of Interest:** Changes in the rate of interest also influence the propensity to consume. For example, if the rates of interest increase people will try to take advantage of the higher rate and thus consume less and save more. This is a normal sequence but it may not be always so. There can be expectations too. A person desirous of fixed income in the future is likely to save less at higher rate of interest than at a lower rate. Thus, change in consumption function due to changes in the rate of interest is uncertain.

Classical economists have pointed towards direct relationship between savings and the rate of interest. In other words, consumption and rate of interest are inversely related. Keynes believes that change in consumption due to changes in rate of interest is unimportant in the short period. It is only in the long-run that the consumption function is influenced to a 'substantial' degree by changes in the interest rates. However, it cannot be denied that the rate of interest has a definite influence when consumers buy consumer durable goods such as television set etc., on an installment basis, because increase in the interest rate will make installment buying costlier to the consumer and thus act as a deterrent to consumption.

(14) Stocks of Durable Goods in Possession: The consumption function of consumers is affected by the stock of durable goods which they currently possess. If the country has enjoyed a long prosperity period then consumers may find themselves possessing various types of durable goods like washing machine etc., worthy of many years of future service. As a result, for some time, the households will spend less on these items and save more at each level of the disposable income.

(15) Holdings of Liquid Assets: The amount of liquid assets in the form of cash balances, savings and government bonds in the hands of the consumers affect the consumption function. Such liquid asset holdings with the people shall have the effect of increasing the sense of security and hence increase consumption. On the other hand, when people do not have any such holdings of liquid assets they are not likely to spend much out of the current income.

Thus, it is clear that more the liquid assets that people have, the greater will be the rate of consumption out of a given income.

Prof. A. C. Pigou was of the view that with a cut in money wages, prices fall and the real value of such liquid assets increases. This tends to shift the consumption function upward. This is called the *"Pigou Effect"*. But it is not necessary for the 'Pigou effect' to take place through money wage-cut. The reason is that an increase in the real value of such accumulated savings takes place directly through a fall in prices and fall in their value when the prices rise (i.e., inflation). In the former case, asset holders will increase their consumption and in the latter case reduce their consumption. However, if the low income groups hold such liquid assets, the tendency is towards increase in the consumption function as their propensity to consume is high.

(16) Demonstration Effect/Duessenbury Hypothesis: According to Prof. Duessenbury the consumption function of a particular section of the community is also affected by what he refers to as *'Demonstration effect'*.

According to Prof. Duessenbury, the consumption standards of low income groups are often influenced by the consumption standards of higher income groups. There is always a deep-rooted desire of the members of the low income groups to imitate the consumption standards of higher income groups. Hence, as soon as the low income group starts consuming goods used by the high income group, the 'richer group' tries to switch over from the consumption of such goods and will opt for still costlier ones and all this results in increasing propensity to save. For example, globalization has narrowed the gap between the developing country and the advanced country which has set in motion the 'demonstration effect' (aping of the west) in the developing countries. The exhibition of Hollywood Films in developing countries like India has resulted in demonstration effect on the richer sections of the people in India.

(B) Subjective Factors

Besides objective factors that determine the propensity to consume, there are certain subjective or psychological factors that affect the consumption function. For example, desire to provide for future needs; desire to bequeath a fortune to one's heirs or merely to satisfy one's miserly instincts.

Keynes has given due importance to the psychological factors in his consumption function which was neglected by Classicists. Although Keynes believed that all the subjective factors did not affect the consumption function, yet there were some which tend to promote consumption and restrict savings, such as desire for a better standard of living, the desire of ostentation, the desire for recognition, etc.

Keynes' describes these factors as *'psychological characteristics of human nature and those social practices and institutions which, though not unalterable, are unlikely to undergo a material change over a short period'*. It implies that the consumption function is stable in the short-run. Thus, if abnormal or extraordinary factors do not intervene (e.g. war) Keynes' concept of propensity to consume may be expected to hold true in actual practice, i.e., under normal conditions the absolute increase in consumption will be less than the absolute increase in income.

Importance of Keynes' Consumption Function

Prof. A. H. Hansen says, *"It is a major landmark in the history of economic doctrines"*. Almost all economists agree that Keynes' consumption function is an outstanding contribution to economic analysis.

This concept has come to acquire a great significance in the modern economic theory for the following reasons:

1. **It throws light on the significance of investment in the employment theory:** According to the Keynes' theory, the two constituents that determine employment are consumption and investment. Thus, if the volume of employment is to be stepped up then both the components, i.e., investment and consumption must be stepped up. But as pointed out by Keynes, in his theory, the consumption function is almost stable in the short-run; hence if employment is to be raised then concentration should be only on investment. In short, investment is the crucial determinant of employment in the short period and should be tackled to promote employment.

2. **Invalidates Say's Law:** The core of Classical economics is Say's Law of Markets i.e., *"supply creates its own demand"*. The Classical economists thus deny the possibility of over-production and mass unemployment. Keynes' consumption function effectively contradicts Say's Law of Market, by his assertion that the marginal propensity to consume is less than unity. It implies that the tendency of the people is to spend less than the full increment in income. Thus, Keynes' could prove all the possibilities of existence of over-production and mass unemployment in the economy. According to Keynes, supply exceeds demand instead of creating demand for it and hence results in over-production and consequently unemployment of factors of production.

3. **Equilibrium at less than full employment:** Keynes' stable consumption function throws light on the fact that there can be under-employment equilibrium in a capitalist economy. According to Keynes the economy, no doubt, reaches its equilibrium but that equilibrium is not accompanied by full employment. This equilibrium can be attained even at "less than full employment" or under-employment. The reason lies in the consumption function (marginal propensity to consume) which is *'less than one'*. In other words, the consumers do not spend the whole of the *increment in income* on consumption and as a result the economy is faced with the problem of under-employment.

4. **It explains the declining tendency of the Marginal Efficiency of Capital (M.E.C) in rich nations:** M.E.C is the expected returns on capital invested. It is observed that in wealthy industrial nations the M.E.C declines because the consumption expenditure fails to rise to keep the consumption at high level. It is true that once the M.E.C of an industry starts declining and this fall can be arrested only by increasing the investment function as the consumption function is stable in the short-run.

   The stability of the consumption function states another too. If the consumption function is stable then the propensity to save is also stable as the propensity to save is an outcome of consumption function. In other words, there is no possibility of reducing savings to the level of available investment opportunities. The economy finds itself confronted with over-savings and the result is fall in M.E.C.

5. **Possibility of permanent over-saving gap:** Keynes' consumption function explains the concept of *'secular stagnation'*. The possibility of over-saving in course of time, in rich industrial nations, leads to stability in the propensity to save. Just as it is not easy to push upwards stable consumption, in the same way, it is difficult to reduce downwards the savings and thus investment opportunities do not grow. The economy is not able to use its savings fully and effectively to step-up the employment. Such a situation Keynes' refers to as 'secular stagnation' and it is purely due to stable consumption function.

6. **It makes clear the 'turning point' of the Business Cycle:** Prior to the publication of Keynes' 'General Theory', many theories on business cycle have been presented. However, none of the theories could furnish any satisfactory explanation to the occurrence of upper and lower 'turning points' of the trade cycle. For the first time it was Keynes' *Consumption Function* that gave a convincing explanation to the 'turning points' of the business cycle.

    Keynes' explains the *upper turning point*, i.e., turning from prosperity to slump due to the marginal propensity to consume being *less than one*. As the boom grows, income expand, people fail to spend on consumption the full amount of the increment of their incomes. This tendency leads the economy's march towards a slump (or downturn from prosperity).

    Keynes' analysis of the *lower turning point*, i.e., an upturn from slump to prosperity also lies in the fact that *MPC is less than one*. When the slump develops, incomes contract, people fail to reduce their expenditure on consumption to the extent of reduction in their incomes. In other words, consumption expenditure is more and savings are less and slump period finally gives way to boom. Thus, Keynes' factor of consumption function (through the concept of M.E.C) enlightens the hitherto 'mysterious' behaviour of the business cycle.

7. **Income propagation from investment (i.e. Multiplier Theory):** 'Leakages' are caused from the newly created income stream due to the reason that MPC (consumption function) is less than one. MPC is less than one as people do not spend the entire increment of income on consumption. And, the magnifying effect of the 'multiplier' goes on shrinking at each round due to these 'leakages'. If 'leakages' were not present it implies that MPC is equal to one and an initial injection of purchasing power would go on and on, magnifying itself, till there was full employment and even inflation.

To conclude, it cannot be denied that Keynes' Consumption Function is an outstanding contribution to the economic theory.

Measures to Raise the Propensity to Consume

Due to certain psychological and institutional factors the consumption function is stable in the short-run. However, in the long-run it is quite possible to raise the consumption function and promote employment level. Following measures have been suggested to raise the propensity to consume in the long-run.

1. *Reduction in taxes*, for example, sales tax, excise duty, etc., would increase the purchasing power of the people. The affordability (due to lower taxes) of the goods would induce people for consumption.

2. The process of *urbanization* would raise the consumption function. It is a fact that the propensity to consume in urban areas is higher than that in the rural areas due to their differences in living standards.
3. A well-devised system of *social security* can be instrumental in raising the propensity to consume. It is observed that during depression, investments and consumption expenditures decline. Hence, during this time a comprehensive system of social security such as, giving of doles and unemployment allowances to the unemployed workers, can help check the decline in consumption expenditure and can stop further deepening of depression.
4. *Easy credit facilities* may be provided to consumer for purchase of durable consumer goods, such as television set, vehicle, etc. It would help in stimulating the demand for such consumer goods.
5. One of a measure suggested to raise propensity to consume is *redistribution of national income* in favour of the poor. The propensity to consume of the poorer class is higher than that of the richer class and if the national income is distributed in favour of their favour then the propensity to consume, in general, can register an increase.
6. *Wage policy* too can help to raise the propensity to consume. It is true that wage policy may not be able to raise the consumption function itself, but there may be an increase in the amount of expenditure on consumption through higher money wages. The reason is that any increase in money wages without any increase in labour productivity would harm the workers more than benefit them. We are aware of the fact that labour productivity cannot be increased in the short-run and thus any attempt to push upwards the money wage in the short-run would bring disastrous consequences for the workers. In the long-run increase in wage policy should be such that it raises the consumption schedule itself by affecting a transfer of income from non-wage groups (e.g. business groups) to wage groups through fiscal measures such as progressive taxation.

4.3 Saving Function: Average and Marginal Propensity to Save

The counterpart of consumption function is the Saving Function, as,

Saving (S) = Income (Y) – Consumption (C)

$S = Y - C$.

Thus, saving is the function of income.

Symbolically, **S = f (Y)**

Here,   S = savings; f = function of; Y = income.

Thus, a saving function can graphically be derived from C+I curve (consumption and investment curve) by plotting savings as a function of income. Income not used is savings and savings are to be invested, hence the equilibrium level of income will be where savings is equal to the given level of investment.

Fig. 4.5 shows the derivation of savings' curve on a given consumption curve.

Consumption and Savings Schedule (in ₹ Crores).

Table 4.4

Income (Y)	Consumption (C)	Savings = (Y − C)
60	70	−10 (dis-saving)
120	120	0 (Break -even point or zero savings)
180	170	50
240	220	50
300	270	50
360	320	50

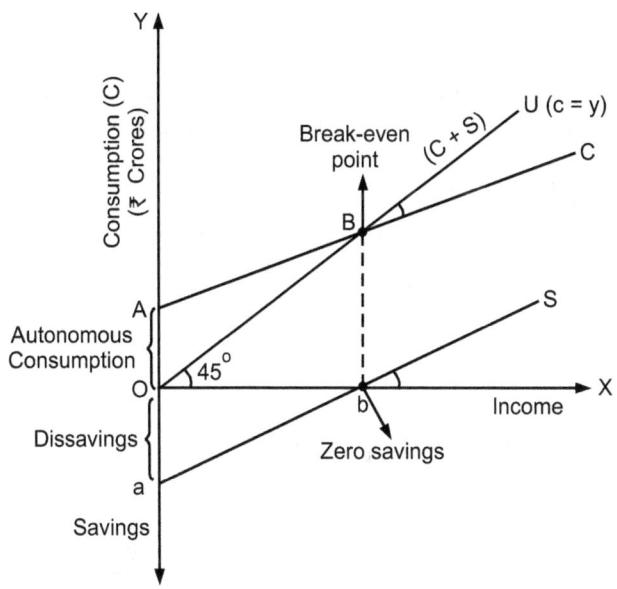

Fig. 4.5 : Derivation of Savings Curve

- OX-axis measures Income (Y)
- OY-axis measures Consumption (C) and Savings (S)
- Curve at 45^0 angle 'U' is which depicts consumption equates income
- Point 'B' shows break-even point where savings are zero.

- OA = Oa which represent autonomous consumption, i.e., where dis-savings are present.
- At B point on the C curve, draw a perpendicular Bb and along ab draw S curve by extending the line.

In short, savings is income that is not used and if consumption is a function of income (other things being equal). Likewise savings is a function of income and can be derived from the consumption function.

Technical Attributes of the Saving Function

Similar to the attributes of the consumption function are the attributes of Saving Function namely, (i) the Average Propensity to Save (A.P.S) and (ii) the Marginal Propensity to Save (M.P.S).

Average Propensity to Save (A.P.S): The average propensity to save (A.P.S) is defined as *"the ratio of aggregate savings to the aggregate income in a given period of time"*.

Thus, the value of A.P.S, for any income level, may be found out by dividing savings by income.

In symbolic terms, $A.P.S = \dfrac{S}{Y}$

Here, S = savings; Y = income.

A.P.S is calculated at various income levels.

It is pointed out that the proportion of income spent on consumption decreases as income increases and on the other hand savings increases. If A.P.C is 100%, 95%, 92%, 90% and 89%, then A.P.S $\left(\dfrac{S}{Y}\right)$ is 0%, 5%, 8%, 10% and 11%.

Table 4.5 : (A.P.S and M.P.S)

Income (Y)	Consumption (C)	APC = C/Y	APS = S/Y or (−APC)	MPC = ΔC/ΔY	MPS = ΔS/ΔY (1 − MP)
140	140	140/140 = 1(100%)	0	−	−
200	190	190/200 = 0.95 (95%)	0.05 (5%)	0.83	0.17
260	240	240/260 = 0.92 (92%)	0.08 (8%)	0.83	0.17
320	290	290/320 = 0.90 (90%)	0.1 (10%)	0.83	0.17
380	340	340/380 = 0.89 (89%)	0.11 (11%)	0.83	0.17

$$A.P.S = \dfrac{S}{Y}$$

Alternatively, $\quad A.P.S. = 1 - A.P.C.$

Or $\quad A.P.S. = 1 - \dfrac{C}{Y}$

Thus, the proportion of income saved increases as the income increases.

The significance of the average propensity to save is that it throws light on what proportion of the total cost of a given output will have to be recovered by the sale of capital goods.

Under given conditions, the relative development of consumer goods and capital goods industries in a nation depends on the A.P.C and A.P.S. It is pointed out that in highly industrialized economies, the A.P.C is low and the A.P.S is high.

Marginal Propensity to Save (M.P.S):

M.P.S is *"the ratio of change in the level of total savings to a change in the level of total income"*. M.P.S, thus, implies the effect of additional income on savings.

M.P.S can be calculated by dividing a change in savings (i.e., increase or decrease in savings), by a change in income (i.e., increase or decrease in income).

In symbolic terms, $\text{M.P.S} = \dfrac{\Delta S}{\Delta Y}$

Here, M.P.S. = Marginal propensity to save;

ΔS = Change in Savings;

ΔY = Change in income.

In Table 4.5 we observe

- M.P.S calculated at the different levels of income (Y).
- Since a linear consumption function has been assumed, therefore, the saving function derived from the consumption function is also linear and hence it is constant at all levels of income (i.e., 0.17).
- We observe that M.P.S is less than one, indicating all income earned is not completely saved.
- It is attributed to Keynes' Psychological law of consumption, i.e., the increase in income is divided between consumption and savings.

It proves that MPS is derived from M.P.C.

$$\text{M.P.S.} = 1 - \text{M.P.C}$$

Alternatively, $\text{M.P.S} = 1 - \dfrac{\Delta C}{\Delta Y}$

To illustrate, if M.P.C is 0.6, then M.P.S will be 0.4 (MPS = 1 − M.P.C) as MPC + MPS = 1. Further, as MPC is always less than 1, MPS always tends to be positive.

Likewise, MPC according to Keynes' is stable in the short-run and also MPS has stability in the short-period.

However, during the cyclical fluctuations, M.P.S may change due to the change in objective factors determining the propensity to save. For example, during the cyclical upswing, the M.P.S will rise while during the downswing MPS will fall.

However, the economic importance of the concept of M.P.S is that it enlightens the division of increase in the income into consumption and savings (ultimately investment). This knowledge assists in the planning of investment to maintain the desired level of income. It also has importance in Keynes' Multiplier theory.

Keynes observes that the propensity to consume is higher in poor people and thus propensity to save is lesser than the rich people. Therefore, in advanced countries M.P.S is high and in underdeveloped countries the M.P.S is low.

Factors Determining the Saving Function (Propensity to Save)

The rate and size of savings is influenced by various factors:

1. **Income Level:** Savings is basically a function of income, i.e., savings increase with an increase in income. Though there is no proportionate relationship between the size of income and savings, it has been empirically proved that there is a correlation between the two. The amount of personal savings depends basically on the disposable income. Hence, with an increase in income, the saving-income ratio rises, i.e., the ratio of $\frac{S}{Y}$ rises. MPS $\left(\frac{\Delta S}{\Delta Y}\right)$ tends to be higher in high-income groups or developed countries, as their per capita income is high and the saving-income ratio is also high. MPS is lower in underdeveloped countries or among low-income group for the same reason that their per capita income is low and the savings-income ratio is also low.

2. **Habit:** A major factor determining our consumption and in turn the saving function are our habits. Taste, preferences, fashion and other psychological factors influence consumption and saving. By nature of his habit when a person is extravagant his savings will be relatively smaller out of a given income. Thus, in general, the total savings in an economy depends upon the habits of the people.

3. **Holding of liquid assets:** If an individual possesses adequate amount of liquid assets like cash balances, bank deposits, etc., then the individual will consume more and save less from the current income. The reason is that he feels secured about his future. Similarly, an appreciation in the value of financial assets also induces people to consume more and save less.

4. **Population growth:** A high growth of population adversely affects the per capita income and hence reduces the savings-income ratio. The age-wise distribution of the population also influences the volume of total savings in the country. The total saving ratio in a community tends to vary with the age-structure of its population,

even with constant per capita income. Total personal savings depends upon the dis-savings of the old, retired people (dependent group) and the savings of the working age group. If the positive savings of the working age group is balanced off by the dis-savings of the retired people to maintain their consumption expenses, then the community's net savings are zero. But, if the savings from the working group is large in proportion to the dis-savings from the dependent group, then the net savings will be positive.

5. **Factors determining consumption:** Savings is that part of the income which is unused. Thus, to know the factors determining savings, we must have knowledge of the factors that influence consumption. According to Duessenbury, the size and pattern of consumption is influenced by:
   - The consumption of certain types of goods required by socially generated needs.
   - These needs can be satisfied alternatively by a range of different kinds of qualitative goods etc.
   - Consumption pattern limited by the budget constraints and the desire to save.

6. **Distribution of wealth and income:** Distribution of wealth and income in the community also determines the total savings. With greater inequalities in the distribution of income, the aggregate savings rate would be high, as the richer section of the society has a higher propensity to save. A nation with low per capita income and equality in the distribution of income would mean low savings rate. Thus, the correction of income inequalities through fiscal and other measures would reduce the savings rate and thus hamper capital formation. But, as social justice, an ideal and fair income distribution is advocated.

7. **Institutional factors:** Institutional or objective factors affect the capacity and willingness of the people to save. For example,
   - *Political stability*, security of life and property encourage the propensity to save more. Likewise, existence of a good banking system, developed capital market, availability of government bonds and securities etc., induce people to save more.
   - *The taxation structure* and government's fiscal policy also influence savings in the economy. For example, progressive direct taxation leads to reduction in personal savings, as the capacity to save is reduced. On the other hand, indirect taxes will force the consumer to spend more on maintaining his living standard. This further leads to reduction in personal savings. Further, high corporate taxation will reduce the net profit of business houses and thus reduce their capacity to save.
   - *Price stability* can lead to more savings and hyper-inflation leads to reduction in savings as money loses its value with the increase in prices.
   - *Windfall gains* increase savings and losses, leading to a reduction in the savings.

8. **Subjective factors:** There are certain subjective factors that motivate people to save and thus increase the personal savings. The savings are :
   (i) To build-up reserves against unforeseen emergencies;
   (ii) To provide for future needs;
   (iii) To enjoy larger consumption in future by high interest rates;
   (iv) To bequeath a fortune;
   (v) To undertake business projects or for speculative activities;
   (vi) To expand business investments;
   (vii) To satisfy miserliness instincts;
   (viii) To enjoy a sense of independence with accumulated savings.

9. **Rate of Interest:** Classical economists believe that savings is a function of the rate of interest, i.e., $s = f(r)$ where, s= savings; f= function of; r= rate of interest. Keynes' believed that savings is a function of disposable income. It is true that savings are part of income and not from rate of interest. However, a high rate of interest gives greater motivation to save. The rate of interest is an important factor in the mobilization of savings.

These are some of the important factors that determine the Saving Function.

Paradox of Savings

Paradox of thrift (or saving) is a macroeconomic concept. The whole and its part are entirely two different things and the characteristics of one do not necessarily pertain to the other. In other words, making *generalizations* for the whole after viewing a part can land us in fallacies. Unfortunately this truth has not been recognized even by some of the leading economists in the past. The failure to recognize this truth has been responsible for some of the gravest errors in economic thinking. The conclusions of *'individual components'* when applied to the *'aggregate'* have led to contradictory situations, which is referred by Prof. Boulding as paradoxes i.e., *Macro-economic paradoxes*. He defines these paradoxes as *"propositions which are true when applied to a single individual but which are untrue when applied to the economic system as a whole"*.

The paradox states that *what is good for an individual need not be necessarily good for the society as a whole*. This fallacy or paradox applies also to the case of savings.

Saving at an individual level is a virtue but at an economy level it is a social evil

The Classical economists argued that savings are productive and essential, as savings lead to capital formation. Thus, savings would increase the productive capacity and the wealth in future. *Savings would lead to more savings*. Examples can be given of saving-conscious families who become richer by being spend thrifts and extravagant families have a bleak future with small or no savings.

Hence, they asserted that savings is a virtue which not only enriches the individual but also the entire nation. They believed that consumption gives rise to satisfaction in the present but renders future losses.

Savings, according to the Classicists, with the flexible rate of interest would equal the investment level in the economy.

It is pointed out by critics that excess savings even at an individual level can be vice, by resulting in under-consumption and fall in demand for goods and services. Savings is a virtue only if it converts itself into productive investments.

Thus, individual savings may be a virtue but savings by the whole economy leads to fallacy or Paradox of Savings.

Keynes severely criticised the classical belief that savings was a virtue for individuals and the same would be true when there is saving at the economy level. Savings by an individual family may enrich that family but it does not conclude that if all families save the nation would be rich.

Let us now explicitly understand as to how this paradoxical situation arises and how more savings would lead to lesser savings in future.

If all individuals in an economy save and if the savings are not being converted into productive investment, (i.e., savings in the nature of a hoarding), it will lead to fall in the aggregate demand for goods and services. With fall in the aggregate demand, over-production would exist. Due to over-production (glut) of goods and services in the market, it will result in unemployment. This would reduce output, employment and income in the economy. With reduced income savings will be of lower level. At the economy level it would result in lesser savings in the long-run.

To conclude, if savings are not matched by corresponding capital formation (investment), there will be reduction in national income. This is Keynes' Paradox of Thrift. It is a paradox because it shows that what seems perfectly correct at the individual level turns out to be completely opposite when applied at the macro level.

Hence, due care should be taken related to the differences between the *individual* and *group* characteristics because failure to do so would lead to dire consequences not only in economics, but also in other social sciences.

Points to Remember

- The consumption function expresses a relationship between two quantities- income and consumption i.e., $C = f(Y)$.
- The consumption function is stable in the short period.
- Keynes propounded the 'Psychological Law of consumption' which forms the basis of the Consumption Function.
- There are 3 propositions to the Psychological Law of consumption are-

- ➤ When income increases, consumption also increases but in a lesser proportion to the increase in income;
  - ➤ Increase in income is divided between consumption and savings;
  - ➤ Increase in income leads to more consumption and savings than before.
- **Keynes' Law of consumption has various implications:**
  - ➤ Invalidates Say's Law of Market;
  - ➤ Importance of investment;
  - ➤ Government interference;
  - ➤ Declining M.E.C.;
  - ➤ Explains turning points of the trade cycle;
  - ➤ Dangers of over-savings;
  - ➤ Explains income propagation.
- **Two technical attributes of the Consumption function are:**
  - ➤ Average Propensity to Consume (APC);
  - ➤ Marginal Propensity to Consume (MPC).
- APC is the ratio of consumption to income i.e. APC = $\frac{C}{Y}$
- MPC is the ratio of change in consumption to the change in income. i.e. MPC = $\frac{\Delta C}{\Delta Y}$
- Various objective and subjective factors determine the consumption function (or the propensity to consume).
- The concept of Consumption Function has great importance in economic theory.
- **There are various measures to raise the propensity to consume-**
  - ➤ Tax reduction;
  - ➤ Urbanization;
  - ➤ Well-devised social security;
  - ➤ Easy credit facilities;
  - ➤ Redistribution of national income;
  - ➤ Wage policy.
- **Savings Function:** Income left unused after consumption is savings. Hence, Savings is a function of income.

  $S = Y - C;$ $S = f(Y).$
- **Technical attributes of the Saving function-**
  - ➤ Average Propensity to Save (APS);
  - ➤ Marginal Propensity to Save (MPS).
- APS is the ratio of aggregate savings to the aggregate income, i.e., APS = $\frac{S}{Y}$ or APS = 1 − APC.

- MPS is the ratio of change in the level of total saving to a change in the level of total income, i.e., MPS = $\frac{\Delta S}{\Delta Y}$ or MPS = 1 − MPC.
- Similar to Consumption Function, Savings Function is also determined by various factors.
- **Paradox of Savings:** Savings at individual level is a virtue but at the economy level is a social evil.

Questions

1. Explain Keynes' Psychological Law of consumption with its limitations.
2. What is meant by Consumption Function? Illustrate it with the help of a schedule and a diagram.
3. Explain the significance of the consumption function in the Keynesian theory of Employment.
4. Explain the various factors which determine the consumption function.
5. Distinguish between average and marginal propensity to consume.
6. What are the determinants of saving?
7. Explain the two attributes of the Saving function: APS and MPS.
8. Write short notes on:
   (a) Consumption Function;
   (b) Saving Function.
9. Explain the macro-economic 'Paradox of Saving".
10. How can Savings Function be derived from the Consumption Function?

Chapter 5...

Investment

Contents ...
5.1 Investment Function - Autonomous and Induced Investment
5.2 Investment Multiplier
5.3 Foreign Trade Multiplier
- Points to Remember
- Multiple Choice Questions
- Questions for Discussion

Learning Objectives ...
➢ To understand an important component of Keynesian theory of employment-investment.
➢ To learn about the main two types of investment function.
➢ To study about the various factors that determines the autonomous and induced investment.
➢ To have knowledge about the working about 'Investment Multiplier'.
➢ To study as to how for an open economy the foreign trade multiplier operates.

Introduction

In ordinary language, investment implies buying of shares, stocks, bonds, etc., which already exist in the stock market. This is *financial or money investment*. It is not real investment as it means a transfer of the existing assets. It does not influence the aggregate expenditure.

By investment, Keynes meant only real investment that adds to capital equipment. For example, construction of public works like dams, roads, buildings, a new plant, inventories, equipment, etc. The 'real' investment of Keynesian type would lead to increase in the level of income, output and employment.

According to *Joan Robinson*, "By investment is meant an addition to capital, such as occurs when a new house is built or a new factory is built. Investment means making an addition to the stock of goods in existence".

5.1 Investment Function: Autonomous and Induced Investment

The second major component of private spending is investment. Investment plays two roles in macroeconomics.

(i) It is a large and volatile component of spending; investment often leads to changes in aggregate demand and affects the business cycle.
(ii) Investment leads to capital accumulation, that is adding to the stock of buildings and equipment which increases nation's potential output and promotes economic growth in the long run.

Thus, investment plays a dual role, influencing short-run output through its impact on aggregate demand and affecting long-run output growth through the impact of capital formation on potential output and aggregate supply.

> *In macroeconomics 'investment' and 'real investment' mean differently. Many people speak of investing when buying a piece of land or any title to property. In economics these purchases are 'financial investments' because what one person is buying someone else is selling and there is investment only when 'real capital' is produced.*

Meaning of Investment Function

In the Keynesian theory of employment, the two components of Aggregate Demand that help increase income, output and employment are

(i) *Consumption demand and*
(ii) *Investment demand.*

The consumption function is more or less stable in the short-run.

If intention is to step-up the income, output and employment, then the economy must place its confidence on the second component of Aggregate Demand Function (ADF) i.e., on investment.

Investment function refers to inducement to invest or investment demand

Classical economists considered investment demand simply as a decreasing function of the interest, i.e., $I = f(r)$ [here I = investment demand; f= function of; r = rate of interest]. But, Keynes gave a strategic role to this variable investment demand that has to be skillfully manipulated to increase employment.

Investment can be-

- Private Investment;
- Public Investment.

The *private investment* is generally *induced investment*. The volume of investment in a private enterprise economy depends upon the factors such as:

(a) The Marginal Efficiency of Capital (M.E.C)
(b) The Rate of Interest.

The *public investment* is an *autonomous investment* i.e., the investment does not depend upon the M.E.C and the rate of interest.

Public investment can be decided upon quite arbitrarily without any reference to either M.E.C (expected profits) or the rate of interest. However, private investment cannot ignore M.E.C and the Rate of interest, when taking decisions on investment.

It is argued that out of these two factors – M.E.C and the Rate of Interest – which one is more important in determining the investment? Normally, the rate of interest does not change much. In fact, it is more or less sticky. It implies that it is the M.E.C (or the expected profit) which determines the volume of investment in an economy. Hence, investment shall increase, if the expected rate of profit (MEC) is high and vice versa. It can be said that *the fluctuations in investment are mainly due to the changes in the MEC.*

Before we discuss the determinants of Investment function, let us understand gross investment and net investment.

Gross Investment is the total amount spent on new capital assets in a year. But, during a span of time capital stock wears out every year and is used up referred to as depreciation and obsolescence. Gross Investment includes expenditure on replacement of the capital assets.

Net Investment is net addition to the existing capital stock of the economy, i.e., it is gross investment minus the depreciation.

> ***Gross Investment = Net Investment + Depreciation***
> ***Net Investment = Gross Investment – Depreciation***

If in any year economy does gross investment to replace the wear and tear (i.e. expenditure done only on 'depreciation') and not on any new capital assets, then there is no addition to the economy's capital stock. It implies that no net investment has been done in that year. And, if gross investment is *even less than depreciation*, it is *disinvestment* in the economy and capital stock decreases.

Thus, for an increase in the real capital stock of the economy, gross investment should be more than only the replacement of the existing capital stock.

Factors Determining Investment

"Investment" in the Keynesian sense does not refer to the purchase of existing bonds, securities or debentures. This is *financial investment* and not real investment. Real investment is *net* addition to the existing capital equipment such as new factories, machines and plants. It is the real investment which gives additional employment to the people.

Gross Private domestic investment or (I) is the domestic component of national investment. The major types of gross private investment are the building of residential structures; investment in business fixed equipment, software, and structures, additions to inventory, etc.

However, in total social investment, besides gross private domestic investment it includes foreign investment, government investment and intangible investments in human capital and improved knowledge.

Why do businesses invest? This simple statement contains following *elements (or following factors)* that are taken into consideration when undertaking investment decision.

1. **Revenue:** An investment will bring the firm additional revenue if it helps the firm to sell more products. It implies that the overall level of output (GDP) will be an important determinant of investment. Investments are low when factories lying idle and firms have relatively little need for new factories. Thus, investments depend upon the revenues that will be generated by the state of overall economic activity. It has been observed that investment is very sensitive to the trade cycle.

2. **Supply price of capital asset:** *The supply price (p) of the asset,* i.e., what the asset is going to cost, is the other factor to be considered while undertaking the real investment. The supply price of an asset is the cost of producing a brand new asset of that kind, not the supply price of an existing asset. The supply price of an asset is also referred to as the *'replacement cost'*.

3. **The prospective yield (y):** is the total *'net'* returns expected from the asset over its lifetime. Net returns imply the 'net' yearly proceeds obtained from the sale of the output produced by the capital asset. The term 'net' implies that out of the gross proceeds the 'running costs' of the asset have to be subtracted to arrive at the net returns. Then, the annual *net returns* expected from the asset during its lifetime are added together. Thus, *the prospective yield of an asset is the aggregate net returns expected from it during its lifetime.*

4. **Costs/ Rate of Interest:** An important determinant of the level of investment is the costs of investing. Investment goods last for many years and estimating the costs of investment is somewhat more complicated than doing so for other commodities. For durable goods, the cost of capital includes not only the price of the capital good but also the interest rate that borrowers pay to finance the capital and the taxes that firms pay on their incomes.

   Investors often raise the funds for buying capital goods by borrowing through mortgaging or in the bond market. *Thus the cost of borrowing is the interest rate on borrowed funds.* In the case of a family buying a house, the interest rate is the mortgage interest rate.

   Further, taxes also determine investments. The taxes play a crucial role in curtailing or extending the corporate profits, thereby discouraging or encouraging investment in the corporate sector. The tax breaks given by government in certain sectors or activities also encourage investments in them.

5. **Expectations:** Another factor in the determination of investment is profit expectations and business confidence. Investment is some sort of gamble at times on the future, a bet that the revenue from an investment will exceed its costs. Thus, investment decisions hang by a thread on expectations and forecasts. It is wise to understand that forecasting can be hazardous and hence businesses spend much energy analyzing investments and trying to narrow the uncertainties about their investments.

To sum up, businesses invest to earn profits and capital goods last for many years, hence investment decisions depend on:
(i) The demand for the output produced by the new investment;
(ii) The interest rates and taxes that influence the cost of the investment;
(iii) Business expectations about the state of the economy.

In choosing among investment projects, firms compare the annual revenues from an investment with the annual cost of capital, which depends upon the interest rate. *The difference between annual revenue and annual cost is the annual net profit. When annual net profit is positive, the investment makes money, while in case it is negative then net profit denotes that the investment loses money.*

All these factors are summed up and Keynes has referred as the *Marginal Efficiency of Capital (M.E.C).*

Marginal Efficiency of Capital (M.E.C)

M.E.C refers to the expected profitability of a capital asset. It may be defined as *"the highest rate of return over cost, expected from the marginal or additional unit of a capital asset".*

(i) In the words of **Kurihara**, *"it is the ratio between the prospective yield of additional capital-goods and their supply price".*

Thus, the M.E.C of a particular type of asset means, "what an investor expects to earn from an additional unit of it compared with what it costs him" (i.e., prospective yield and the supply price).

(ii) **Keynes** states, *"MEC, as being equal to that rate of discount which would make the present value of the series of annuities given by the returns expected from the capital asset during its life, just equal to its supply price."*

That is, the MEC of a particular type of asset is the rate at which the prospective yield expected from the additional unit of that asset is to be discounted if it is to equal the supply price of the asset.

Thus,   Supply Price = Discounted Prospective Yield

In symbolic terms,
$$R_c = \frac{Q_1}{(1+r)_1} + \frac{Q_2}{(1+r)_2} + \frac{Q_3}{(1+r)_3} \cdots \frac{Q_n}{(1+r)_n}$$

Here, R_c = supply price or replacement cost of the new capital asset;

$Q_1, Q_2, Q_3 \ldots Q_n$ represents the expected annual returns from the capital asset;

r= rate of discount which will make the present value of the series of annual returns just equal to the supply price or replacement cost of the capital asset.

Thus, r = rate of discount or the marginal efficiency of capital.

However, the values of Q's are not necessarily the same each year. In a dynamic economy, the annual returns from the *capital asset* (Q's) are not necessarily the same each year. It is very rare that the annual returns are the same each year. Thus, there will be some *discount rate (r)* which will bring the two sides of the equation into equality with each other.

The term $Q_1 \div (1 + r)^1$ is the present value of the yield (annually) to be received at the end of the first year discounted at the rate of r for that year. Suppose the rate of discount (r) to be 10 percent, each rupee which is expected per year hence, is worth 90.91 paisa now. (This is calculated as ₹ 1 divided by 1.10). Hence, 90.91 paisa invested at 10 percent will grow to ₹ 1 in one year.

Now, for $Q_2 \div (1 + r)^2$ is the present value of the yield expected at the end of the second year discounted at the rate of r. At the same 10% each rupee (after two years), it is worth 82.65 paisa (this can be obtained by dividing 1/- by $(1.10)^2$ i.e., 1.21). In other words, 82.65 paisa invested now at 10% will be ₹ 1 in two years time. In this way, we can discount the present value of the various yields so as to bring their aggregate into equality with the current supply price of the capital asset.

Arithmetic Illustration:

Let us take a simple arithmetic example to understand the meaning of r (or M.E.C) as the rate of discount. Suppose, the supply price or the cost of replacement) of a capital asset is ₹ 50,000/- and its life is 3 years. In the course of these three years, the asset is expected to yield a series of annuities (or yields) like 1st year: ₹ 11,000/-, 2nd year: ₹ 24,200/- and 3rd year: ₹ 26,620/-. These three annuities added together are equal to ₹ 61,820/-. But the present value of each yield is to be found out by discounting the expected future value. Obviously, if we take 10% as the rate of discount (or the M.E.C) then the supply price becomes equal to the discounted prospective yield. The value of r being 0.10 (i.e., 10%), 1 + r is 1.10. According to the formula,

$$R_c = \frac{Q1}{(1+r)_1} + \frac{Q2}{(1+r)_2} + \frac{Q3}{(1+4)_3}$$

Substituting the values: $₹ 50,000 = \frac{₹ 11,000}{(1.10)_1} + \frac{₹ 24,200}{(1.10)_2} + \frac{₹ 26,620}{(1.10)_3}$

$$= \frac{₹ 11,000}{(1.10)} + \frac{₹ 24,200}{(1.21)} + \frac{₹ 26,620}{(1.331)}$$

₹ 50,000 = ₹ 10,000 + ₹ 20,000 + ₹ 20,000

= ₹ 50,000.

Since 10% is the rate which equates the present value of expected annuities from the asset (₹ 10,000 + ₹ 20,000 + ₹ 20,000) with the supply price (₹ 50,000), it should be taken to be the Marginal Efficiency of Capital (M.E.C).

From the above discussion one simple point is to be understood, i.e., so long as the supply price is greater than the prospective yield of an asset, the investor would not think of taking up such as investment project. It is only when the *'net'* prospective return is *greater than* the supply price that he shall agree to take up the investment project.

Investment Demand Curve

M.E.C is determined by the prospective yield of an asset and its supply price. *Private investment is very much affected by the M.E.C*

Let us discuss as to how M.E.C is affected by the investment demand or by the volume of investment. To be more precise, the influence of the volume of investment in a particular asset depends on its M.E.C

The M.E.C of an asset will progressively fall as the investment in that asset increases, due to the following reasons:

(i) The M.E.C of an asset will fall as more and more units of that asset are produced, just as the price of a good falls and more units are put in the market for sale.

(ii) Alongwith the fall in the prospective yield, the supply of such an asset is likely to go up if more units of such an asset are produced due to the rising costs in the industry which produces these assets.

Illustration:

Lower M.E.C with an increased investment can be illustrated as follows:

Table 5.1 : Diminishing Marginal Productivity (Efficiency) of Capital

Investment (in ₹)	M.E.C (%)
1,000	5
2,000	4
3,000	3
4,000	2
5,000	1

In **Table 5.1** when the investment is ₹ 1,000, the MEC is 5 percent. As the investment go on increasing from ₹ 1,000 to ₹ 5,000, the MEC goes on declining from 5 percent to 1 percent respectively. If the rate of interest is 3 percent, then only ₹ 3,000 will be invested and if the rate of interest falls to 2 percent then the investment will be ₹ 4,000. Thus, the M.E.C and the rate of interest are closely related to each other and they are *inversely proportionate* to each other.

Diagrammatic Illustration

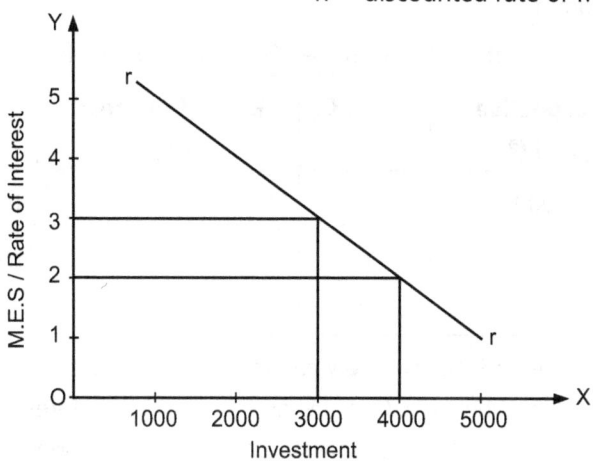

OX-axis measures investment;
OY-axis measures M.E.C
rr = discounted rate or M.E.C curve.

Fig. 5.1 : Investment

M.E.C which determines investment and rate of interest are inversely related to each other. The M.E.C curve slope downwards from left to right indicating an inverse relationship between investment and the rate of interest. Thus, given the M.E.C curve (or the schedule), the investment will depend upon the current rate of interest. For instance, at 3 percent, the capital investment is ₹ 3,000 and at 2 percent the invested capital is ₹ 4,000.

M.E.C and the Rate of Interest

The volume of private investment in a capitalist economy depends upon two factors, namely, (a) the *M.E.C and (b) the Rate of interest.*

(a) M.E.C depends on the supply price and the prospective yield of the capital asset;
(b) Rate of Interest is determined by the demand for and supply of money.
  ➤ *On demand side* the rate of interest is determined by the liquidity preference of the people.
  ➤ *On supply side* the rate of interest is determined by the supply of money available in the economy.

Investment is undertaken after weighing the M.E.C of a particular capital asset against the current rate of interest (i.e., expected returns from the capital asset with the cost of that capital asset).

> **When M.E.C is greater than the rate of interest, fresh investments will be undertaken till M.E.C = rate of interest.**

Illustration

The relationship between M.E.C and the rate of interest can be illustrated with the help of a schedule and a diagram.

Table 5.2 : Relationship between M.E.C and the Rate of Interest

Supply Price (₹)	Prospective yield (₹)	M. E. C	Rate of Interest (%)	Impact on Investment
50,000	2,000	4	4	Neutral
40,000	2,000	6	4	Favourable
50,000	2,000	4	5	Unfavourable.

In Table 5.2, it is observed that the new capital asset yields an annual constant return of ₹ 2,000. In the first case, when M.E.C is 4% and the rate of interest is 4%, the effect on investment would be neutral. No new investments would be undertaken as there are no gains out of it.

In the second case, new investments are *favoured* by investors as M.E.C is 6% and the rate of interest is lower, i.e. 4%.

In the third case, M.E.C is 4% (expected returns) which is lower than the rate of interest (cost of capital asset) which is 5%. It is clear that the investors would suffer loss if they proceed with new investments and hence an *unfavourable* case.

Thus, the private investment is determined by M.E.C and the rate of interest. Of the two factors, M.E.C is subject to greater fluctuations and the rate of interest is more stable in character.

Position and Shape of the Investment Demand Curve

M.E.C is inversely related to the volume of investments. The position and shape of the investment demand curve plays an important role in determining the volume of investment.

- If the investment demand curve (M.E.C curve) is relatively *interest-elastic* (i.e., responds to rate of interest) then a slight fall in the rate of interest will result in a great expansion in the volume of investment.

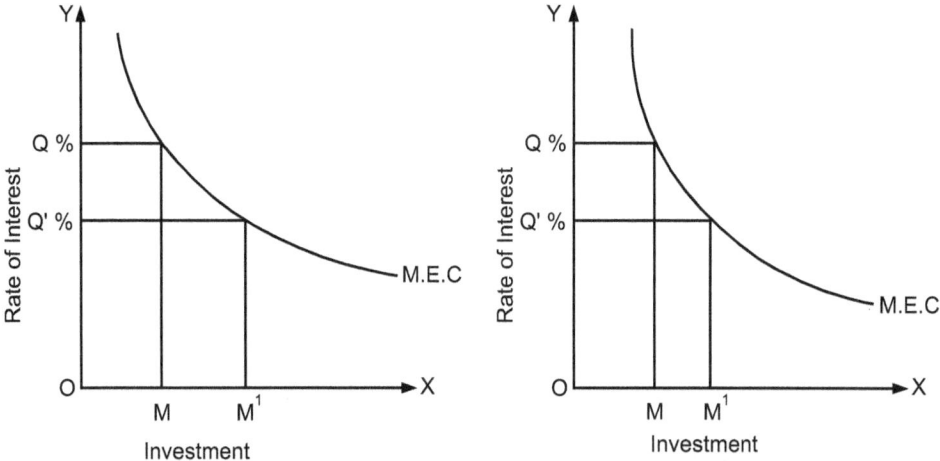

Fig. 5.2 : M.E.C is Relatively Elastic   Fig. 5.3 : M.E.C is Relatively Inelastic

- If the investment demand curve (M.E.C curve) is relatively interest-inelastic (i.e., does not respond to a greater extent to the rate of interest) even a great fall in the rate of interest may not lead to any increase in the volume of investment.

Fig. 5.2 shows the M.E.C curve to be *interest-elastic*. At Q interest rate, the volume of investment is OM. At a lower rate of interest, OQ'% a huge increase in volume of investment is seen, i.e., OM^1.

In **Fig. 5.3**, M.E.C curve is *interest-inelastic*. At Q interest rate, the volume of investment is OM. At lower rate of interest of OQ'%, smaller increase (in relation to the fall in interest rate) in investment is undertaken, i.e., OM^1.

- With the rate of interest remaining the same, an increase in the M.E.C leads to an increase in investment.

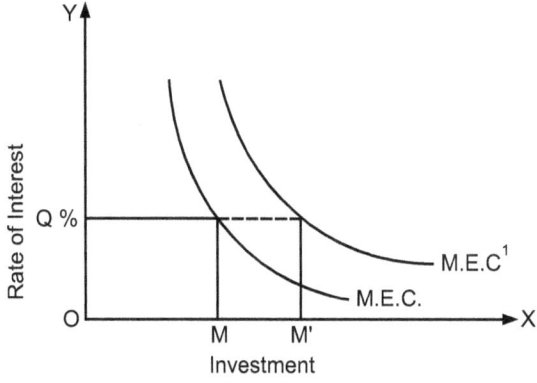

Fig. 5.4 : Change in MEC on Investment

Fig. 5.4, the rate of interest remains constant at OQ%, but M.E.C has increased to MEC^1. Thus, the volume of investment increases from OM to OM^1.

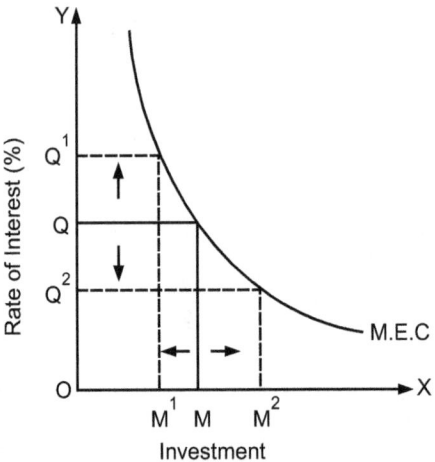

Fig. 5.5 : Change in Interest Rate on Investment

Fig. 5.5 shows that when there is no change in M.E.C but the rate of interest changes (increases or decreases) it leads to a change in the volume of investment.

When the interest rate increases from OQ to OQ^1, volume of investment falls from OM to OM^1. And, when the rate of interest falls to OQ^2, the volume of investment expands to OM^2.

M.E.C is considered in relation to a *'particular'* capital asset (i.e., returns from a particular capital asset), but in *'general'* it is considered for an economy. M.E.C, in *'general'* means the M.E.C of the most profitable asset in the economy.

To sum up the Investment Demand curve (M.E.C curve):

- Of the two factors – the supply price and the prospective yield – which influence the M.E.C, it is the *supply price* which is considered as stable and fixed in the short period. The reason is that production conditions do not change so readily in the short period and hence the supply prices of capital assets do not undergo changes in the short period.
- Keynesian economics is a short-period analysis, hence the first factor determining Investment demand is assumed as *given or fixed*.
- Thus, if there are fluctuations in M.E.C, then it due to variations in the prospective yield of capital assets.
- The instability of M.E.C in a capitalist economy is the direct outcome of the instability of the prospective yield.

Let us now discuss the prospective returns of capital assets.

- The prospective yield of capital assets is the most unstable factor operating in capitalist economy. Why is it so unstable and uncertain?

- The reason is that the expected returns imply returns in future that are expected, but future itself is uncertain, unforeseen and incalculable. Thus, anything which is related to the future can neither be certain nor stable.
- Despite its high degree of uncertainty, the entrepreneur does attempt to calculate the prospective yield of a capital asset, by considering all the possible foreseeable factors. According to Keynes, in estimating the prospective yield of contemplated assets, the entrepreneurs are influenced by business expectations.

Factors Influencing M.E.C

A large number of factors, short-run and long-run, determine and influence the Marginal Efficiency of Capital (M.E.C) in a private enterprise economy.

(A) Short-Term Factors

(1) **Cost and Prices:** The future behaviour of costs and prices has a strong influence on M.E.C For instance, if the costs are expected to fall and the prices are expected to rise in the future, the expected returns from the venture will increase. On the other hand, if the costs are expected to rise and prices to fall in the future,, M.E.C will receive a set-back and as a result the volume of investment will fall.

(2) **Future Expectations of Demand:** M.E.C depends to a great extent on the expected demand for the products in the economy. For example, if the demand for the goods is expected to be high in the future, M.E.C will step up and as a result investment will increase. On the other hand, if the demand for the goods is expected to fall in the future, M.E.C will be low and the investment will be low.

(3) **Current State of Affairs:** Current expectations influence the volume of investment. The rates of return on 'current' investment influence the future business expectations. Businessmen, while taking decisions on new investments are guided by the current state of affairs in business, e.g., prices, costs, etc. They tend to evaluate how these factors will work in the future. In short, if the current rates of returns are high, M.E.C is expected to be high for new projects of investment.

(4) **The Consumption Function:** A rise in the propensity to consume will cause an upward shift in M.E.C and in the volume of investment. The reason is that, the demand for investment goods is partly derived from the demand for consumer goods.

(5) **Change in the Income Level:** Investment is income-elastic, i.e., investment is directly related with the changes in the level of income through the accelerator. For example, sudden changes in income due to windfall gains or unexpected losses, imposition of heavy taxes or tax concessions, influence M.E.C and ultimately the investments. An increase in the income level raises investment and decline in the income level discourages investment.

(6) Conducive Business Environment: The entrepreneurs in a private enterprise economy are often subject to alternating waves of *optimism* and *pessimism* which influence M.E.C and investment. For example, during the period of *optimism*, the entrepreneurs *over estimate* the rates of return on future investments and boost the M.E.C of capital assets. On the other hand, during the period of *pessimism* when the rates of return are *under estimated*, it lowers M.E.C of capital assets.

(B) Long-Run Factors:

(1) Growth of Population: A rapidly growing population means a rapid increase in the demand for all types of goods – consumption and investment goods. This invariably raises M.E.C in the private enterprise economy. In contrast, a declining population has an opposite effect on M.E.C

(2) Technical Progress: An improvement in the techniques of production in industry generally boosts new investment on the part of entrepreneurs. For instance, a new discovery or new invention in the production technique makes it essential to install costly machinery or plant in the industrial enterprise.

(3) Opening-up of New Areas: The development of new areas in a country requires heavy investment in all sorts of fields such as transport, banking, irrigation, agriculture, housing, etc.

(4) **Level of Current Investment:** The rate of current investment in any particular industry has a significant influence on M.E.C For instance, if the rate of current investment in an industry is already high, then there is little scope for any further investment in such an industry. If a large number of textile mills are being set-up, then new entrepreneurs will hesitate to invest in such an industry, until and unless demand for textiles is expected to be exceptionally high in future.

(5) **Political Climate:** Political conditions also affect the inducement to invest. If there is political instability in the country, the inducement to invest may be affected adversely. While, a stable government creates confidence in the business community whereby the inducement to invest is raised.

Criticism of the Concept of M.E.C

M.E.C as a concept has come in for severe criticism from many critics.

1. **No fixed meaning:** It is criticised that Keynes has failed to adhere to any fixed meaning of M.E.C concept. Keynes has used the term 'Marginal Efficiency of Capital' (M.E.C) in so many different senses that it becomes difficult to keep track of them.

2. **Ambiguities of the concept:** Prof. Hazlitt points out the ambiguities of the concept. He suggests that it would have been better if Keynes had dropped this term and substituted it for any of the other terms that are already in use. Among the terms in use are, 'the marginal productive yield', 'utility', 'efficiency of capital' etc. Keynes has used the vaguest one, i.e., Marginal Efficiency of Capital (M.E.C).

3. **Inconsistency of the terms:** Keynes' concept has been criticised on the inconsistency of the terms. It is said that Keynes failed to recognize that rates of interest were as much governed by expectations as was M.E.C. In other words, Keynes included the M.E.C in the realm of *dynamic economics* and the rate of interest in the realm of *static economics*. If the M.E.C embodied expectations, then so did the interest rate. To assume otherwise was to assume that entrepreneurs were inflected by their expectations but the lenders were not. It is like assuming that lenders (not assuming the prices of future), were not intelligent and the borrowers were intelligent.

4. **Ignored 'economies':** In his analysis Keynes ignored the discussion of the 'economies' which may influence the shape of investment demand schedule, in either case.

5. **Inadequate explanation:** Keynes has inadequately explained the determination of the shape of investment demand function. Fluctuations in the profitability of capital in relation to its productivity are totally ignored in Keynes' theory.

6. **Incorrect Assumption:** According to Saulnier, Keynesian analysis of the investment function is related to the rate of interest and the M.E.C as Keynes assumed that wages equal the marginal productivity of labour. And, if this assumption is removed, the rate of wages becomes an important element in this theory.

Critics conclude that Keynes' concept of M.E.C is incomplete, inconsistent, contradictory and ambiguous.

Autonomous and Induced Investment

New investments can be classified as:

1. Autonomous investments.
2. Induced investments.

The distinction between the two kinds of investments can be made with reference to the neo-classical *investment function*. The general form of investment function is given as follows:

$$I = f(y, i)$$

Here,
I = investment;
f = function of;
y = income;
i = rate of interest.

The investment that responds to changes in income, i.e., investment increases with increase in income (y) and decreases with change in the rate of interest (i) is called as *induced investment*. Since, y is assumed to remain constant in the short-run, investment function is given as:

$$I = f(i)$$

Thus, investment which is influenced by the consumption expenditure, rate of interest and business expectation is "induced investment". In short, induced investment is profit or income motivated. And, factors like prices, wages and interest changes, which influence profits also influence induced investment. Likewise, demand also influences it. When income increases, demand for consumer goods increases and to meet this demand, investment increases. Thus, induced investment, in the long-run, is a function of income, i.e., $I = f(y)$ or investment is *income-elastic*. The investment fluctuates (increase or decrease) with the rise or fall in income. This can be illustrated in **Fig. 5.6 below.**

OX-axis measures income.

OY-axis measures investment.

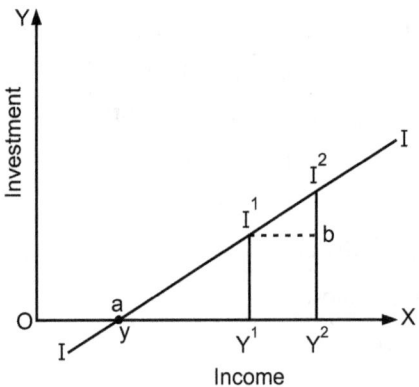

Fig. 5.6 : Shows Induced Investment

II is the investment curve. It shows '*induced*' investment at various levels of income.

Induced investment is zero at OY income, as II intersects X-axis at a. When income rises to OY^2, induced investment, which is income-elastic, also increases to I^2Y^2. And, fall in income to OY^1 reduces induced investment to I^1Y^1.

Induced investment may be further classified into: (a) the Average Propensity to Invest (API) and (b) the Marginal Propensity to Invest (MPI).

API is the ratio of investment to income, i.e., API = $\frac{I}{Y}$. For instance, if the income is ₹ 50 crores and investment is ₹ 5 crores, then API = $\frac{I}{Y}$ or $\frac{5}{50}$ = 0.1. In the above Fig. 5.6 the average propensity to invest at OY^2 income level is $I^2Y^2 \div OY^2$

MPI is the ratio of change in investment to the change in income, i.e., MPI = $\frac{\Delta I}{\Delta Y}$. For instance, if the change in investment (ΔI) is ₹ 2 crores and the change in income (ΔY) is ₹ 10 crores, then

$$\text{MPI} = \frac{\Delta I}{\Delta Y} \text{ or } \frac{2}{10} = 0.2$$

In the above Fig. ..... $\frac{\Delta I}{\Delta Y} = I^2 b \div Y^1 Y^2$

Autonomous Investment is the investment caused by the factors other than the level of income and interest rate. It means that autonomous investment is independent of changes in income and is an independent decision of the business units. In fact, income and interest rates are not only determinants of investment. There are other factors called as *external or exogenous factors*. They are long-run factors that bring changes in the economy, such as:

(i) Innovations in techniques or production;
(ii) Future expectations;
(iii) Invention or discovery of new raw materials;
(iv) Invention of new production processes;
(v) Discovery of new markets;
(vi) Increase in public expenditure;
(vii) Growth of population and its purchasing power, etc.

Investment caused due to these factors is called *autonomous investment*. Investment in houses, roads, public buildings, electric supply etc. is dependent upon social factors like the rate of growth of population, the rate of economic growth, etc. Similarly, the discoveries of new techniques and their application to business are also the result of investment that goes into research. All these types of investment are long-run investments. Such investments are largely autonomous.

To conclude, autonomous investment is independent of the level of income and thus is income-elastic. It is not influenced by changes in demand. It is influenced by exogenous factors, such as innovations, inventions, growth of population and labour force, social and legal institutions, weather changes, war etc.

Investment in economic and social overheads, whether made by a public or a private enterprise, is *autonomous investment*. Expenditure on social and economic overheads includes expenditure on road, canals, schools, hospitals etc. Since investment on these projects is generally associated with public policy, autonomous investment is regarded as public investment.

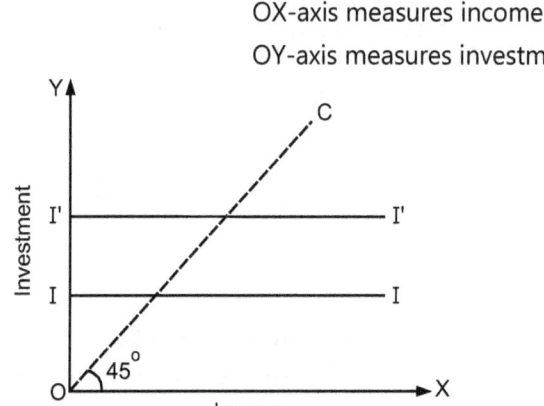

Fig. 5.7 : Shows autonomous investment

Autonomous investment is shown as a curve parallel to the OX-axis as II curve.

It indicates that at all levels of income, the amount of investment, OI remains constant. The upward shift of the curve to I'I' indicates an increased and steady flow of investment, at a constant rate OI', at all levels of income. However, for purposes of income determination, the autonomous curve is superimposed on C curve in a 45^0 line diagram.

5.2 Investment Multiplier

Introduction

With the concept of Marginal Propensity to Consume (MPC) is closely connected the concept of the *Multiplier*. It is considered as one of Keynes' path breaking contribution to economic analysis. The concept of multiplier was first developed by R. F. Khan in his article *"The Relation of Home Investment to Unemployment"* (1931). Khan's multiplier was the 'Employment Multiplier'. Keynes took the idea from R. F. Khan's employment multiplier and formulated the 'Investment Multiplier'.

The Investment Multiplier

Keynes considers his theory of multiplier as an integral part of his theory of employment.

The multiplier expresses the relationship between an initial increment in investment and the final increment in aggregate income. Thus, *the multiplier is the ratio of the change in income to the change in investment.*

The investment multiplier (K) has been defined as *"a ratio of increment in income (ΔY) to an increment in autonomous investment (ΔI)"*

It points to the fact that when there is an increment in investment, income will increase by an amount which is K times the increment of investment.

In the words of *Hansen*, Keynes' investment multiplier is the coefficient relating the increase of investment to an increase of income.

Thus, $$K = \frac{\Delta Y}{\Delta I}$$

Alternatively, $$\Delta Y = K \times \Delta I$$

Here, Y = income, I = investment; Δ = denotes change (increase or decrease); K = the multiplier.

It shows as to how many times the effect of an initial change in investment is multiplied by causing changes in the aggregate income.

Whenever an investment is done in the economy, the effect is to increase aggregate income not only by the amount of the original investment, but by something much more than it. The reason is simple, the original investment increases income not only in the industries where the investment is made, but also in certain industries whose products are demanded by men employed in investment industries.

The size of the Marginal Propensity to Consume (MPC) decides the size of the multiplier, as the two are closely related to each other. Thus, "higher the marginal propensity to consume higher shall be the size of the multiplier and vice versa. In fact, the size of the multiplier can be derived from the MPC.

The multiplier is equal to the reciprocal of 1 minus the MPC.

Thus, $$K = \frac{1}{1 - m}$$

Here, K = multiplier; m = marginal propensity to consume (MPC).

Hence, if the m (marginal propensity to consume) is known to us, K can be determined according to this formula.

Illustration:

Suppose, the MPC is $\frac{1}{2}$, then $K = \frac{1}{1 - 1/2} = \frac{1}{1/2} = 2$.

The multiplier can be also derived from the Marginal Propensity to Save (MPS) and it is the reciprocal of MPS, therefore $K = \frac{1}{MPS}$ or $K = \frac{1}{S}$

Here, K = multiplier; MPS or S = marginal propensity to save.

> MPC + MPS is equal to 1

If the MPC is deducted from 1, we are left with the MPS. Hence, it is said that we can obtain K provided we know either the MPC or MPS.

Let us suppose that the MPC is $\frac{9}{10}$, by deducting $\frac{9}{10}$ from 1, we get $\frac{1}{10}$ which is the marginal propensity to save. The reciprocal of $\frac{1}{10}$ is 10 and this is the multiplier. Hence, *the multiplier is the reciprocal of the Marginal Propensity to Save (MPS) which is always equal to 1 minus the Marginal Propensity to Consume (MPC).*

MPC very rarely is zero. It means nothing is spent by the consumers out of the increased incomes. In other words, the whole increase of income is saved and the multiplier is 1. In such a case, if the new investment is ₹ 10 crores in public works and the MPC is zero; it means that the whole of ₹ 10 crores is saved, the multiplier is 1 and the aggregate income increases only by ₹ 10 crores.

The other limiting case is when MPC is 1. It implies that the consumers spend the whole of the increment of their incomes on consumption and *nothing in saved* (MPS = zero). This will result in an explosive situation, for example, investment of ₹ 10 crores in public works. The men who are employed will receive ₹ 10 crores and shall spend the whole of it on consumer goods. Other workers who receive increased incomes shall also spend them. In this way, ₹ 10 crores shall emerge and re-emerge and result in an infinite increase in income. Such a situation is rare but can be witnessed during hyper-inflation, as the multiplier will be *infinity*.

> MPC = zero; and MPC = 1, both the situations are rare.

The multiplier can never be 1 or infinity. It generally varies between 1 and infinity, i.e., the multiplier is greater than zero but less than 1.

Table 5.3, gives values of the multiplier which correspond to certain values of the MPC.

Table 5.3 : Derivation of the Multiplier

MPC $\left(\frac{\Delta C}{\Delta Y}\right)$	MPS $\left(\frac{\Delta S}{\Delta Y}\right)$ (or MPS = 1 − MPC)	K (Multiplier (Coefficient)
0	1	1
1/2	1/2	2
2/3	1/3	3
3/4	1/4	4
4/5	1/5	5
8/9	1/9	9
9/10	1/10	10
1	0	α (Infinity)

Numerical Illustration

The actual process of multiple expansion of income brought about by increased expenditure on consumption goods as a result of new investment is shown below. Suppose that n investment of ₹ 10 crores is made in a public works project and the MPC is ½. It means that the multiplier is $2 \left[K = \frac{1}{1-m} \right] \left[K = \frac{1}{1-1/2} \right]$. Hence, an investment of ₹ 10 crores will lead to an aggregate income of ₹ 20 crores. **Table 5.4** explains the working of the multiplier.

Table 5.4: Working of the Multiplier

(in ₹ Crores)

Round		Increment in investment (ΔI)		Increment Income (ΔY)
1		10	=	10
½	×	10	=	5
$(1/2)^2$	×	10	=	2.50
$(1/2)^3$	×	10	=	1.25
$(1/2)^4$	×	10	=	0.62
		Total	=	19.37

In the *first round*, the income shall increase by ₹ 5 crores, MPC being ½, the first set of income recipients will spend only 50 percent of their income. In the *secondary round*, income shall increase by ₹ 2.50 crores (it is ½ of ₹ 5 crores). In the *third round*, income increases by ₹ 1.25 crores (it is 50 percent of 2.50 crores) and in the *fourth round*, income rises by 0.62 crores (it is ½ of 1.25 crores). Finally, the aggregate income will have increased to ₹ 20 crores (i.e., 2 times of the original investment as K = 2). In the above arithmetical example, it is to be noted that the whole process of income propagation is spread over time. It implies that the income does not increase to ₹ 20 crores all at once and simultaneously. If each round takes 5 months and 4 rounds are involved, then it will take 20 months for an investment of ₹ 10 crores to increase income by ₹ 20 crores. However, Keynes has ignored the 'time lags' in this process of income propagation.

To conclude, *the size of the multiplier varies directly with the size of the MPC. Thus, if Marginal Propensity to Consume (MPC) is high, higher shall be the multiplier (K) and vice versa.*

Diagrammatic Illustration

The concept of multiplier can be illustrated graphically. Suppose that the MPC in a community is ½ or the MPS is ½ and the multiplier (K) is 2. Further, suppose that the community which is already investing a sum of ₹ 30 crores now decides to increase the investment by another ₹ 10 crores. Since the multiplier is 2, the income of the community shall increase by ₹ 20 crores as a result of additional investment of ₹ 10 crores.

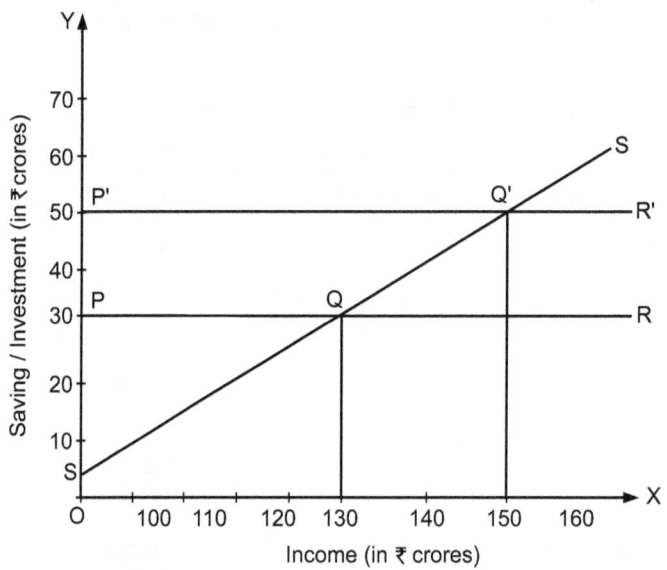

Fig. 5.8 : Multiplier

In **Fig. 5.8**, PR represents the original investment of ₹ 30 crores. SS represents the saving curve. The additional investment of ₹ 10 crores is represented by P'R'. The distance between the two curves PR and P'R' is ₹ 10 crores. Q was the original point of equilibrium between saving and Investment and the income of the community is ₹ 130 crores. With an additional investment of ₹ 10 crores, the new investment curve P'R' intersects the saving curve (S) at the new equilibrium point Q' and the income increases by 150 crores (K is 2, therefore from ₹ 130 crores to ₹ 150 crores). Thus, with an additional investment of ₹ 10 crores, the income has increased by ₹ 20 crores.

The theory of investment multiplier bears a significant amount of truth. It is true that an increase in investment has secondary consequences that result in an increase in income larger than the initial increase in investment. However, certain difficulties arise from the use of the multiplier concept. For example, in the above illustration it has been assumed that everyone had MPC is ½ (50 percent). This is not very realistic assumption. Because, varying conditions are likely to produce varying MPC. In such conditions it is difficult to estimate the value of the multiplier. Thus, the theory of the multiplier is subject to certain limitations.

Limitations of the Multiplier

The multiplier is based on certain assumptions. Non-fulfillment of these assumptions will hamper the effective operation of the multiplier theory. Following are the limitations of the multiplier principle:

1. **No change in MPC:** To achieve the actual value of the multiplier, it is essential to assume no change in MPC during the working of the multiplier, as the multiplier depends on the MPC. It is assumed that the value of the multiplier will not change, when MPC undergoes a change.

2. **No time lags in the successive rounds of consumption:** To achieve the full value of the multiplier, it is assumed that there are no time intervals between the receipt of income and spending of it. It means, the consumers should immediately spend the income as soon as they receive it. This is not realistic, as in reality; there is always a time lag between the receipt of income and spending of that income, even if the time interval is of short period. It is obvious that longer the time interval between the receipt and the spending of the income, weaker will be the operation of the multiplier, i.e., smaller will be its value.

3. **Existence of less than full employment:** The multiplier assumes that there is the existence of involuntary unemployment in the economy. Because, so long as there is involuntary unemployment, i.e., less than full employment, in the economy, income, output and employment will continue to expand as a result of the operation of the multiplier. But, after the full employment stage, additional investment will only increase the prices (inflation) and not output, income and employment.

4. **No investment from induced consumption:** It is assumed that the accelerator principle does not operate and that the investment increases only by the original amount. If the accelerator is allowed to operate then the value of the multiplier would be far greater and would be achieved at an earlier stage in the process of income propagation.

5. **Maintenance of additional investment:** To achieve the full value of the multiplier, it is essential that the various increments are repeated at 'regular' intervals. In case of failure to do so, it will not be possible to raise the income to the multiplier, i.e., multiplier effect will not be observed. And, any break in the continuity of investments would bring a fall-back in the national income to the original level. Thus, new investment is indispensable for the operation of the multiplier.

6. **Availability of consumer goods:** The success of the working of the multiplier depends upon the availability of consumer goods. If consumer goods are available in adequate quantity, the multiplier will continue to work and new income would increase. But, if consumer goods are not available then the income recipients will not be able to spend as much on consumption goods as they would desire.

7. **Net increase in investment in the economy:** It means that an act of investment in one sector should not be off-set by an act of disinvestment in some other sector of the economy. If it happens so, then there shall be no net increase in investment and it is possible that the operation of the multiplier will be obstructed as increase in investment in the public sector is neutralized by fall in private investment.
8. **Existence of a closed economy:** It is necessary to assume the existence of a closed economy in the country in question. Thus, the multiplier assumes that the country in question has no trade relations with the outside world. If the concerned country has trade relations with other countries, it is possible for the multiplier to be of lesser value. For example, if the concerned country enjoys an export surplus, there will be net addition to the income stream and the value of the multiplier would be greater than its anticipated value. On the other hand, if the country is faced with import surplus, there will be a leakage from the income stream and the value of the multiplier may turn out to be lesser than its anticipated value.

To conclude, the multiplier principle will operate to the full extent only if these assumptions are actually realized in practice. Thus, these assumptions give rise to a lot of limitations of the multiplier principle.

Conditions for the Successful Operation of the Multiplier

Following are the conditions essential for the effective operation of the multiplier:

1. **Availability of excess capacity in consumer goods' industries:** For the complete operation of the multiplier, it is necessary that there exists excess and unutilized capacity in the consumer goods industries. The reason is that, in case excess capacity exists, an increase in investment would result in an increased demand for consumer goods. This increased demand would be met by using this unutilized or surplus capacity in the consumer goods industries. More workers would be employed in such industries and the multiplier would operate.
2. **Elastic supply of capital:** It would be activated when the multiplier theorem is working. An increase in investment would provide more employment to the workers. This is possible when there are no bottlenecks in the supply of capital, raw materials and other resources for the purpose of business expansion.
3. **Industrialised economy:** One of the conditions for the working of the multiplier is the existence of an industrialized economy in the country. In an agricultural economy, the multiplier does not operate fully. Existence of industrialized economy is essential as:
    - The demand for industrial consumer goods is higher in an industrialized than in an agricultural economy. Whether it is public or private investment, it results in a greater demand for industrial consumer goods in as industrialized economy rather than in an agricultural economy.

- The agricultural output depends more on natural factors than on the industrial output. Adverse natural forces may actually reduce agricultural output despite increase in investment.
4. ***Absence of voluntary unemployment:*** An essential condition for the working of the multiplier is the existence of involuntary unemployment in the economy, i.e., absence of any voluntary unemployment. Involuntary unemployment is when the workers cannot find jobs even though they are willing to accept the ruling wage-rate. Thus, an increase in private or public investment (by increasing the demand for consumer goods) would result in an increase in the level of income, output and employment. The multiplier will fail to operate, if involuntary unemployment does not exist. This is because the increase in investment after full employment stage will result in increasing only the price level (inflation) rather than the volume of employment.

Leakages in the Working of the Multiplier

It is clearly stated that the MPC is rarely 1 (i.e., 100 percent). It means that the whole of the increment in income is not spent on consumption. If it were so, then full employment would be attained. But, as pointed out, the MPC is seldom 1. The reason is that there are several leakages from the income stream. If MPC is ½ , then ½ of the new income leaks out of the income stream and only the remaining ½ is spent on consumption. These are as follows:

1. **Price rise:** Due to price inflation, a good amount of increased income may be dissipated on higher prices instead of encouraging consumption, income and employment.
2. **Repayment of debts:** A part of the new increment of income may be used by the income recipients to pay-off old debts and thus have no effect on consumption.
3. **Idle cash deposits:** A portion of the increased income may be saved and held back in the form of idle bank deposits which would not promote the consumption function.
4. **Savings:** This is an important leakage in the process of income propagation as; it is well-known that MPC is rarely 1. In actual practice, people do not spend the entire increment in income on consumer goods and a part of it is saved. The 'saved' part of the increased income 'filters out' of the income stream, assuming that the savings are not converted into investments. This leakage in the form of savings limits the value of the multiplier. Thus, *higher the propensity to save lower shall be the value of the multiplier.*
5. **Purchase of old stocks and securities:** A portion of the new income may be used in the purchase of old stocks and securities from others who fail to spend the proceeds on consumption.

6. **Purchase of imported goods:** The part of the income that is spent on the purchase of imported goods does not add to domestic income and employment. Such a spending on imported goods will have no effect on the consumption of domestic goods and hence is certainly a 'leakage' from the domestic income stream.
7. **Taxes and savings:** Taxes and corporate savings determine the MPC of the people and have inevitable repercussions on the multiplier value. As taxes increase, they reduce the purchasing power of the people and hence it is a 'leakage' from the income stream. In the same way, undistributed profits of business Corporates represent a leakage as they are not available (in the form of dividends) to the shareholders to be spent on consumer goods.

To the extent that these leakages from the income stream can be 'plugged', the initial increase in investment would have greater *multiplier effect* on the income propagation process.

Despite the above limitations, the multiplier is a very useful tool for economic analysis.

Reverse Working of the Multiplier

It is quite possible that the multiplier may work in the 'reverse' direction. Suppose that there is a net reduction in investment to the tune of ₹ 10 crores and with MPC being 0.5 the multiplier is 2 and hence the total fall in income would be ₹ 20 crores.

With reduction of ₹ 10 crores in the first round, the men engaged in investment industries will reduce their consumption expenditure by 50 percent. Similarly, in each subsequent round, men will go on reducing their expenditure by 50 percent until the total income has decreased by ₹ 20 crores (as the multiplier is 2).

Thus, higher the value of the multiplier, greater shall be the reduction in the aggregate income.

A nation with higher MPC and lower MPS will suffer more from the reverse working of the multiplier. Higher MPC is better to a nation when the multiplier works in forward direction. A high multiplier would subject the economy to a more shocking decline of income whenever there is a fall in the aggregate investment. However, the picture is not so gloomy and pessimistic as *MPC is generally less than unity (i.e.1) or MPC is not infinity.*

Hence, it can be said that just as consumers do not spend the entire increase in income on consumption, likewise they do not reduce the consumption expenditure by the full extent of the decrease in income. If the MPC was equal to 1, then the reverse working of the multiplier would result in complete collapse of the economy.

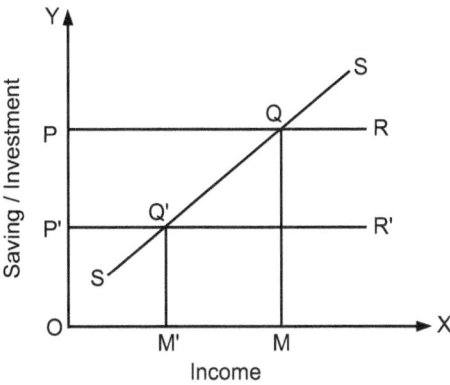

Fig. 5.9 : Reverse Working of the Multiplier

In Fig. 5.9 SS is the MPS curve (1/2) multiplier is 2. The SS curve is intersected by the PR curve at point Q. The equilibrium level of income is OM at QM. The investment falls from OP to OP' (i.e., by ₹ 10 crores). The income also declines from OM to OM' and a new equilibrium Q'M' is established. The fall in income MM' is double the fall in investment of PP'.

Significance of Keynes' Multiplier

The Multiplier has become part and parcel of the Keynesian theory of employment. In fact, it is the 'centre-piece of the macroeconomic theory'. It is considered as an important theoretical concept as it focuses on *investment* as the major dynamic element in the economy.

(i) It has highlighted the *importance of public investment*, particularly during depression and unemployment. A small increase in public investment leads to a large increase in income, output and employment.

(ii) The multiplier principle helps the government *in formulating an appropriate employment policy* during depression.

(iii) The concept of multiplier indicates that employment is directly created by investment and also shows that *income was generated throughout the economic system,* just like a stone thrown in water causes ripples in the water.

(iv) The concept of multiplier *helps in analyzing the course of the trade cycle* and also assists in devising an anti-cyclical policy to iron-out business fluctuations in the working of the economy.

(v) The multiplier principle has revolutionized the modern economic theory and also *helped in policy-making at the state level.*

(vi) The multiplier principle highlights the importance of *deficit-budgeting*. During depression, increased public expenditure takes place through public investment programmes by creating a budget deficit. This will help in increasing the income and employment.

Criticism of the Multiplier

Keynes' concept of the Multiplier has been subjected to severe criticism.

(i) Hazlitt refers to this concept as *"a strange concept about which some Keynesians make more fuss about than anything else in the Keynesian system"*. He bluntly points out that there is *never any precise, pre-determined or mechanical relationship* between investment and income.

(ii) The multiplier rests on an *assumption* which is *not at all realistic*, namely, that there is already *existing unemployment* in the economy. Critics point out and question as to why Keynes should assume mass unemployment as a 'general situation' and full employment as a 'special situation'.

(iii) Another *unrealistic assumption* of Keynes' multiplier is that *part of the community's income is not spent and is 'hoarded'*. Keynes assumed that the unconsumed income is not invested. It is the propensity to consume that determines the multiplier and what is not spent on consumption is not spent on anything at all, i.e., it is hoarded. This statement of the principle is in contradiction to what Keynes had said earlier that saving and investment were identical. According to Keynes what is saved must be invested so that savings and investments are equal. The acceptance of the multiplier concept gives rise to the problem of inequality between savings and investments. Thus, according to Hazlitt, Keynes' concept of the multiplier is not in conformity with the definition of Savings and Investment given in the *'The General Theory'*.

(iv) *Prof. D. H. Robertson, A. P. Lerner and R.M. Goodwin* points out that Keynes' multiplier does not take into account the effect of induced investment. It is a one-sided theory while dealing with the theory of income propagation, as the multiplier considers only the effects of increase in consumption consequent upon increase in income, but takes no note of the effects of increase in consumption on investment.

(v) *Prof. Stigler* has criticised the multiplier as the *fuzziest part of Keynes' theory*.

(vi) According to Prof. Hutt, Keynes' has done great intellectual harm by putting forward the multiplier theory.

But despite these scathing criticisms, the multiplier principle has considerable practical applicability to macroeconomic problems.

5.3 Foreign Trade Multiplier

Introduction

An open economy is conceptually one, which has economic transactions with the rest of the world. In fact an open economy is a realistic model. It is difficult to name an economy of the modern world which has no economic transactions with any other country.

Foreign trade and transactions of a country affect its macro-variables and thereby the equilibrium level of its national income, particularly when foreign transactions account for a significant proportion of its GNP (Gross National Product).

Like Consumption, Investment and Government (C, I, G- the three components of aggregate demand), exports of goods and services constitute a part of the aggregate demand in an economy and its effect on the economy is also the same. The difference is that C, I, G originate within the economy and is called *domestic demand*, but the demand for exports which originates outside the economy is called the *external demand*.

Foreign Trade Multiplier

The two important extensions of the multiplier theory are the balanced budget multiplier and the foreign trade multiplier. The 'Foreign trade Multiplier' is discussed below.

The foreign trade multiplier is also referred to as the 'export multiplier' and it operates like the investment multiplier of Keynes. As exports increase, there is an increase in the income of all those people who are associated with the export industries, this in turn creates a demand for goods. However, the income propagation is dependent upon their Marginal Propensity to Save (MPS) and the Marginal Propensity to Import (MPM). The value of the 'foreign trade multiplier' depends inversely upon these two marginal propensities. That is, *smaller* these two propensities, *larger* will be the value of the multiplier.

To explain the process of multiplier, let us suppose the exports (X) of the country increase, i.e., the exporters will sell their products to foreign countries and receive more incomes. To meet the foreign demand for their products, they will engage more factors of production and increase the output. The factors will earn income and this process will continue and the national income increases by the value of the multiplier.

The value of the multiplier depends on the value of MPS and MPM and this relationship is an inverse one (i.e., the two propensities and the export multiplier).

Algebraically, the foreign trade multiplier can be derived as follows:

Assume the national income identity in an 'open' economy, thus:

$$Y = C + I (X - M)$$

Here,
- Y = National income;
- C = Total consumption;
- I = Total investment;
- X = Exports; and
- M = Imports.

(X-M) implies that *'net'* earnings are added to the national income.

The above relationship can be solved as:

$$Y - C = I + (X - M)$$

Since,
$$S = Y - C$$

Hence, the above formula can be rewritten as-

$$S = I + (X-M)$$

At equilibrium level,
$$S + M = (I + M)$$

Hence, at the equilibrium levels of income, the sum of savings and imports (S+M) must equate to the sum of investment and exports (I + X).

When an economy has an external sector (i.e., when the economy is open), the total investment (I) is divided into domestic investment (I_d) and the foreign investment (I_f).

Now,
$$I = S$$

And this 'I' is $I_d + I_f = S$ ... (i)

Foreign investment (I_f) is the difference between exports and imports, thus,

$$I_f = X - M \quad \text{... (ii)}$$

Now substituting (ii) into (i), we have

$$I_d + X - M = S$$

Alternatively,
$$I_d + X = S + M$$

This is the equilibrium condition of national income in an open economy. The foreign trade multiplier represented by K_f is equal to:

$$K_f = \frac{\Delta Y}{\Delta X}$$

and
$$\Delta = \Delta S + \Delta M$$

Dividing both sides by ΔY, we get

$$\frac{\Delta X}{\Delta Y} = \frac{\Delta S + \Delta M}{\Delta Y}$$

Or
$$\frac{1}{K_f} = \frac{\Delta S + \Delta M}{\Delta Y} \qquad \left(\text{Since } K_f = \frac{\Delta Y}{\Delta X}\right)$$

Or
$$K_f = \frac{\Delta Y}{\Delta S + \Delta M}$$

Thus,
$$K_f = 1 \div \frac{\Delta S}{\Delta Y} + \frac{\Delta M}{\Delta Y} \qquad \text{(since dividing by } \Delta Y\text{)}$$

Hence,
$$K_f = \frac{1}{MPS + MPM}$$

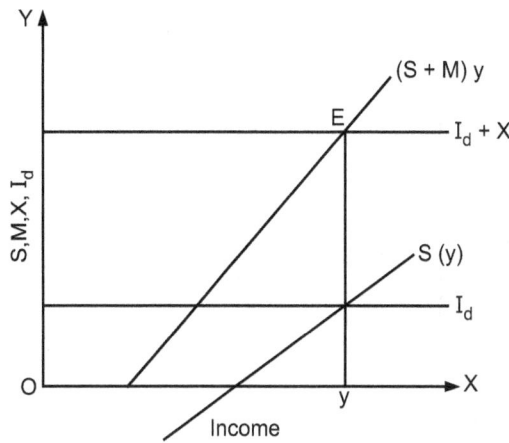

Fig. 5.10 : Shows the equilibrium level in the economy

S(y) represents the saving function.

(S+M) is the saving plus import function.

I_d = Domestic investment

I_d + X= Export plus domestic investment.

(S+M) and (I_d + X) functions affect the equilibrium level of national income (Y), where savings (S) equals domestic investment and exports equals imports.

In the above analysis, the foreign trade multiplier (K_f) has considered only one country, however in reality countries are inter-related with each other through trade.

A country's foreign trade (exports and imports) influences the income of the other country which in turn affects the foreign trade and income of the first country. This is referred to as *foreign repercussion or the back-wash effect*. Thus, smaller the country in relation to its trading partner, negligible will be the foreign repercussions and conversely foreign repercussions will be high in the case of larger nations as a change in the income of such a country will have significant foreign repercussions.

Illustration: Assume two countries A and B.

Table 5.5 : Influence of Foreign trade on Income

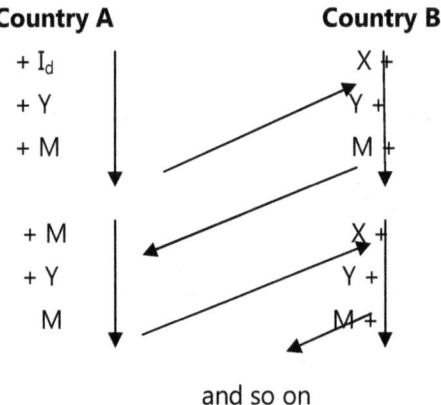

and so on

In **Table 5.5**, we observe that when domestic investment Id increases in country A, it increases its exports to country B. Country A's income increases (represented by + Y). It encourages country A to import more from Country B, it increases demand for country B's exports (X+). As a result, the income in Country B increases (Y+). Hence, Country B imports more (M+) from Country A. As the demand for Country A's exports increases, its income increases further. This is the back-wash effect (or repercussion) for Country A.

Diagrammatic Illustration

These stages of the *back-wash effect* can be explained graphically:

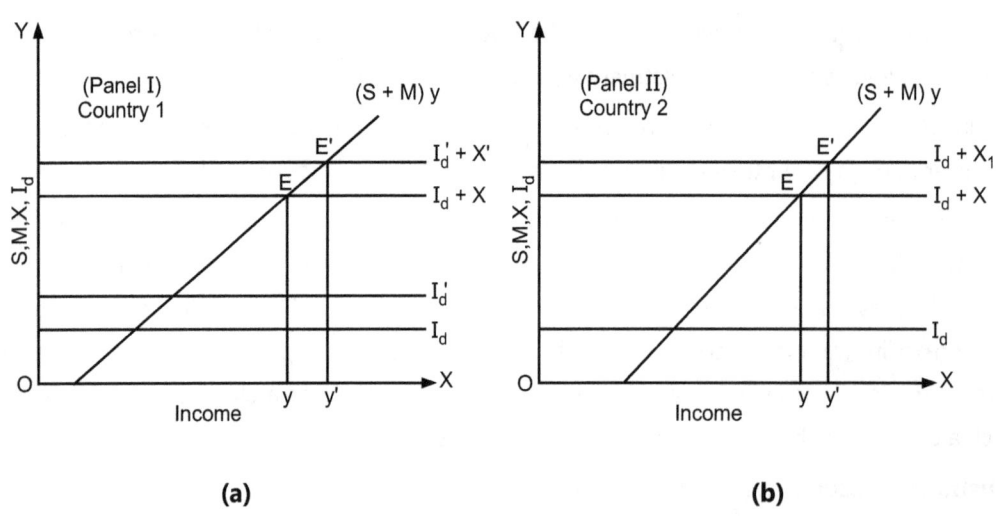

(a)   (b)

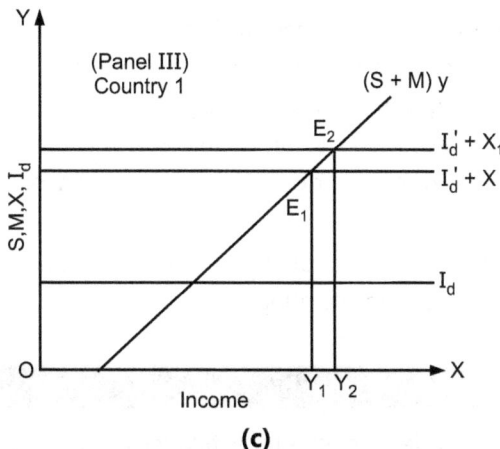

(c)

Fig. 5.11 : Stages of the Back-wash Effect

In **Fig. 5.11**, we observe:

Panel I: Domestic investment (I_d) in Country A increases from I_d to I_{d1}. This results in an upward shift in the $I_d + X$ schedule to $I_{d1} + X$. The new equilibrium point is at E^1, which shows increase in income from OY to OY_1.

Panel (II): As the total income increases, the demand for imports from Country B also increases. This means a rise in exports of Country B. This is depicted in Panel (II) of **fig.5.11** when the $I_d + X$ schedule of Country B shifts upwards as $I_d + X_1$. As a result, the national income of Country B increases from OY to OY_1 at the higher equilibrium level i.e., E_1.

Panel (III): As the income of Country B increases, its demand for imports from Country A also increases. This results in the back-wash effect and thus the repercussion is in the form of increase in the demand for exports of Country A. This is shown in Panel (III) of Fig. 5.11 where $I_d + X$ schedule (of Panel I) shifts upwards to $I_d + X_1$ and as a result the total income rises further from OY_1 to OY_2.

To conclude, this is the process how the foreign repercussions in one country affect its own national income and that of the other country which, in turn, again influences the national income of the first country with greater force, via the back-wash effect.

Critical Evaluation:

The foreign trade multiplier is based on certain assumptions which make the analysis unrealistic.

(i) The analysis is based on the *assumption of full employment*. But, in reality there is less than full employment in every economy. Thus, the foreign trade multiplier does not find clear expression in an economy with less than full employment.

(ii) The analysis is *applicable to a two-country model*. If there are more than 2 nations, it becomes a complicated affair to analyse the foreign back-wash effect of this theory.

(iii) The foreign trade multiplier *assumes no time-lags* and hence is unrealistic.

(iv) The analysis is based on the *assumption that exports and investment* (I_d and I_f) are independent of changes in the level of income. This is unrealistic because a rise in exports does not always lead to an increase in the total income. In fact, certain imports such as that of capital goods have the impact of increasing the income of the country.

Despite these limitations and short-comings the foreign trade multiplier is a useful tool of economic analysis and serves in formulating policy measures.

Points to Remember

- Investment in bonds, securities, stocks, etc., is financial investment.
- Keynesian investment is real investment i.e., investment in capital equipment, construction of public works, etc.
- Investment function refers to the inducement to invest, (or investment demand).
- **Private investment depends upon two factors:**
    (a) The Marginal Efficiency of Capital (MEC).
    (b) The rate of interest.
- Private investment is Induced investment.
- Public investment is Autonomous investment.
- **Factors determining Investment are:**
    (a) Supply price of the capital asset;
    (b) Expected rate of profit from the capital asset during its lifetime;
    (c) Rate of interest.
- All these factors are summed up as MEC.
- **MEC depends upon two factors:**
    (a) The prospective yield from the capital asset;
    (b) The supply price of the capital asset.
- MEC of an asset falls as successive units of that asset are produced.
- With the fall in the prospective returns, the supply price of such an asset is likely to go up, if more units of such an asset are produced due to rising costs in the industry which produces these assets.
- Private investment depends upon:
    (a) MEC, which depends upon the supply price of the capital and prospective return of the capital asset.

- (b) Rate of interest, which depends upon the liquidity preference of the people and the supply of money available in the economy.
- Factors influencing MEC can be classified into: short-term and long-term factors.
- Keynes' concept of MEC has been criticised as incomplete, inconsistent, contradictory and ambiguous.
- **New investment can be classified as:**
  (a) Autonomous investment; (b) Induced investment.
- *Autonomous investment* is determined by long-term goals and is free from income and profit level in the economy.
- *Induced investment* is income and profit motivated.
- *Investment Multiplier:* It is the ratio of the change in the income to the change in investment.
- **Symbolic terms :** $K = \dfrac{\Delta Y}{\Delta I}$

  K= multiplier, ΔY = change in income; ΔI = change in investment.
- Multiplier size depends on the M.P.C.
- Multiplier is equal to the reciprocal of 1 minus the M.P.C.
  Therefore, $K = \dfrac{1}{1 - m}$
- MPC + MPS= 1, therefore, MPS can be derived when MPC is known and vice versa.
- **MPC has two limiting cases:**
  (a) The MPC is rarely zero; (b) MPC is rarely 1.
- The multiplier is based on many assumptions which turn out to be its limitations.
- Despite various criticisms, the multiplier has great significance in the economic theory.
- *Foreign Trade Multiplier* is also referred to as 'export multiplier'.
- The value of the foreign trade multiplier depends inversely upon 2 marginal propensities – (a) the Marginal Propensity to Save (MPS) and (b) the Marginal Propensity to Import (MPM).

Multiple Choice Questions

1. Which of the following is not real investment?
   (a) Inventories
   (b) Construction work
   (c) Share capital of the company
   (d) New capital goods.

2. The demand for investment at different interest rates is represented by the term:
    (a) Marginal Efficiency of Capital
    (b) Marginal Efficiency of Investment
    (c) Marginal Productivity of Capital
    (d) Prospective Yield of Capital Assets
3. For the purpose of investment, the prospective yield in relation to supply price should be:
    (a) Less
    (b) Indifferent
    (c) Equal
    (d) More
4. The relationship between MEC and the prospective annual yield is:
    (a) Inverse
    (b) Direct
    (c) Negative
    (d) None of the above
5. Total investment *minus* replacement investment is equal to ....
    (ANS. net investment).
6. The purchase of existing bonds or securities is ....investment.
    (ANS. financial).
7. The investment which does not depend upon variations in income is known as .... investment.
    (ANS. autonomous investment).

Answers:
    1 - (c), 2 - (b), 3 - (d), 4 - (b)

Questions for Discussion

1. What do you understand by 'Marginal Efficiency of Capital'? What are the factors that influence it?
2. 'The size of the multiplier varies directly with the size of MPC'. Discuss.
3. What conditions must be fulfilled to enable the multiplier to operate? Discuss in this context the various limitations of the multiplier?

4. Enumerate the various leakages which create obstacles to the full operation of the multiplier.
5. Critically examine the doctrine of the multiplier.
6. Bring out the distinction between Induced Investment and Autonomous Investment.
7. Write in brief, the meaning of Investment function.
8. What factors determine Investment?
9. Explain the relationship between Marginal Efficiency of Capital (M.E.C) and Rate of Interest, with the help of a diagram.
10. Discuss the factors influencing M.E.C
11. Critically examine the Foreign Trade Multiplier.

Chapter 6...

Trade Cycle

Contents ...
6.1 Nature and Characteristics of Trade Cycle (Business Cycle)
6.2 Phases of Stages Trade Cycle (Business Cycle)
6.3 Control of Trade Cycle
6.4 Inflation - Meaning, Causes and Control
6.5 Deflation
- Points to Remember
- Multiple Choice Questions
- Questions for Discussion

Learning Objectives ...
➢ To understand about the cyclical fluctuations in business activities.
➢ To know about the different phases or stages of a typical business cycle.
➢ To classify the different causes of upswing and downswing in cyclical fluctuations.
➢ To study and have knowledge about the different measures to control business cycles.
➢ To learn about the different types of inflation and the measures to control the hyper-inflation.
➢ To understand the impact of inflation on the various sections of the society.

Introduction

The short-term variations in economic activity are known as business cycles or business fluctuations. Understanding business cycles has proved to be one of the most durable problems in all of macroeconomics. What causes business fluctuations? How can government policies reduce their virulence? Economists were largely unable to answer these questions until 1930s. At that point, it was the revolutionary theories of J. M. Keynes that pointed to the importance of the forces of aggregate demand in determining business cycles.

6.1 Nature and Characteristics of Trade Cycle (Business Cycle)

The term *business cycle or economic cycle* refers to economy-wide fluctuations in production, trade and economic activity in general over several months or years in an economy organized on free-enterprise principles.

The effect of upswings and downswings in economic activity is felt quite intensely because of the ever increasing business activity and the strong inter-relations between different sectors of an economy and between various economies.

During the Great Depression of 1930s, the ill effects of the wide swings in business activity were almost devastating. It was also noticed that after Great Depression there was 'no natural recovery' of the economic activity. The deliberate measures that were adopted for the recovery of the world economies needed a scientific understanding of the swings in the activity.

> *In the working of a market-oriented economy there has been witnessed the existence of alternating periods of prosperity and depression generally referred to as "business cycle". The British economists refer to it as "trade cycle". The business cycle is associated with sweeping fluctuations in economic activity, such as production, prices, employment, etc.*

In recent years economic theory has moved towards the study of economic fluctuation rather than a 'business cycle'- though some economists use the phrase 'business cycle' as a convenient shorthand.

For Milton Friedman calling the business cycle a "cycle" is a misnomer, because of its non-cyclical nature. Friedman believed that for the most part, excluding very large supply shocks, business declines are more of a monetary phenomenon.

The business cycle is the upward and downward movements of levels of Gross Domestic Product (GDP) and refers to the period of expansions and contractions in the level of economic activities (i.e., business fluctuations) around its long-term growth trend.

These fluctuations occur around a long-term growth trend, and typically involve shifts over time between periods of relatively rapid economic growth (an expansion or boom), and periods of relative stagnation or decline (a contraction or recession).

Business cycles are usually measured by considering the growth rate of real GDP. Despite being termed cycles, these fluctuations in economic activity can prove unpredictable.

MEANING OF ECONOMIC CYCLE

A business cycle is such a complex phenomenon and economists have so far not been able agree upon a common definition for business cycle.

W.C. Mitchell says, "Business cycles are a type of fluctuations found in the aggregate economic activity of nations that organize their work mainly in business enterprises. A cycle consists of expansion occurring at about the same time in many economic activities followed by similarly general recessions, contractions and revivals which merge into the expansion phase of the next cycle; this sequence of change is recurrent but not periodic......". Thus, in this definition the economist insists upon a measure of regularity in cyclical fluctuations.

In the words of **Prof. Keynes**, *"A trade cycle is composed of periods of good trade characterized by rising prices and low unemployment percentages, altering with periods of bad trade characterized by falling prices and high unemployment percentages."* Thus, two indices have been stressed by Keynes, namely, prices and unemployment, for measuring the *upswing* and *downswing* of the economic activity.

According to **Benham**, *"A trade cycle may be defined, rather badly, as a period of prosperity followed by a period of depression. It is not surprising that economic process should be irregular, trade being good at some time and bad at others."*

Characteristics of Business Cycles:

- Trade cycles are the *wave-like fluctuations* in economic activity as reflected in the basic economic variables like employment, income, output and price-level.
- These fluctuations are *cyclical* in nature.
- The sequence of changes in business cycle, i.e., recovery, prosperity, depression and recession, *recur frequently and in a fairly similar pattern*.
- The rhythm on the *periodicity* between the cycles needs to be similar.
- Expansion and contraction in a business cycle are *cumulative in effect*.
- Business cycles are a type of *fluctuations found in the aggregate economic activity* and not in any single firm or industry. In fact, the cyclical changes are in the overall economic environment affecting all the business entities. Thus, business cycles are *all pervading in their impact*.
- Prof. Knight identified 5 distinguishing features of business cycles, as under:
- (a) The duration between two major cycles is 6 to 12 years. A 'minor' cycle has duration of 3 to 4 years and then these cycles make to a 'major' cycle.
- (b) The empirical studies show that during a period of prosperity the business activity is usually 10% to 25% above the long-term trend, while during depression it is 5% to 25% below the trend.
- (c) Often, prosperity takes twice as much time to develop as the depression.
- (d) The phases and their sequence are same in all cycles.
- (e) It has been observed that if the boom is high the succeeding depression will also be severe. However, the reverse may not be correct, i.e. severe depression is not followed by a high boom period.

It can be summed up as, (i) in business cycle, there are cyclical changes in the general price level. But, whether the beginning of prosperity or depression, changes are at first in the prices of stocks and shares; (ii) After the changes in prices of stocks and shares, it is changes in the wholesale prices and in the volume of production, followed by changes in the interest rate and wage rates; (iii) amongst the commodities, the prices of raw materials change (rise or fall) before those of final foods; (iv) in general, in prosperity or depression, the retail prices lag behind the wholesale prices.

Types of Cyclical Fluctuations:

It is essential to distinguish between secular trend, random fluctuations, seasonal changes and cyclical fluctuations.

The *secular trend* represents long run changes in business activities which occur slowly and are spread over a number of years. Such long-run changes are the result of factors like improvement in production techniques, change in population, etc.

Random fluctuations are a result of events like labour strike, power cut, drought, flood, etc., which occur suddenly and are unpredictable. Effect of these events on the economy is limited to the period of occurrence of the event, as there is no regularity in their occurrence.

From the factors causing fluctuations, it can be said that, neither the secular trend nor the random variations in economic activity can form the part of trade cycle.

The *Seasonal changes*, which are short-run oscillations with regularity, can be mixed up with cyclical fluctuations. But the basic difference between the seasonal changes and cyclical fluctuations is that the seasonal variations repeat themselves each year, for instance, demand for cotton clothes during summer, umbrellas and other rainwear during rainy season, depending on the season each year. While, cyclical fluctuations have a longer life span. The seasonal fluctuations have easier predictability and adjustability in business than the cyclical fluctuations.

Major and Minor Cycles: Major cycles (Juglar cycles) may be defined as the fluctuations of business activity occurring between successive crisis. The term 'crisis' may be understood here to mean the major 'breakdowns' or 'downturns' that interrupt from time to time the relatively even equilibrium of economic activity. Thus, the major cycles constitute the intervals between successive major downturns or business activity or between major recessions. It has been established from the records of business fluctuations that each major cycle is made up of two or three minor cycles. The upswing of business in the major cycle is often interrupted by minor downswings. In the same way, the downswings of economic activities in the major cycle may be interrupted by minor upswings. The difference between major and minor cycles was observed by Prof. J. Kitchin and the minor cycles are sometimes referred to as *Kitchin cycles*.

Building cycles: It has been discovered that the building industry is also subject to fluctuations of a fairly regular duration. There are upswings and downswings in the building activity. The average of the building cycles is 18 years – just twice in the length of the business cycles.

Kondratieff Cycles: (Long Waves): The long waves in economic activity were discovered by the Russian economist, Kondratieff. Hence these long waves are called Kondratieff Cycles. On the basis of statistical data pertaining to the period 1780-1920, he was able to establish $2^{1/2}$ long cycles in England and France, each full cycle being of the duration of 60 years.

To conclude, the major fluctuations in economic activity include 3 kinds of cycles- (i) the minor or short cycles (Kitchin cycles- duration of 40 months); (ii) Major (Juglar cycles) composed of 3 minor cycles, duration of 10 years and finally (iii) the Kondratieff cycles (long waves) composed of 6 Juglar cycles and duration of 60 years.

6.2 Phases/Stages of Trade Cycle (Business Cycle)

A typical or standard business cycle is characterized by five different stages or phases- depression, recovery (or revival), prosperity (or full employment), boom (or overfull employment) and recession.

These stages of business cycle recur with some sort of regularity and are uniform in case of different cycles. However, the periodicity of different phases of trade cycles and their time interval differ between cycles. For instance, a cycle may have a periodicity of about 5.5 years in case of advanced nations, while it may be about 8.5 years in case of less developed countries. The time interval also differs. Though the periodicity and time interval between cycles may differ, but a typical business cycle depicts the five phases or stages

Depression: It constitutes the first phase of a trade cycle. If unchecked, depression is a natural consequence of the recession. The process of falling prices, demand and employment gather momentum. It is a period in which business activity in the country is *far below the normal*. It is a period characterized by a sharp reduction of production, mass unemployment, low employment, falling prices, falling profits, low wages, shrinking credit, high rate of business failures, and an atmosphere of all-round pessimism and despair.

- A decline in output or production is accompanied by a reduction in the volume of employment;
- During depression all construction activities come to a standstill;
- The consumer goods industries are not so much affected by unemployment as the basic capital goods industries;
- The costs are 'sticky' and do not fall rapidly as prices and the manufacturers suffer huge financial losses;
- With the fall in prices, the relative price structure is distorted;
- The prices of agricultural goods and raw materials fall to greater extent than the prices of finished manufactured goods. Thus, the agriculturists are hit more than the manufacturers.
- Thus, depression is characterized by low prices, idle funds with banks, mass unemployment and slack trade.

The two longest depressions in the U.S history were those of 1873-1879 (65 months) and 1929-1933 (44 months).

Revival/Recovery: This is the phase of revival of demand for goods and services. Revival period implies increase in business activity after the lowest point of the depression has been reached. During this stage, there is slight improvement in economic activity. The pessimism and despair of the preceding period is replaced by an atmosphere of all-round cautious hope.

- The entrepreneurs begin to feel that economic situation was, after all, not so bad as it was in the depression stage. This leads to further improvement in business activity;
- The upward movement of business activity is slow, production picks up, construction activity is revived and there is a gradual rise in employment.
- This is a period when the industrialists and the businessmen repay the loans taken by them from the banks earlier and the frozen stocks held by the banks are released. This leads to further improvement in business activity.
- Once the recovery starts, it results in a snowballing process for investment. The demand rises and provides the much needed stimulus to the producers to produce more. Attracted by rising profits, the sellers stop their conservative buying and plan building larger stock of goods to take advantage of an anticipated rise in prices. Thus, the business inventories also start rising slowly.
- The speed, with which the expansion of business activity takes place in response to a given initial increase in investment, would depend upon the multiplier effect.

The recovery continues until business activity reaches approximately the same level that it had achieved before the decline set in. The more severe the depression, the more rapid will be the recovery, as the rate of recovery is generally related directly to that of the preceding depression. However, the rate of recovery depends upon the strength of the forces which initiated the recovery. The revival/recovery may be due to two reasons: (i) change in business psychology in favour of optimism; and (ii) fresh public investments, innovations, changes in production techniques, investment in new regions, exploitation of new sources of energy, etc.

Prosperity (or Full Employment): In this period there is a general feeling of optimism among businessmen and industrialists.

- This stage is characterized by increased production, high capital investment in basic industries, expansion of bank credit, high prices, high profits, a high rate of formation of new business enterprises and full employment.
- During this stage there is a great incentive for new investment, even though interest rates, wage rates and raw material prices are higher.
- As a result, producers tend to produce more than the amount they can sell at present. Therefore, producers start procuring additional capital goods to expand production according to their anticipated future demand. The capital goods industry experiences a sharp upturn in its business activity.
- The longest sustained period of prosperity occurred in the U.S.A., between 1923 and 1929 with some minor interruptions in 1924.

Boom (or Overfull Employment): This is a phase of rapid expansion in business activity to new high marks, resulting in high stocks and commodity prices, high profits and overfull employment.

- The prosperity phase of the business cycle does not end up with a stable state of full employment. The peak of prosperity may lead to over-optimism in business psychology resulting in over-full employment of resources and raw material, leading to inflationary rise in prices.
- Such a situation signifies the end of prosperity and leads to the emergence of *boom*. The continuance of investment even after the stage of full employment results in a sharp inflationary rise of prices. The undue optimism among businessmen and industrialists puts additional pressure on the factors of production which are already employed, causing a sharp rise in their prices.
- Soon a situation develops in which the number of jobs exceed the number of workers available in the market. It is referred to as *overfull employment*.
- Profits touch a new high and the businessmen and industrialists are attracted by it and further increase their capital investments. This adds fuel to fire.
- Prices rise sky-high and runaway inflation raises its head, tempo of the boom reaches new heights. It is an atmosphere of *over-optimism* all around.
- The phase of boom has inherent seeds of recession in the form of structural constraints of the economy. The constraints can manifest it in various forms, such as: (a) bottlenecks begin to appear in the various sectors of the economy; (b) factors of production become scarce, causing further spurt in their prices; (c) consumption fails to rise due to increasing commodity prices and stability in marginal propensity to consume beyond a point of income increase. Consequently, there is piling of inventories, as the sales lag behind production; (d) the cost calculations of the businessmen and industrialists are completely upset and they become over-cautious.
- They now begin to move away from new projects, stop expansion of units. Thus, it prepares the ground for the next phase of trade cycle, i.e., recession. It is rightly said that a boom is inevitably followed by a bust.

Recession: This is the stage in which over-pessimism takes the place of over-optimism. Prices collapse and confidence is rudely shaken. In other words, there is a collapse of confidence.

- It is a period that witnesses panic, fear and hesitation on the part of the businessmen. The failure of some businesses creates panic among the industrialists and businessmen.
- The banks suddenly discover that they have expanded their deposits a little too far. They get panicky and begin to withdraw loans from business enterprises, as such more enterprises fail.

- Construction activities slow down; unemployment appears in basic, capital goods industries. This initial unemployment spreads to other industries too.
- Profit margins decline as costs start overtaking prices. There is a struggle for solvency among the businessmen.
- The recession has a cumulative effect. Once a recession starts, it goes on gathering momentum and finally assumes the shape of depression that is the first phase of business cycle.
- A severe recession was witnessed in the year 1957-58 in the U.S.A.

The above-mentioned phases of a business cycle can be illustrated in Fig. 6.1.

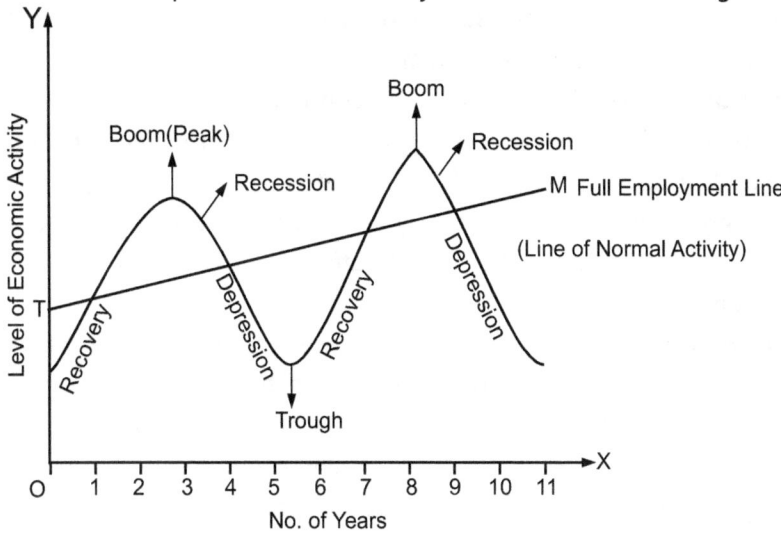

Fig. 6.1 : Phases of a Trade Cycle

In this Fig. 6.1, TM is the full employment line. There are two stages above this line of activity- boom in the upswing and a recession in the downswing. Below this full employment line, we have two stages of the trade cycle- recovery in the upswing and depression in the downswing. The business cycle, as shown in the Fig. 6.1, passes through five stages, starting with depression, then recovery, full employment, boom (peak), and recession and ultimately ends up again with depression.

Any typical business cycle passes through these five stages. However, it does not imply that every business cycle passes through these five stages in the *same* order. There is a possibility that the recovery stage may be followed by the recession stage without the business cycle entering into the prosperity and boom stages. This type of behaviour of trade cycle was witnessed in the U.S.A. in 1937. We cannot even say about the duration or length of the various stages of the business cycle. For instance, the depression stage can be a prolonged one followed by a quick recovery or vice versa.

Factors Causing Alternate Swings in Business Activity:

A common phenomenon of a capitalist economy is the existence of boom and depression. In such an economy, the 'free enterprise' economy is motivated by 'profits'. Production is undertaken with profit as an objective. In the short-run, production can fall short or exceed in relation to the demand. The main causes for the occurrence of business cycles are:

1. **Credit Activities:** Banking operations play a vital role. By expanding and contracting credit creation, changing ratio of cash deposits to total deposits, the banks can change the volume of money supply in the economy. These activities contribute to the cyclical movements in the economy.
2. **Production pattern:** Changes in proportion between capital goods and consumer goods production results in shortages or surpluses in commodity supply, causing boom or depression situation in the economy.
3. **Purchasing power:** If the purchasing power does not match to the expansion or contraction of production, the market suffers from imbalances, causing economic fluctuations.
4. **Profit motive:** The profit in the market makes the producer too optimistic. He is under a constant illusion regarding the exact nature and volume of demand. As a result, if the retail trade is fast moving, the producer magnifies the tendency by expanding production with over-optimism and contributes to boom in raw material and labour markets. On the other hand, if the retail trade slacks, the over-cautious producers immediately reduce his output and bring a downfall in the demand for raw material and labour.
5. **Human psychology:** The human psychology contributes to the occurrence of business cycle. The optimism and pessimism attitude gives rise to an endless chain of boom and depression.
6. **Weather changes:** The changes in weather contribute to the emergence of business cycles. These changes affect agricultural goods and the prices of those basic goods which the working class in a society consumes. In turn, it influences the wage rate, cost of raw material, etc., thus contributing to the fluctuations in the business activity.

Factors Causing Recession

1. **Weather Fluctuations:** In an agrarian economy, a fall in agricultural production due to bad weather influences the economy. A rise in prices of agricultural goods, purchasing power declines and demand for agro-based raw material also declines. This is a situation of over-all recessionary effect on the economy.

2. **Aggregate supply more than aggregate demand:** When during the phase of rising prices firms become enthusiastic in relation to investment, cost calculations get disrupted, resulting in over-investment. Thus, supply exceeds demand, prices fall, inventories increase and profits fall.
3. **Supply of money:** Changes in money in an economy does influence business activity. When the banks provide liberal credit facilities, there is expansion of credit and the business activity also expands. However, when the apex bank (central bank) realizes that the credit by the banks expands its reasonable limit, it starts imposing restrictions on credit creation facilities. Money becomes costly, adversely affects the business activity, consequently a situation of recession.
4. **Decrease of public expenditure:** In India, public sector shares a substantial part of the total investment in the economy and has strong linkages with the rest of the economy. In such a situation, with decrease in the rate of investment in public sector slows down the growth of related sectors. If this continues to happen for some time, it can lead to the emergence of recessionary trends.

Factors Causing Inflation
1. **Demand-pull Inflation:** When aggregate demand for goods and services exceeds their aggregate supply, it pulls the product price upwards. When the firms respond to the excess demand by producing additional quantity of goods and services required, this creates demand for additional resources. And, since producers compete with each other for these additional resources the cost of inputs to the firms also goes up, which in turn induces the firms to further raise product prices.
2. **Cost-push Inflation:** Strong trade unions use their collective power to force the firms to pay additional wages which may be in excess of additions to productivity. Industries, having such trade unions, face rising wages and other costs, leading to cost-push inflation. Further, increased money-income with the workers pushes up the demand for goods, causing a price rise. Soon the workers find that their increased purchasing power is not adequate to maintain their standard of living and a fresh demand for rise in wages triggers. In this manner, a rising wage-spiral would emerge.
3. **Profit push Inflation:** In an economy, there are firms with varying degrees of market power. Profit-push inflation results when firms having strong market power try to increase profits only by a price rise, with no cost decline.

Adverse Effects of Business Cycles
- During the upswings-recovery and expansion phases- individual firms gain as demand, prices and profits increase. And, during recession the firms lose.

- However, during expansion phase, the firms start experiencing sharp rise in prices of raw materials, high rentals, wages, etc. And at advanced stage of expansion phase, the firms find markets highly competitive.
- The recession period lands the firms in great difficulty, as demand falls, old orders get cancelled, prices fall, and inventory levels goes up. Banks call back their credits. For this, firms have to sell their goods even at a loss. The element of overhead cost to the firm also contributes to loss. A lot of capacity remains excess during the stage of depression.
- Since business cycles cannot be eradicated, all that is possible is to reduce the ill effects of cyclical fluctuations. The remedies may be of two types:
- (a) The preventive measures which tend to eliminate the causes that breed economic crises; and (b) The curative measures that improve upon the ill-effects of the cyclical fluctuations.

THEORIES OF BUSINESS CYCLE (Causes of Inflation)

Keynes' Theory of Business Cycles:

According to Prof. Keynes, the operation of the business cycle is due to the fluctuations in the volume of investment, and these fluctuations in investment are considered to be due to fluctuations in the marginal efficiency of capital (MEC).

- The volume of private investment depends upon two factors: (a) the rate of interest, and (b) the marginal efficiency of capital (MEC). Since the rate of interest is quite stable in nature, hence the variable factor is MEC which determines the volume of private investment.
- MEC, in turn, depends upon two factors: (a) the prospective yield, and (b) the supply price of the capital asset. In the short period the supply price of the capital asset is quite fixed and therefore it is fluctuations in the prospective yield which ultimately determine the MEC.
- A rise in MEC, by leading to an increased investment, creates more employment and output and income in the economy. It initiates the period of prosperity and with the working of the multiplier it leads to emergence of boom. On the other hand, decline in MEC, through decreased investment, leads to unemployment and contraction of income and output. It initiates the period of depression and with the *reverse* operation of multiplier leads to slump in the economy.

Illustration of the Phases of Trade Cycle:

- It is a period of *expansion* and the business activity is progressively expanding. There is optimism in the businessmen about the future and are expecting higher profits. The MEC is rapidly rising. The rate of interest is sort of stable, so it is profitable to set up new enterprises. The process of expansion continues till the peak of boom is reached. At this stage, certain economic forces become active and exert pressure on the M.E.C. in the downward direction. (a) with process of expansion costs of production start rising due to increasing scarcities of material and equipment and the rising costs depresses the M.E.C. (b) the expansion has led to abundance of output, thus lessen the yields (or returns) below expectations. Thus, these two factors depress M.E.C. Since the businessmen are sensitive to the fall in M.E.C., they adjust their activities accordingly.

- **The period of *depression and revival*:** For some time the M.E.C. remains at a low level and the revival of economic activity is slow. However, M.E.C. does not remain low for ever. As time passes, it tends to move up. The question is how does M.E.C. revive? (a) as time passes, the existing machinery and plants become worn-out and obsolescent and need to be replaced, thus there arises a demand for new machinery and plant. (b) with the passing time the surplus stocks of other goods also get exhausted. These two factors promote new business activity. The costs are also considerably cut down due to fall in the prices of raw materials and equipment and wage costs also go down. All these activities *tone up* the M.E.C. leading to progressive expansion of the economy.

The real contribution of Keynes' theory of the trade cycle is that it explains the **turning points**, i.e., the lower as well as the upper turning points of the economic cycle. These turning points earlier to Keynes' theory were not well explained. For example, the upper turning point, prosperity to depression, was attributed to the inability of the banking system to give additional loans to the needy borrowers. Keynes explains this *downturn* in the context of M.P.C., according to which the expenditure on consumption goods does not increase in proportion to the increased income of the community. This sets a limit to the expansion of the output of consumption goods. This fact reacts upon the M.E.C., which tends to move now in the downward direction.

Likewise, the lower turning point, from depression to prosperity was earlier explained as liberal lending of the banking system. However, to Keynes, the most important cause for the *upturn* in M.P.C., which states that the expenditure of the community does not decrease in the same proportion as decrease income of the community. This sets a limit to the downward contraction of the output of consumption goods and this fact reacts in favour on the M.E.C., which now tends to move in the upward direction.

Thus, Keynes, by putting forward his concept of consumption function, could explain fairly satisfactorily the turning points of the trade cycle.

Critical Evaluation:
1. Prof. Hazlitt criticizes Keynes for attributing the economic crisis to a sudden collapse in the "marginal efficiency of capital". Hazlitt comments that Keynes M.E.C., is a very vague term and can give rise to several possible meanings.
2. Keynes' advocacy of a cheap money policy or low interest rates as a remedy for economic crisis has been relished by the critics. The criticism is that a cheap money policy encourages excessive borrowing, excessive credit expansion, and various types of distortions in the economy. It might lead to a policy of perpetual inflation, for the only way to keep the interest rate low is by a constant expansion of the money and credit supply.
3. Keynes' suggested for government intervention and a "socially controlled rate of investment" as a weapon to combat depression and unemployment. Critics point out that the socially controlled rate of investment would amount to putting the entire economy in the hands of government officials who are neither perfectly rational, nor completely informed, nor incorruptible. Critics point out that Great Britain had to pay a price for it.

HICK'S THEORY OF BUSINESS CYCLES:

Prof. J. R. Hicks attributes the operation of cyclical fluctuations to the combined action of the multiplier and accelerator.

Hicks' theory of economic cycle is based on certain assumptions as stated below:

(a) The theory assumes progressive economy in which autonomous investment increases at a constant rate so that the system remains in a moving equilibrium.
(b) It assumes constant values for the multiplier and the accelerator.
(c) The magnitudes of saving and investment coefficients are such that a displacement from equilibrium path will tend to cause a movement away from equilibrium.
(d) Full employment of resources act as a ceiling to the expansion of an economy.
(e) The rate of decrease in the accelerator is limited by the rate of depreciation in the downswing.
(f) Consumption of current period is a function of the income of the previous period. Likewise, induced investment in the current period is a function of change in output of the previous period. In other words, the relation between the multiplier and accelerator is treated in a lagged manner.
(g) The theory assumes that the average capital-output ratio is greater than unity and that gross investment does not fall below zero.

Hicks' model is based on warranted rate of growth, the consumption function, autonomous investment, an induced investment function, and the multiplier-accelerator relation.

The *warranted rate of growth* is the rate which will sustain itself. It implies that real investment and real saving are taking place at the same time (it is consistent with saving-investment equilibrium).

Consumption in period 't' is regarded as a function of income (y) of the previous period (t -1). The consumption lags behind income and hence multiplier is treated as a lagged relation.

Autonomous investment is not related to the growth of the economy, i.e., it is independent of changes in the level of output.

Induced investment is a function of the growth rate of the economy, i.e., it is dependent on changes in the level of output.

Accelerator is based on induced investment which together with *multiplier* brings about an upturn.

According to Hicks' there are two types of investments – autonomous and induced investment. *Autonomous investment* is that investment which is determined independently of existing economic conditions, such as, national income level or consumption. It is an exogenous factor that arises from public investment, increase in population, change in technology. This type of investment starts an expansion of employment and output. Its force is expressed in the *multiplier*. Induced investment is determined by past changes in the income level or of consumption level, and is a reaction to increase or decrease in the aggregate demand. It is an endogenous factor, a reaction to changes started by autonomous investment. Its force is expressed in the *accelerator*.

According to Hicks', the cyclical fluctuations in business activity is caused by autonomous investment (through the multiplier) and induced investment (through accelerator).

Illustration: The economic system which is in equilibrium is subject to sudden disturbance in the form of autonomous investment. The income and output will rise to the extent of the multiplier. This expansion will result in induced investment through accelerator, which gives rise to further expansion of income (multiplier) and further induced investment (accelerator), and so on.

In the *upswing*, output rises faster than equilibrium rate. Investment increases beyond its normal rate. The expansion of income and output will continue till it reaches the *ceiling* determined by full employment. The expansion is checked when the expanding output and income reaches its upper limit and thus slows down the rate of expansion. The rate of induced investment is reduced because the spurt of autonomous investment was short-lived. Now, the multiplier-accelerator mechanism operates in a *reverse* way- falling investment reducing income, reduced income reduces investment, and so on. The output may decline downwards below the equilibrium level to a greater extent than it rose above it due to the reverse working of the multiplier and the accelerator.

Diagrammatic Illustration:

Due to a close relationship between the level of money income and the volume of investment, for every level of investment, there is the corresponding level of money income and the ratio of money income to investment is determined by the combined action of the multiplier-accelerator (or the leverage).

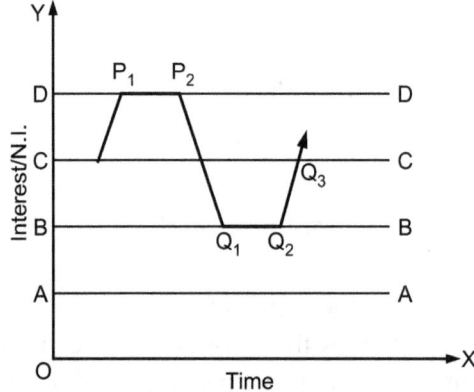

Fig. 6.2 : The Leverage

- Prof. Hicks assumes that autonomous investment grows annually at the rate given by the slope AA.
- With given the size of marginal propensity to consume (mpc), the multiplier and the autonomous investment together determine the equilibrium level of income represented by BB. BB is referred to as *floor line* by Prof. Hicks.
- When the national income grows along the floor line BB, there is bound to be some induced investment through the working of the accelerator.
- The line CC shows the equilibrium time path of national income determined by autonomous investment and the leverage- the combined working of the multiplier and the accelerator.
- DD represents full employment ceiling and shows the maximum national income or output at any period of time.
- The economy starts from C and will be moving along the path CC and the equilibrium will be determined by the growing level of autonomous investment and the leverage.
- Suppose the economy reaches the point P_0 along the CC path. Further, suppose that there is an outburst of investment activity due to some government expenditure and will push the economy above the CC path after the point P_0.
- The autonomous investment results in increase in national income which will further cause induced investment through the working of the accelerator. The increase in induced investment will cause the national income to increase by a magnified amount through the multiplier.

- Hence, due to combined effect of the multiplier and the accelerator, the national income will rapidly expand along the path P_0P_1 but this expansion will inevitably stop at P_1 because P_1 is located on DD line which is the full employment ceiling and the national income cannot expand beyond the DD line. All the factors are fully employed and additional output is out of question.
- DD line grows upward in a gentle manner at the rate of autonomous investment AA. P_0P_1 line slopes upwards in a steep manner.
- When the economy reaches P_1 on DD line, it will grow at the rate with autonomous investment increase. Since the national income has now ceased to grow at a rapid rate, the induced investment through the accelerator falls off in course of time.
- The fall in induced investment starts a contraction in the level of income and investment activity. From P_2, the level of national income moves downwards to CC and the multiplier works in reverse direction. The fall in national income will not stop on touching the line CC, but will continue moving downwards till it reaches the point Q_1.
- The economy will be slipping down from P_3 to Q_1. But it will not slip down beyond Q_1, as the floor line has been reached. The economy may creep along the floor line BB from Q1 to Q_2. In this process, there is a growth in the level of national income and the rate of growth starts once again leading to induced investment.

Hicks' explanation of the business cycle is accepted by the majority of economists. That is, the theory enjoys general acceptance among the present day economists. However, this theory is not free from criticism –

- The assumption that the multiplier and accelerator remain constant during the various stages of the economic cycle is unrealistic.
- Likewise, the rate of consumption cannot remain constant during the different phases of economic cycle.
- Further, the assumption that the capital-output ratio, which influences the size of the accelerator, remains constant is untrue.

REAL BUSINESS CYCLE THEORY

Within the mainstream of economics, Keynesian views have been challenged by 'real business cycle' models in which fluctuations are due to technology shocks.

This theory is most associated with Finn E. Kydland and Edward C. Prescott. They consider that economic crisis and fluctuations cannot stem from a monetary shock, but for an external shock, such as an innovation. Thus, the underlying idea of this theory is to study business cycles with the assumption that they were driven entirely by technology shocks, rather than by monetary shocks or changes in expectations.

According to real business cycle theory, the *ups* and *downs* are caused by technology or other similar shocks to the supply side of the economy.

The theory highlights the importance of *supply side* of business in causing economic fluctuations. This theory associates business cycles with rational expectations, and lays down the idea that markets generally function very smoothly; thus any *ups* and *downs* in economic activity must reflect the outcome of rational decisions made by many individuals.

Over the period since the Industrial Revolution, technological progress has had a much larger effect on the economy than any fluctuations in credit or debit.

The theory postulates that with an invention of productivity (a device that would increase production), entrepreneurs will increase investment, expand output and employ more people. This would bring in *boom* conditions in the economy. On the other hand, there may be times when new advances are lacking, or productivity is low, and at this point entrepreneurs will rationally choose not to produce and the economy may witness *recession*. Hence, in the downturn, the rate of technology slows down, marginal productivity of workers falls, real wages fall; people react to the change in real wage in a rational manner by shifting their work and leisure decisions over time.

In other words, as per the theory, the economy will be busier in high productivity times than in low productivity times. When there is a technological shock raising real wages, people work more to leisure, causing output to surge; and when there is a technological shock lowering real wages, people withdraw from work, output falls. This pattern is referred to as booms and recession.

A very interesting suggestion from the proponents of this theory is that although booms are more welcome than recessions, there is no need to react to either, as they represent the best use of the opportunities available.

Real business cycle theory has been categorically rejected by a number of mainstream economists in the Keynesian tradition. The theory has not attracted much empirical support. Many economists find this theory unbelievable and argue that it is very difficult to observe the technological shocks that are at the crux of this explanation.

Politically- based Business Cycle:

Another set of models tries to derive the business cycle from political decisions. The *partisan business cycle* suggests that cycles or fluctuations result from the successive elections of administrations with different policy regimes. For example, Regime X adopts *expansionary policies*, resulting in growth and inflation, but is voted out of office when inflation becomes unacceptably high. The replacement, Regime Y, adopts contractionary policies reducing inflation and growth, and the downwards swing of the cycle. It is voted out of office when unemployment is too high, being replaced by Regime Z.

The political economic cycle is an alternative theory stating that when an administration of any kind is elected, it initially adopts a contractionary policy to reduce inflation and gain a reputation for economic competence. It then adopts expansionary policy in the lead upto the next election, hoping to achieve at the same time low inflation and unemployment on the Election Day.

The political business cycle theory is explained by Michal Kalecki, who discussed the reluctance of the entrepreneurs or businessmen to accept government intervention in the matter of employment. Persistent full employment would mean increasing workers' bargaining power to raise wages and to avoid doing unpaid labour, potentially hurting profitability. In recent years, proponents of the "electoral business cycle" theory have argued that incumbent politicians encourage prosperity before elections in order to ensure re-election and make the citizens pay for it with recessions afterwards.

Real Estate Business Cycle:

Henry George identifies land price fluctuations as the primary cause of most business cycles. The theory is generally ignored in most of today's discussions, despite the fact that the two great economic contractions of the last 100 years – 1929-1933 and 2008-2009 both involved speculative real estate bubbles.

Henry George observed that one of the factors that is absolutely necessary for all production – land – has an inherent tendency to rise in price on an exponential basis as the economy grows. The reason for this is that the quantity of land (natural resource) is fixed in supply, while its quality is improved due to improvements such as economic development of the surroundings. Investors see this tendency as the economy grows and they buy land ahead of the boom areas, withholding it from use in order to take advantage of its increased value in the future.

Since housing and commercial real estate provide collateral for a large part of lending, there is a tendency for real estate price to rise faster than the rate of inflation in business cycle upswings.

Speculation in land concentrates profits in landholders and diverts economic resources to speculation in land, squeezing profits away from production that has to occur on this land. According to Henry George, land speculation is always the cause of economic downturns. Land speculation slows the economy in two ways: it increases production costs by making land in general more expensive as well as decreasing productivity by denying access to the best locations and lowering "potential output".

Measures to Control Business Cycles

The trade cycles, by creating cyclical fluctuations in business activity, do a great deal of harm to the smooth and orderly progress of society. Therefore, efforts should be made to check the operation of the business cycle. As regards the long waves (i.e. long business cycles), it is not possible to check them. Long waves are inevitable in a capitalist society. But something can definitely be done to mitigate the ravages of the short business cycle.

(a) Preventive Measures: Certain preventive measures that can be suggested are:
- There can be a good check on the market's over-optimism and over-pessimism (that cause cyclical fluctuations), if equilibrium is maintained with the appropriate information on demand and supply.
- Taking care that: (i) inventories do not increase or decrease excessively; (ii) financial commitments do not exceed financial resources; (iii) plant and equipment increase at a steady rate.
- The overhead cost per unit of output should not be allowed to go up.
- Due to lack of demand during depression, the firms are generally less careful in accepting orders, which can be ruinous for the firm.

(b) Curative Measures: These measures assist in smoothening the cyclical fluctuations as under:-
- Proper monitoring of costs and reduction in costs can to a great extent overcome the problem of recession.
- Changes in quality and nature of the product can help raise the demand.
- Firms can also change their marketing methods and strategies to adjust to new situations.
- The firms can utilize the time period of depression to plan for the introduction of new products as the stage of recovery starts.
- To overcome the difficult time of depression the firm can utilize a part of its retained profits.

(c) Government Policies: Two types of policies are pursued by the State to combat the inflationary and deflationary tendencies in the economy. These are called stabilization policies, which include (1) Monetary Policy; (2) Fiscal Policy.

Monetary Policy:
- Whatever may be the cause of the short business cycle it is always *aggravated* by the monetary factors. The monetary factors may not cause the business cycle, but once the cycle occurs, these factors *aggravate* it.
- Monetary inflation, by leading to higher prices, higher profits and an optimistic outlook, strengthens the upswing of the cycle. On the other hand, monetary deflation, by leading to lower prices, lower profits and a pessimistic outlook, reinforces the downswing of the cycle.
- To check the cyclical fluctuations, caused by monetary factors, the government may evolve a suitable monetary policy to deal with the situation.

- So far as money supply is concerned, its undue expansion could be checked by insisting upon a proper and adequate cover against note issue. And, as regards the bank credit, the Central Bank could utilize the various weapons of control- quantitative as well as qualitative measures.

The Quantitative measures are bank rate, open market operations, reserve ratios, moral suasion, etc., to control cyclical fluctuations. By raising the *bank rate*, central bank makes borrowing costlier; as a result commercial banks borrow less from the Central bank. In turn the commercial banks raise their lending rate, which reduces the money supply in the economy. Reduction in money supply reduces demand for goods and services in the economy, resulting in the check on price rise. *Open market operations* refer to sale and purchase of securities by the central bank. To control inflation, the central bank sells securities in the open market, reducing reserves of commercial banks, restricting the capacity of the banks to lend. This reduces money supply and checks price rise. The Qualitative or selective credit controls are used to encourage or discourage specific types of credit for particular purposes.

During *recession*, the State uses the monetary policy in opposite direction. For example, the central bank should lower the bank rate, making the borrowing by commercial banks cheaper. Again, in the open market operations, the central bank should buy the securities, thereby raising money supply in the economy. The central bank can use some selective credit control measures, particularly lowering margin requirements which would help in encouraging greater business activity.

- Whenever there is a tendency towards an overexpansion of business activity, the Central Bank should utilize its weapons to check and control expansion of credit. On the other hand, whenever there is a tendency towards an undue slackening of economic activity, the Central bank should utilize its weapons to ensure an adequate expansion of credit. To combat inflationary trends in business activity, the bank rate weapon is increasingly used in recent years in countries like Great Britain and the U.S.A.
- Thus, monetary policy plays an important part in curbing cyclical fluctuations and contributing to economic stability.

Limitations of Monetary Policy:

Anti-cyclical monetary measures can become effective only within the following limitations:

1. **Cash-holdings of the Banks:** If the banks in the country have large amounts of cash or other semi-liquid assets like treasury bills, government securities, etc., credit controls by the central bank become less effective. Thus, monetary measures are not very successful in controlling prosperity-bred inflation.

2. **Velocity of the Circulation of Money:** The velocity of the circulation of money is beyond the control of the central bank. So, during the prosperity period, even if the total supply of money is controlled, the velocity of the circulation of money may increase and expenditure may continue to rise.
3. **Non-banking Financial Intermediaries:** The Central Bank can control credit creation by commercial banks, but there are various non-banking financial intermediaries like Chit Funds, Nidhis, various financial corporations, and mutual funds etc., which also make loans available. The credit supplied by all such institutions to industry and commerce is beyond the control of the Central Bank.
4. **Management of Public Debt:** The responsibility for the proper management of public loans rests with the Central Bank of every country. If, during open market operations, large number of government securities is sold in the market, their prices fall. Under these circumstances, when the government floats new loans, the people contribute to these loans cautiously.
5. **Varying Effectiveness:** The monetary measures affect different sectors of the economy differently. Many a times, the producer's goods industry producing durable goods continues to get credit even when restrictions on credit are imposed by the Central Bank. But, small scale industries, agriculture and such other fields may be starved off credit. If this happens, the internal balance of the economy is disturbed and new problems arise.

The various monetary measures may be effective in curbing inflation, but starting recovery is very difficult. Thus, it has been observed that monetary measures have shown some success in curing deflation or depression as other factors like the business environment etc., are equally important for the entrepreneurs to invest during period of depression.

Fiscal Policy: Monetary policy taken alone may not suffice to check cyclical business fluctuations. Therefore, it is suggested that monetary policy should be properly integrated with a suitable fiscal policy to achieve the desired results.

Fiscal policy refers to the deliberate changing of taxes and government spending for the purpose of keeping the actual GNP close to the potential full employment GNP. It is inflationary situation when the potential GNP exceeds, while it is recessionary situation when the actual GNP falls short of potential one.

Keynes and the Keynesians, such as, Alvin Hansen and others, have recommended *compensatory finance or compensatory fiscal policy* to bring about stabilization of business activity.

In recent times, Government activity has expanded so much that government is now in a position to exercise a very great influence on the total volume of output in a country. Therefore, it is suggested that the government should regulate its activities in a manner to *offset* the cyclical fluctuations in private business activity.

The three main instruments of fiscal policy – *taxation, expenditure and borrowing*- can be used by the state to achieve its purpose.

In the event of *downswing* in the economy, the government should at once enforce its three instruments of fiscal policy to check the downtrend and ensure stability in the economy. In such a situation,

(i) **Taxation:** The government should not levy any new taxes on the public. Even the existing taxes should be reduced to a great extent. With lesser imposition of taxes, it leaves more money in the hands of the people who should be encouraged to spend it on buying additional goods and services and would offset the downtrend of the business activity.

(ii) **Spending:** At the same time, the government itself should embark on a vast spending programme to stimulate business activity in the economy. The government should initiate public works projects of various kinds, such as construction of roads, canals, parks, schools, hospitals, etc., involving expenditure of money and involving additional employment of labour. These projects should be initiated at the first sign of depression in the economy. It would help in avoiding the falling effective demand and business activity.

(iii) **Borrowing:** The funds to finance the public works projects should be obtained either by printing more paper money or by borrowing from the banks. The deflationary effect of reduced business spending can be offset by creating more money in circulation. At such times, the government should follow deficit budgetary policy which will further increase the flow of income into the economy. Public borrowing can also be employed by the government as an instrument to fight depression and unemployment. The deficit in the government budget can be partly met by public borrowing and these borrowings should be from people with whom the funds lie idle. The idea is to use the funds through borrowing for productive purposes.

On the other hand, when the economy recovers and the phase of prosperity sets in, the government should follow an exactly opposite policy of fiscal measures, in terms of taxation, spending and borrowing. It should raise the existing taxes; even levy new ones to check private spending. The state itself should reduce its spending on public works projects. It should retire paper money and pay off its debts to the banks and the public, which would reduce the money in circulation. During the period of boom the government should follow the policy of *surplus budgeting*.

Thus, a compensatory fiscal policy followed by the government would help to maintain a circular flow of income in a manner that would bring stabilization in the economy.

Limitations of Fiscal Policy:
1. High rates of taxes have a disincentive effect on the desire to work, thus, taxation instrument should be implemented with great care.
2. Many of the public spending projects such as hospitals, hydro-electricity projects, etc are such, that they cannot be kept waiting for depression to set-in in the economy.
3. Increased purchasing power (when tax rates fall) must be spent by the people. If they save it, the aggregate demand will not change. Similarly, increased taxes should not be accompanied by 'dissaving' by the people.
4. By convention, taxes can be changed only at the time of the annual budget. Frequent changes are resented and opposed by the people.

(a) Automatic Stabilizers: At the discretion of the government are the monetary and fiscal policies, as such they demand a certain amount of alertness and promptness on the part of the government to enforce them at the right moment- right amount of taxation, right amount of spending to offset the cyclical fluctuations. Therefore, the economists recommend the introduction of a number of *automatic stabilizers, i.e., built-in stabilizers*, to deal with the fluctuations in economic activity.

- An Automatic Stabilizer is an economic shock absorber that helps smooth the cyclical business fluctuations of its own accord, without requiring any deliberate efforts on the part of the government.
- The federal progressive income tax, in U.S.A. is so devised that people in high income group are taxed at a progressively higher rate than those in the low income group. For instance, a person of high income may have to pay a tax of 50 percent, whereas a person with a low income may have to pay 5 percent of his income.
- Such a type of *progressive taxation*, i.e., one which increases with increase in income of the person, tends automatically to offset cyclical fluctuations, because in an *upswing*, when incomes are rising, people would pay more taxes to the government. Higher taxation would leave lesser disposable income with the public and thus help in curbing private expenditure. In the *downswing*, when incomes are declining and tax percentage falls, people would pay less tax to the government, leaving more disposable funds in the hands of the people to them to spend more.
- Another automatic or built-in stabilizer in the U.S.A. is *unemployment insurance*. During the period of *prosperity* the employers pay taxes to the government at higher rates and at the same time government does not pay any doles or unemployment allowances to the unemployed persons, as during the peak period there is hardly any unemployment. Therefore, money accumulates with the government. To that extent (people not getting any unemployment allowances) the private spending is checked. During the period of *depression*, the government lowers the taxes, pays out unemployment allowances to the unemployed persons, thereby making available more spending power to the people, which automatically tend to offset the reduction in the circular flow. Consumer's spending power is encouraged and curbs the recessionary pressures.

- The two measures- progressive taxation and built-in stabilizers- have played an important role in the prompt reversal of fluctuations since Second World War.

The fiscal policy or discretionary policy involves a certain amount of delay in reacting to the new situation. On the other hand, the built-in stabilizers are superior as they go into action immediately whenever the economy is faced with economic fluctuations. However, the shortcoming of this automatic stabilizer is that they provide only a *partial* solution to the problem.

The empirical studies conducted in the U.K. and the U.S.A. suggests that automatic stabilizers can control at the most 50 percent of the economic fluctuations in the economy. Hence, it is necessary to supplement the automatic stabilizers with discretionary policy to secure effective and lasting stability in the nation's economy.

(b) Other Anti-Cyclical Measures: Some of the other measures which can be utilized for controlling business cycles are:

1. **Price Controls:** Imposing control on prices, declaring and maintaining support prices during depression and imposing a ceiling on prices during prosperity, are important contra-cyclical measures.
2. **Employment Assistance:** Starting employment exchanges or short-term technical courses etc., are also termed as 'automatic stabilizers' and can be successfully utilized as anti-cyclical measures.
3. **Purchase and Sale of Commodities:** To combat cyclical fluctuations, the government may purchase different commodities at a fixed price, when the prices of different goods start falling because of depression. In this way, the government prevents an excessive fall in prices. Similarly, the government may sell these commodities at a fixed price during inflationary period and thus, check excessive increase in prices. This measure becomes more effective especially in the case of essential commodities like food grains, clothes, etc.

To sum up, we can say that, the understanding of the business cycles brings forth basic faults which arise in the mechanisms that bring about equilibrium in the economy and keep it stable. One such fault is under-consumption. At high levels of income, people save more than they are expected by the businessmen to save and this result in a deficiency of demand causing a downturn. Secondly, when private investments suddenly fall, it causes a multiplier effect in reverse and imparts a speed to the cycle. During expansion, investment is buoyant and feeds on induced demand created by the multiplier effect. At a moment when it surpasses the point where resource supplies become inelastic and inflation sets in.

Both the *investment function* and *consumption function* are the major components of aggregate demand. If we have to cure the situation and succeed in achieving the major objectives of full employment, economic stability and price stabilization; we must work on these two components of aggregate demand. During recession, demand should be encouraged and it must be stabilized when the economy has reached full-employment level. Thus, at this stage, we should curtail aggregate demand when prices pick-up and are all set to cross the safe boundary. If aggregate demand remains unstable, the state should come forward to intervene in view of the major objectives mentioned above. In short, whichever policy intervention is done, it should focus at demand management. The instruments of such an intervention can be anti-depression (aimed at arresting the downswing of demand) or anti-inflationary (aimed at containing inflationary forms of expansion). Thus, these instruments are made to work in such an anti-cyclical manner.

6.4 Inflation: Meaning, Courses and Control

Introduction

In the modern times, inflation is a global phenomenon. There is hardly any country in the capitalist world today which is not afflicted by inflation. Inflation, in the popular mind, is generally associated with rapidly rising prices which cause a fall in the purchasing power of money. But, the term 'inflation' is a highly controversial term. Different economists have offered different definitions of inflation. The persistent inflation and the problems associated with it have claimed more attention of the economists than any other macro-economic problem. This has led to a great increase in the literature on inflation.

Meaning of Inflation

Broadly speaking, inflation means a considerable and persistent rise in the general price level over a long period of time. The term 'inflation' has widely attracted the attention of the economists all over the world, but despite that, there is no generally accepted definition. Some frequently quoted definitions of inflation are considered below:

Definitions of Inflation:

- According to **Prof. Crowther**, Inflation *"is a state in which the value of money is falling, i.e., prices are rising."*
- However, **Crowther's** definition is not complete. This definition has been criticised on the following grounds:

(a) Crowther terms every increase in the price level as inflationary. This has harmful consequences for the economy. However, an increase in the price level during the depression period is not inflationary and has no adverse effects on the economy.

(b) Crowther's definition stresses more on the symptoms rather than the causes of inflation. It is observed that a rise in prices is the effect and not the cause of inflation.

Hence, this definition fails to explain the rise in price from time to time.

- *Prof.* **Hawtrey** defines inflation as the *"issue of too much currency."*

This definition too is unsatisfactory. It does not offer a clear criterion of the term "over-issue of currency."

- According to **Pigou**, *"Inflation exists when money income is expanding more than in proportion to the increase in earning activity."*

- In **Prof. Kemmerer's** words, inflation is defined as *"too much currency in relation to the physical volume of business being done."*
- **Prof. Coulbourn** has also stressed on the same point as he says, *"Inflation is too much money chasing too few goods."*
- **Prof. Goldenweiser,** *"Inflation occurs when the volume of money actively bidding for goods and services increases faster than the available supply of goods."*

In the above definitions, the general spirit is to define Inflation as-

- A situation in which supply of money increases at a rate much faster than the supply of real output.
- The rise in the price level is caused by an increase in the supply of money.
- The increase in the supply of money is the cause and rise in the price level is the effect.

Thus, these definitions do not capture full implications of the inflationary situation. The cause and effect relationship between the supply of money and the price level was reversed in Germany after the First World War. The hyper-inflation which was witnessed in Germany in the post-war could not be explained by the normal cause and effect relationship between supply of money and the price level as mentioned in the above various definitions.

These definitions consider inflation as a purely monetary phenomenon. The recent definitions of Cambridge economists, including Pigou and Keynes, have analysed inflation – a phenomenon of full employment.

According to Keynes, an inflationary rise in the price level cannot take place before the point of full employment. Keynes explains that every expansion of money supply does not result in a rising price level so long as there are unemployed resources in the economy. It is only after the economy has attained full employment that the price level will increase. In other words, an expansion of money supply before the point of full employment will go on to increase the output and employment and not the price level. Thus, according to Keynes, the rise in the price level after the point of full employment is *true inflation*. Any rise in the price level, before the point of full employment, can occur due to certain bottlenecks in the expansion of output in the economy. However, this is not true inflation and it can be referred to as semi-inflation, i.e., inflation that is pre-full employment.

According to Hicks, "our present troubles are not of a monetary character". *Johnson* defines inflation as "a sustained rise in prices". *Shapiro* defines it as "a persistent and appreciable rise in the general level of prices". According to Brooman inflation "is a continuing increase in the general price level." All these definitions clearly point out that the Modern economists do not consider money supply alone as the cause of inflation.

From the various definitions, the term 'inflation' can be summarised as-

(a) Inflation is a phenomenon or rising prices. However, every rise in price is not inflationary.
(b) Inflation is a sustained rise in prices.
(c) Inflation is a general and dynamic phenomenon. It is general as it is not limited to only a particular sector of an economy. It is dynamic in nature and severity. Inflation occurs over a period of time.
(d) True inflation is witnessed only after reaching the full employment level.
(e) Inflation is characterised by an excess of demand or an increase in costs or the occurrence of both.
(f) Neo-Classicists define inflation as a monetary phenomenon. According to *Friedman*, "*inflation is always and everywhere a monetary phenomenon.....and can be produced only by a more rapid increase in the quantity of money than output.*"
(g) Modern economists do not agree that money supply alone is the cause of inflation. *Hicks* say, "Our present troubles are not of a monetary character." *Johnson* defines inflation as a sustained rise in prices.
(h) However, it is essential to understand that a sustained rise in prices may be of various magnitudes and accordingly, different names have been given to inflation based upon the rate of rise in prices:
   - Creeping Inflation- price rise of less than 3% per annum;
   - Walking Inflation- price rise between 3 to 7% per annum, but less than 10%.
   - Running inflation – price rise between 10 to 20 % per annum;
   - Hyper-inflation – price rise from 20 to 100 % per annum. It is runaway or galloping inflation.

Nature of Inflation

Economists have defined inflation in various ways. Broadly speaking, it appears that there are two approaches to the global phenomenon of inflation.

1. The Quantity Theory Approach: The quantity theory of money points out that the increase in the quantity of money causes an inflationary rise in the price level. The economists who support this approach are Hawtrey, Coulbourn, and Goldenweiser. They believe that inflation is purely a monetary phenomenon.

The objections that have been raised against this approach are:-

(i) This approach does not adequately explain hyper-inflation which took place in Germany in the post-war period. It was observed that it was the rise in the price level which caused an increase in the supply of money.

(ii) This approach has failed to produce solution for an economy which suffers from depression and unemployment. It is pointed out by the critics of this approach that an expansion of money supply in such an economy may not necessarily result in an inflationary rise in the price level.

2. The Excess Demand Approach: This approach has been put forth by Lord Keynes and other Cambridge economists. According to them, inflation is that situation in which the total demand for goods exceeds the total supply of goods at current prices. Thus, the only cause of inflation is the existence of a persistent excess demand in the economy.

There is practically no difference between these two points of view about inflation because when the total quantity of money increases, the money income of the people increases and this leads to an increase in demand in the form of money. This brings about a difference between demand and supply at current prices and hence there is inflation.

Approaches to the Theory of Inflation

Historically, a great deal of economic literature was concerned with the question of what causes inflation and what effect it has. There were different schools of thought to the causes of inflation can be divided into o broad areas: Quality theories of inflation and Quantity theories of inflation.

Currently, the quantity theory of money is widely accepted as an accurate model of inflation in the long run, i.e., the inflation rate is essentially dependent on the growth rate of money supply in relation to the growth of the economy. However, in the short and medium term, inflation may be affected by supply and demand pressures in the economy, and influenced by the relative elasticity of wages, prices and interest rates.

Keynesian economics proposes that changes in money supply do not directly affect prices, and that visible inflation is the result of pressures in the economy expressing themselves in prices.

Thus, there are two main approaches to the theory of inflation- (A) The Quantity Theory of Money Approach and (B) The Excess Demand Approach.

(a) **The Quantity Theory of Money Approach:** *According to this approach, it is the increase in the quantity of money which causes an inflationary rise in the price level.* Prof. Hawtrey, Goldenweiser, Coulbourn advocate this approach- they look upon inflation as a purely phenomenon.

Limitations:
(i) This approach does not adequately explain the phenomenon of hyper-inflation which took place in Germany in the post-war period. However, it was pointed out that the rise in the price level was the cause and the increase in the money supply was the result.

(ii) This approach does not hold good to economies suffering from depression and unemployment. An expansion of money supply in such an economy instead of raising the price level will actually increase output and employment.

(b) **The Excess Demand Approach:** Prof.Keynes and other economists of Cambridge School have developed this approach. According to this approach, *"Just as the price of any good is determined by the demand for it and the supply of it, so also the general price level is determined by the total demand for and total supply of the group of goods concerned."* Thus, it is the total demand for goods exceeds the total supply of goods at current prices or it is the existence of a persistent excess demand in the economy that causes inflation.

Excess Demand is due to various situations like:

1. **Planning Period:** The situation of excess demand can arise during a period of developmental planning. The demand for investment goods invariably goes up under the influence of developmental planning and results in increase in the general price level in the economy.

2. **War Period:** During the war period, the government expenditure definitely goes up, resulting in a substantial increase in the demand for various goods and services. Consequently, price level shows a rising trend during war period.

3. **Period of Rapid Improvement in Technology:** Technological development requires fresh investments in the various sectors of the economy and hence it increases the demand for investment goods of various types.

4. **Decline in Supply:** Excess demand can arise when the total supply of goods and services declines for whatever reasons.

There is no fundamental difference between the two approaches; however the excess demand approach is more popular than the quantity theory of money approach.

Causes of Inflation

When there is a difference between the aggregate supply and the aggregate demand, there is a rise in prices. But, why there is a difference between the aggregate demand and aggregate supply? This can be explained with the help of causes of inflation.

(a) **Increase in Demand:** the phenomenon of excess demand for goods and services can arise in a number of situations, as believed by Keynes and other monetarists such as:

1. **Increase in Public Expenditure:** An increase in the public expenditure as a result of the outbreak of war or developmental planning invariably causes an increase in the demand for goods and services in the economy. This is an important reason that gives rise to the emergence of excess demand for goods and services in the country.

2. **Increase in Private Expenditure:** When optimism prevails in the business world, businessmen are eager to spend more money on capital goods and this in turn brings about an increase in the demand for consumer goods. This is because there is an increase in the income of the people who work in the capital goods industries. Therefore, they are in a position to spend more and thus there is an increase in the demand for all types of goods.

3. **Increase in Foreign Demand:** An increase in the foreign demand for the country's products (i.e. export), reduces the stock of goods available for domestic consumption. It is obvious that when more commodities are exported to foreign nations, less is available for domestic consumption. It creates a situation of shortages and scarcity in the economy, giving rise to inflationary pressures.

4. **Reduction in Taxation:** Reduction in the taxes levied by the government causes excess demand in the economy. With reduction in taxes, it results in an increase of the purchasing power in the hands of the public. With this excess purchasing power, people buy more of goods and services for private consumption.

5. **Repayment of Internal Debts:** When the government repays past debts, more purchasing power is placed at the disposal of the people. They use it for buying goods and services for consumption purposes. This leads to an increase in the aggregate demand in the economy.

6. **Population growth:** A rapidly growing population results in raising the level of aggregate effective demand for goods and services in a country. It acts as an inflationary force and consequently raising price levels.

7. **Existence of Black Money:** People spend such easy money extravagantly on luxurious items and thus lead to rapidly rising prices.

8. **Deficit Financing:** When the government resorts to deficit financing by borrowing from the public and by printing new notes in huge quantity. It raises the aggregate demand in relation to the aggregate supply.

9. **Cheap Money Policy:** The bold policy of credit expansion leads to an increase in the supply of money which results in a rise in demand for goods and services.

10. **Rise in Consumer Spending:** when consumer spending increases, it increases the demand for goods and services. Increased consumer spending can be due to any reason, for instance, easy credit facility etc.

(b) Decrease in Supply: The factors which leads to reduction in the supply of goods and services are as under:-

1. **Natural Calamities:** Natural calamities such as floods, drought, earthquake, etc., adversely affect the supplies of agricultural products. They cause shortage of food products, raw materials and thereby results in inflationary pressures.

2. **Scarcity of the Factors of Production:** At times the economy of a country may be faced with shortages of factors of production such as labour, capital equipment, raw materials etc. These shortages reduce the production of goods and services for consumption purposes. In fact, the shortage in the factors of production causes a serious obstacle to any effort to increase production in the country.

3. **Industrial Disputes:** Trade Unions resort to strikes and if they happen to be unreasonably prolonged, they force the employers to declare lock-outs. As a result, the supply of goods is reduced.

4. **Imbalanced Production:** If the emphasis is placed on the production of comfort and luxury goods and essential and consumer goods are neglected in the country, it creates shortage goods in the market and causes inflation.

5. **Operation of the Law of Diminishing Returns:** When industries in the country use old and obsolete machines and outdated methods of production, the law of diminishing returns operates. This results in the rise of the cost per unit of production, raising the prices of products and causing inflation.

6. **Hoarding by Merchants:** When traders and merchants know that there is a short supply of any commodity, they will purchase and stock large quantities of these commodities. The stocks of essential goods often go underground during a period of inflation and rising prices, causing further scarcity of these goods in the market.

7. **Hoarding by Consumers:** It is not only the traders and merchants who resort to hoarding, but during inflation it is the individual consumers who also hoard essential goods to avoid payment of higher prices in the future. Thus, the consumers hoard essential commodities to ensure the uninterrupted supply of these commodities.

Types of Inflation:

On basis of speed with which the price level rises in the economy, the classification of inflation is as follows:-

(1) **Creeping Inflation:** It is creeping inflation when the price rise is very slow like a creeper or a snail. The price level rises approximately by 2% annually. It is the mildest type of inflation and sometimes government resorts to it to make the economy dynamic. This inflation works as a tonic for developing economy. The slow rise in prices stimulates industry and trade. On account of its stimulating effect some economists welcome it for the economic development of a backward economy. There are some economists who support creeping inflation in the form of a slow and gradual rise in prices to keep the economy away from stagnation. Creeping inflation must be controlled effectively in time before it is too late because if proper control is not exercised over creeping inflation, it may assume alarming proportions with the lapse of time.

(2) **Walking or Trotting Inflation:** Under walking inflation, the rate of increase of the price level acquires greater speed and rapidity. The price level rises at approximately 5% annually. Walking inflation, like creeping inflation, if not well handled can assume dangerous form of inflation.

(3) **Running Inflation:** When the prices rise rapidly like the running of a horse at a rate of speed 10 to 20 percent annually, it is called as running inflation. In case, the government fails to curb running inflation in time, it may easily develop into galloping inflation.

(4) **Galloping or Hyper Inflation:** When prices rise at double or triple digit rates from more than 20 to 100 % annually or even more, it is hyper-inflation. This is the most dangerous type of inflation. Here the prices rise every minute and there is no upward limit to which the price level may rise in course of time. Prof. Keynes refers this type of inflation as 'true inflation' and it occurs after the point of full employment has reached. There are two classic examples of galloping inflation in recent history: (a) the Great Inflation of Germany, after the First World War, and (b) the Great Chinese Inflation after the Second World War.

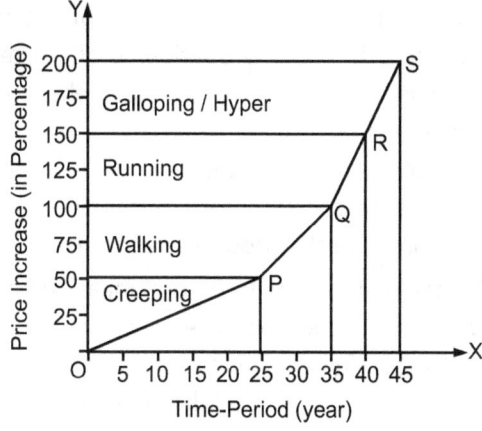

Fig. 6.3 : Inflation based on speed

In Fig. 6.3 the OX-axis measures the time-period or the years and the increase in price level (in percent) is shown on the OY-axis.

In the first period of 25 years, the prices of goods rise by 50% and the OP line represents *creeping inflation*. In the second period of 10 years, the prices have gone up by 50%. The PQ line represents the *walking inflation*. *Running inflation* is shown by the QR line. In the fourth period the price rises by 50% comprising three years in duration and it is shown by RS line. This is *galloping or hyper-inflation*. Thus, in a total period of 43 years, all the four types of inflation take place in succession and the price level rises by 200% during the entire period.

(1) **Comprehensive and Sporadic Inflation:** It is *Comprehensive* Inflation when the prices of all commodities register a rise in the economy. Normally, when there is inflation, it is generally comprehensive inflation. If inflation is sectoral, it is *sporadic* inflation. Only the prices of few commodities may rise upwards due to physical bottlenecks that impede any attempt to increase the production of goods.

For instance, failure of rains may lead to failure of bumper crops and upward trend in the prices of foodgrains. Sporadic inflation can be dealt effectively if government resorts to price controls on the affected goods.

(2) **Open and Repressed Inflation:** It is *Open Inflation* when the government takes no steps to check the rise in the price level. This inflation is allowed to continue unchecked without any attempts on the part of the government to correct it. Under open inflation, the market mechanism is allowed to work itself out fully without restrictions imposed by the government. The market mechanism can afford to pay a higher price for it, hence this mechanism distributes scarce factors among competing industries. The hyper-inflation experienced by Germany after the First World War is an example of open inflation. *Repressed Inflation* is when the government actively intervenes to check the rise in the price level. The government may resort to price controls and rationing of scarce commodities. The administration of controls on prices and rationing of scarce goods is an inseparable feature of repressed inflation. Hence the side effect of this type of inflation manifests itself in the form of profiteering, black-marketing, hoarding and corruption on a large scale. It distorts the production activity from essential to non-essential industries. The reason is that the prices of essential goods are statutorily fixed, while those of non-essential goods are left free and uncontrolled.

(3) **Full and Partial Inflation:** This classification of inflation has been explained by Prof. Pigou. It is *Partial Inflation* when the price level rises slightly due to the expansion of money supply in the pre-full employment stage. This slight rise in price level and expansion in money supply goes to mobilize the idle resources in the economy. It results in more employment and output. However, increase in the money supply even after the point of full employment leads to a sharp uninterrupted rise in the price level with no increase in output and employment. Such a situation is a case of *Full Inflation*.

(4) **Peacetime, Wartime and Post-war Inflation:** On basis of 'time' we have this classification of inflation. When the price level increases during peace time, it is *peace-time inflation*. It is the result of increased government expenditure on developmental projects in the economy. In underdeveloped economies when such projects are undertaken, it results in inflation, referred to as peace-time inflation. During war time, the increase in the output of goods and services does not keep pace with the expansion of money supply. An inflationary gap inevitably emerges resulting in rising price level. This inflation arises during a period of war, hence *war-time inflation*. *Post-war inflation* generally takes place immediately after the end of hostilities and the suppressed demand springs up due to relaxation of price and physical controls by the government.

(5) **Currency Inflation and Credit Inflation:** On the basis of 'factors' which cause inflation there can be currency, credit, profit-induced, deficit-induced, wage-and scarcity-induced inflation. Inflation caused by excess supply of money in relation to the available output of goods and services, it is *Currency inflation*. The excessive supply of money is faced with a limited supply of goods and services and results in inflationary rise in price level. When Government encourages an expansion of credit without expanding the supply of money in circulation, it is known as *Credit Inflation*. The main objectives of Credit Inflation are: (i) to mobilize financial resources for developmental plans; (ii) to expand production; (iii) to reduce the burden of indebtedness of the farmers.

(6) **Profit-induced and Deficit-induced Inflation:** Sometimes the production costs start declining, and as a result the government resorts to artificial means to stop the trend of falling prices. In such a situation, the prices continue to stay at the old levels as the prices do not go up and are also not allowed to fall down. Prof. Keynes refers this inflation as *Profit-induced Inflation*. When government's income does not match its increased expenditure consequent upon the outbreak of the war, it results in *deficit-induced inflation*. The government is not able to cover the deficit by resorting to new taxes and public borrowings. To finance the deficit the government resorts printing new currency, this is deficit-induced inflation. To finance its developmental plans, government of underdeveloped economies resort to the printing press and it results in deficit-induced inflation.

(7) **Wage-Induced Inflation:** When the workers organize themselves into powerful trade unions and force the employers to increase their wages, this pushes up the production costs, increases the price level upward. This is wage-induced inflation.

(8) **Scarcity-Induced Inflation:** It is also known as production inflation. When the supply of money does not increase but the supply of goods decreases due to natural calamities, the prices moves upward. It is inflation due to scarcity of commodities.

(9) **Mark-Up Inflation:** This type of inflation is due to the peculiar method of pricing of goods and services adopted by the huge business organizations operating in that country. The gigantic business organizations calculate their production costs first and then add to these costs a certain mark-up to yield the targeted rate of profit on their capital investment. The mark-up is on the high side and adds to inflationary pressure in U.S.A. The higher the demand, the greater is the size of the mark-up.

(10) **Ratchet Inflation:** Under ratchet inflation, the prices in certain sectors are not allowed to fall, i.e., are held in a fixed position, even when there are strong reasons for the prices to decline. Sometimes, it may happen so that the aggregate demand

in the economy is not high but in certain sectors the aggregate demand is excessive and low in others. In sectors having high aggregate demand the prices would register a rise in prices and in other sectors the prices show a decline. But the prices are not allowed to fall in accordance with the low aggregate demand due to resistance from the industrialists and trade unions. Thus, the prices in the excess-demand sectors rise and are not allowed to fall in the deficit-demand sectors, consequently the net result is a rise in the general price level. This is known as 'ratchet inflation'.

(11) **Stagflation:** Since the 60's a new type of inflation had come into vogue in the post-war period. This is *Stagflation*. It is not inflation in the strict Keynesian sense as according to Keynes inflation is accompanied by *overfull* employment. The present day inflation is quite different from the traditional inflation. Today, 'Stagflation' is a global phenomenon. It is inflation accompanied by stagnation on the development front- high prices and high unemployment go hand in hand. The whole Western world particularly U.S.A., Britain, Italy and even developing countries like India have fallen prey to this most vicious type of inflation. Even the Keynesian measures to arrest inflation like budget surpluses, higher taxes and spending cuts have not been successful; in fact they have aggravated the problem of unemployment. Any measure undertaken to ease the situation of unemployment through increased capital investment adds to the inflation. Today, the world stands between the devil of inflation and the deep sea of unemployment.

(12) **Sectoral Inflation:** When the rise in prices is not general but restricted to a particular sector of the economy, it is *Sectoral Inflation*. Sectoral inflation, if not taken care of, it can spread to all the sectors of the economy. For example, during 1979-80 due to drought conditions agricultural prices shot up. But this sectoral (agricultural sector) inflation did not remain confined to the agricultural sector for long as the manufacturers had to push the prices higher due to higher cost of raw materials and increased wages.

(13) **Imported Inflation:** Inflation which is caused in a country due to the operation of external inflationary pressures transmitted to the country concerned through foreign trade. For example, when a country depends heavily on imported goods and services, any inflationary pressure originating in foreign country is bound to have its repercussions on its domestic economy.

(14) **Demand-Pull Inflation: (Demand Inflation):** *Demand inflation is caused by an increase in the aggregate effective demand for goods and services in the economy.* Demand inflation is direct result of an excess of aggregate effective demand over the aggregate supply of goods and services.

The process starts this way- the increase in the supply of money leads to fall in the rate of interest and thus increases the demand for investment in the economy. With investment demand increases the demand for factors of production; in turn the factors of production receive money income for the services rendered by them. With increased money income, there is an inevitable rise in the expenditure for consumption goods. Thus, it is the increase in the demand for services of factors that lead to increase in their money incomes and it becomes natural on part of the factors of production to spend additional amounts on consumption goods. Since the economy was operating already at full employment, hence increase in investment expenditure results in inflation caused by increase in demand. The increased in investment expenditure and consumption expenditure creates a situation of shortage of goods and services, increasing imports, rising wages, increasing employment, increasing profit margins, etc. These all are indicators of presence of demand inflation.

During the war period, the people generally keep postponing their purchases due to overall shortages of commodities in the economy. And, as soon as the war is over the longstanding demand for goods increases. Thus, this type of demand inflation generally arises in the postwar period. The demand inflation can be tackled by the government by curtailing unnecessary demand through the adoption of monetary and fiscal methods.

The Monetarists emphasise the *role of money as the principal cause of demand-pull inflation.* According to Friedman, inflation is always and everywhere a monetary phenomenon that arises from a more expansion in the quantity of money that the total output in the economy. Since the demand for money is fairly stable and excess demand for goods and services is mainly the outcome of increased money supply in the economy. Increased demand for goods, caused by increased money income raises the demand for labour. The workers demand higher wages, input costs and prices rise. Thus the money supply expansion works through output before inflation starts.

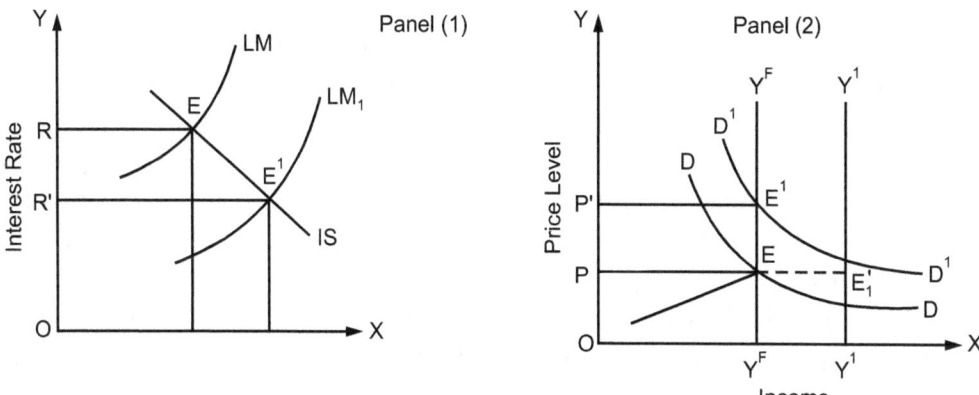

Fig. 6.4 : Shows the Quantity Theory Version of Demand-pull Inflation.

- Y^F is the full employment level of income which is depicted by price level P in Panel (2) and by intersection of IS and LM curves at E in Panel (1) at OR rate of interest.
- LM curve shifts to the right, i.e., LM_1 with the increase in the quantity of money. LM_1 intersects IS curve at E^1 and the equilibrium level of income rises to Y^1 and this lowers the rate of interest to OR^1.
- The increase in demand is shown by shift in aggregate demand curve from DD to D^1D^1 and the excess demand is to the extent of EE_1 (= Y^FY^1) in Panel (2).
- The vertical curve S is the fixed supply curve and the excess demand raises the price level to P^1.
- The rise in price level reduces the value of money, so that the LM_1 curve shifts to the left LM.
- Excess demand will not be eliminated until D^1D^1 curve cuts supply curve S at E^1. This will result in rising of price level to P^1 (panel 2) and restoring original equilibrium position to E (Panel 1).

To sum up, demand-pull inflation is caused by increases in aggregate demand due to increased private and government spending, etc. Demand inflation encourages economic growth since the excess demand and favourable market conditions will stimulate investment and expansion.

(1) Cost Inflation-(Supply Inflation): It is also called as "Supply shock inflation", and is caused by a drop in aggregate supply (potential output). This may be due to natural disasters, or increased prices of inputs. For example, a sudden decrease in the supply of oil, leading to increased oil prices, can cause cost-push inflation. Producers for whom oil is a part of their costs could then pass this on to consumers in the form of increased prices. Another example arises from unexpectedly high insured losses, either legitimate or fraudulent.

Thus, Cost inflation is generally caused by three factors: (a) an increase in wages; (b) an increase in the profit margins; and (c) imposition of heavy commodity taxes.

(a) These days labour is organised and using their collective strength they dictate their own terms to the employers. Powerful trade unions get the wages pushed up even without an equivalent increase in the productivity of the workers. This attempt on the part of the trade unions to push up the wages invariably causes cost inflation in the economy.

(b) Cost inflation is also caused when the industrialists push up their profit margins and then the prices cannot remain at their old levels. However, it is more the wage-push than the profit-push element that is significant in causing cost inflation. The reasons for it are that (a) profit constitutes a small part of the total price of the commodity. Thus, even if it is raised a little, it may not really bring a huge difference in the price of the commodity. (b) the industrialists generally do not like to raise profit margin beyond a certain limit as they fear losing customers. Thus, the wage-push element is an important cause of cost-push inflation. It is more so because the industrialists should never be prepared to absorb the increase in wages by lowering down their own profit margins. Hence, any increase in the wages of the labour will lead to increase in price level and ultimately to cost inflation. When the cost inflation is due to wage-push factor, it has its effect gradually in all the sectors and does not remain confined to a particular sector or an industry. When cost inflation arises in one particular industry, it soon spreads to the other sectors of the economy because the various sectors are linked closely with each other. The output of one industry may serve as an input for another industry. Thus, cost inflation starting in one industry soon becomes all-round phenomenon for the economy.

(c) The government may impose heavy taxes on different commodities. For example, it can be V.A.T.or now it is Local Body Taxes (LBT). In seller's market the producers can easily shift the tax burden on to the shoulders of the consumers along with a margin of their own. This causes cost inflation in the economy.

Implications of Cost-Push Inflation are: (a) It is associated with unemployment. Thus, some percent of unemployment is to be tolerated if inflation is to be controlled to an extent; (b) But, if the government is committed to a policy of full employment then it has to tolerate wage increase and hence cost-push inflation; (c) if the government attempts to increase aggregate demand during periods of the employment, it may lead to increase in wages instead of raising output and employment.

(2) Demand-pull and Cost-push Inflation: It can be referred to as "built-in" inflation. It is often linked to the "price/wage spiral". It involves workers trying to keep their wages up with prices (above the rate of inflation), and firms passing these higher labour costs on to their customers as higher prices, leading to a 'vicious circle'. This inflation is also referred to as 'hangover inflation' as it reflects events in the past.

Thus, the two concepts are not exclusive concepts. Demand inflation, when it once starts, may soon land the economy into cost inflation. Let us see how this action and reaction takes place. An increase in the prices of consumption goods is definitely accompanied by the demand for higher wages by the workers. The prices of raw materials too show an upward trend under the impact of demand inflation. Naturally, an increase in wages and in the prices of raw materials will lead to the emergence of cost-push inflation in the economy. Hence, it is very difficult to draw a clear-cut line between the two types of inflation and describe them as exclusive types of inflation. In fact, each one strengthens the other. Increasing commodity taxation, rising wages, falling profit margins, frequent devaluations of domestic currency (in efforts to push up the exports) are important pointers to the cost-push inflation in the economy.

Of the two types of inflations, it is easier to tame demand inflation than the cost-push inflation. That is, demand inflation can be tackled by adopting various types of monetary and fiscal measures to suction out (take away) the surplus purchasing power from the hands of the public, but cost inflation is difficult to be tackled by these two measures. This is because; any attempt to cut down wages by the authorities will be met by stiff resistance on the part of the workers.

To conclude, the theory of inflation would be complete only if the demand side and supply side are well-integrated to provide a viable explanation of the phenomenon of rising prices.

Effects of Inflation

An increase in the general level of prices implies a decrease in the purchasing power of the currency. That is, when the general level of prices rises, each monetary unit buys fewer goods and services. The effect of inflation is not distributed evenly in the economy, and as a consequence there are hidden costs to some and benefits to other from this decrease in the purchasing power of money. For example, with inflation, those segments in society which own physical assets, such as property, stock, etc., benefit from the price/value of their holdings going up, while those who seek to acquire them will need to pay more for them. Their ability to do so will depend on the degree to which their income is fixed. For example, increase in payments to workers and pensioners often lag behind inflation, and for some people income is fixed. Increases in the price level (inflation) erode the real value of money (the functional currency) and other items with an underlying monetary nature.

A period of prolonged and continuous inflation results in the economic, social, political and moral disruption of the society. The effects of inflation can be discussed under various sub-headings, such as, (1) Effects on Production; (2) Effects on Distribution; (3) Non-economic Effects; and (4) Other Consequences.

(1) Effects on Production: The effects of inflation on production are very important. As long as the economy has not reached full employment and inflation is proceeding at a mild rate, it may be helpful to an economy as it mild increase in prices acts as stimulant to the producers. An expansion of money supply in an underemployed economy will result in a gradual rise in the prices. The cost of production increases at a lower rate than the prices. This results in greater profit margins and optimistic conditions for entrepreneurs. Investments rise, generating more income and employment till full employment is reached. But, after full employment, any expansion of money supply is very harmful for the economy. Thus, it is the hyper-inflation that disrupts the smooth functioning of the economy. The adverse effects of inflation on production are as follows:

(a) Runaway inflation results in a serious depreciation of the value of money and discourages savings, which in turn give a serious setback to capital accumulation.
(b) Inflation disrupts the smooth functioning of the price mechanism, thereby creating an all-round confusion in the economy.
(c) Due to reduced capital accumulation, the investment will suffer resulting in low volume of production.
(d) The volume of production may also decline due to business uncertainty which may discourage entrepreneurs from taking business risk in production.
(e) It is not only the volume of production that suffers but the pattern of production may also undergo changes. Hyper-inflation may result in diversion of productive resources from the essential goods industries to the luxury goods industries. As a result, there is further shortage in supply of consumer goods for the common man.
(f) During hyper-inflation, it is a seller's market. This leads to serious deterioration in the quality of goods produced in the economy.
(g) Traders and consumers resort to hoarding of essential goods. Traders do so to earn higher profits or sell scarce goods in the black market. Consumers resort to hoarding of essential goods for fear of paying higher prices in the future.
(h) Hyper-inflation gives rise to speculative activities due to the uncertainty generated by persistent rise in price level.
(i) With the continuous rise in prices, the value of money falls. It drives out the foreign capital invested in the country.
(j) In due course of time, runaway inflation results in a flight of domestic currency due to the constant depreciation in the value of money.

To sum up, high or unpredictable inflation rates are regarded as harmful to an overall economy. They add inefficiencies in the market, and make it difficult for companies to budget or plan long-term. Inflation can act as a drag on productivity as companies are forced to shift resources away from products and services in order to focus on profit and losses from currency inflation. Uncertainty about the future purchasing power of money discourages investment and saving. And inflation can impose hidden tax increases, as inflated earnings push tax-payers into higher income tax rates unless the tax brackets are indexed to inflation.

(2) Effects on Distribution: Inflation has a deep impact on the distribution of income and wealth in the society. The flexible income groups, such as businessmen, merchants and traders are always the gainers in an inflationary period. On the other hand, the fixed income groups such as workers, salaried employees, teachers, pensioners, etc., are always the losers due to the inflationary rise in prices. Thus, inflation is unjust. It throws the economic burden on the weakest shoulders.

(a) **Debtors and creditors:** During inflation, debtors are gainers, while the creditors are the losers. The reason is that, the debtors while repaying their debt return less purchasing power to the creditors than what they have actually borrowed and in this way; the creditors receive less in real terms and are losers during the inflationary period.

(b) **Fixed-income group:** Persons who live on past savings, pensioners, interest and rent receivers suffer the most during an inflationary period as their incomes remain fix while the prices rise sky-high.

(c) **Salary and wage earners:** They suffer during inflation as wages and salaries do not rise in the same proportion as the cost of living rises. If the salary earners and workers are well-organized into powerful trade unions, they may not suffer to a great extent during inflation. However, if they are unorganized, they are great sufferers as their wages and salaries may not increase in proportion to the cost of living.

(d) **Businessmen and Entrepreneurs:** Manufacturers, traders and merchants are gainers during inflation. They experience windfall gains as the prices of their stocks and inventories rise. They also benefit as the prices of their products rise, but the costs are quite 'sticky' and do not rise rapidly. In this way, inflation converts the entrepreneurs into 'profiteers'.

(e) **Investors:** Investors in shares (or equities) are gainers, while investors in fixed interest-yielding bonds and debentures do not benefit much. Income from bond and debentures remain fixed. The middle-class investors generally invest in bond and debentures and thereby stand to lose as they find their savings largely wiped out as a result of the depreciation in the value of money. On the other hand, the rich-class investors invest in equities and benefit during inflation.

(f) **Farmers:** During inflation, farmers are generally the gainers. The prices of the farm products increase more in proportion to the cost incurred by them. Moreover, farmers are generally debtors, thus they repay in terms of lesser purchasing power. However, small farmers do not really gain during inflation as they hardly have surplus to dispose-off in the market.

To sum up, inflation redistributes income and wealth from those on fixed nominal incomes, such as some pensioners whose pensions are not indexed to the price level, towards those with variable incomes whose earnings may better keep pace with inflation. This redistribution of purchasing power will also occur between international trading partners. Where fixed exchange rates are imposed, higher inflation in one economy than another will cause the first economy's exports to become more expensive and affect the balance of trade. There can also be negative impacts to trade from an increased instability in currency exchange prices caused by unpredictable inflation.

(3) Non-Economic Effects:
   (a) Inflation is socially unjust and inequitable for the society as it favours the affluent class. This creates a sense of grievance among those who are adversely affected by inflation.
   (b) Social conflict is seen in the society which can have serious political consequences by creating political instability.
   (c) Inflation gives a serious blow to business ethics and morality.
   (d) Attracted by quick profit, deterioration sets in the quality of products. Businessmen may also resort to adulteration and other anti-social tactics to boost up their profits.
   (e) The general morality of the people in the country suffers, resulting in all-round corruption in the country.
   (f) Inflation thus not only disturbs the smooth functioning of the economy but prepares the ground for social and political upheavals.

(4) Strengthening of Cost-Push Inflation: High inflation can prompt employees to demand rapid wage increases, to keep up with consumer prices. In the cost-push theory of inflation, rising wages in turn can help fuel inflation. In the case of collective bargaining, wage growth will be set as a function of inflationary expectations, which will be higher when inflation is high. This can cause a wage spiral. *In a sense, inflation begets further inflationary expectations, which beget further inflation.*

(5) Other Consequences: Inflation poses a serious danger to underdeveloped countries. The less developed countries require huge capital resources for their speedy economic development. However, during inflation, savings are discouraged and hence capital accumulation in the economy suffers. Inflation also discourages the inflow of foreign capital into the country. With reduced capital resources, an underdeveloped country finds it difficult to set up its progress towards economic development. Inflation encourages speculative activities in the economy.

Hyper-Inflation: If inflation gets totally out of control, it can grossly interfere with the normal workings of the economy, hurting its ability to supply of goods. Hyperinflation can lead to the abandonment of the use of the country's currency, leading to the inefficiencies of barter.

   (1) Reallocation of Resources: A change in the supply or demand for a good will normally cause its relative price to change, signalling to buyers and sellers that they should re-allocate resources in response to the new market conditions. But when prices are constantly changing due to inflation, price changes due to genuine relative price signals are difficult to distinguish from price changes due to general inflation, so agents are slow to respond to them. The result is loss of efficiency in allocation.

(2) **Shoe Leather Cost:** Hyper inflation increases the opportunity cost of holding cash balances and can induce people to hold a greater portion of their assets in interest paying accounts. However, since cash is still needed to carry out transactions, this means that more "trips to the bank" are necessary in order to make withdrawals, proverbially wearing out the "shoe leather" with each trip.

(3) **Menu Costs:** With hyper inflation, firms must change their prices often to keep up with economy-wide changes. But often changing prices is itself a costly activity in two ways: explicitly- the firms need to print new menus, or implicitly- firms need extra time and effort needed to change prices constantly. For example, firms dealing in imports- with exchange rate changing everyday at hyper speed between rupee and the strong currencies like dollar, euro and pound- the menu cost is high.

(4) **Business Cycles:** According to the Austrian economists, the most damaging effect of inflation is that inflation sets off business cycle. The artificially low interest rates and the associated increase in the money supply lead to reckless, speculative borrowing, resulting in clusters of mal-investments, which eventually have to be liquidated as they become unsustainable.

Control of Inflation

A variety of methods and policies have been used to control inflation. Inflation is caused by the failure of aggregate supply to match with the increase in the aggregate demand. To check and control an inflationary boom, three lines of action are suggested.

(A) Monetary Measures: These measures include increase in discount rates, sale of government securities in the open market, increase in reserve ratios and implementation of selective controls to cure inflationary credit boom. These methods are adopted by the Central Bank of the country.

(1) **Increase in Bank Discount Rates:** To arrest inflation, the Central Bank increases the rediscount rates. This action leads to an increase in the cost of borrowing funds for business and consumer spending, thus discouraging excessive activity based on borrowed funds.

When the rediscount rates rise, bank rates rise. Bank rates are interest rates charged by the commercial banks. An increase in bank rates tends to discourage borrowings by businessmen and consumers from banks resulting in a fall in the intensity of inflationary pressures in the economy.

However, this measure suffers from the following limitations:

(a) If the bank rates do not rise with the rise in rediscount rates, there may be no decline in the business and consumer borrowing. In this way, the inflationary pressures will continue.

(b) For the rediscount rates to be an effective anti-inflationary instrument, the commercial banks should have no easy access to additional reserves. For example, the commercial banks which are in possession of large amounts of short-term government securities can increase their reserves by selling these securities to the Central Bank or converting mature securities into cash, rather than approaching the Central Bank.

(c) Rise in rediscount rates will fail to check inflation if non-bank holders, like insurance companies of government securities were to convert their holdings into cash. This would increase the velocity of money due to increased cash balances. It is a general tendency on part of the holders of fixed-income-yielding assets, to cash when prices are rising and value of money is falling.

(2) Selling of Government Securities: To check inflationary boom, government resorts to sale of government securities in the open market through the Central Bank. When public purchases them and pays for these securities, the banks' reserves with the Central Bank are reduced and they adopt a *'dear'* and *'restrictionist'* credit policy in relation to business requirements. With restricted and tight money conditions in the market, further growth of inflationary boom is curtailed.

Following are the limitations when operating this instrument:

(a) This instrument may be ineffective if the commercial banks are able to increase their reserves by selling their stocks of government securities to the Central Bank.

(b) The non-bank holders of government securities too, in the absence of other buyers, sell them to the Central Bank and deposit the proceeds with commercial banks. This would increase the reserves of the commercial banks and make ineffective the sale of the government securities by the Central Bank.

(c) The impact of gold may also reverse the anti-inflationary effect of this instrument.

(d) This instrument may be off-set by increased borrowings from or increased sales of treasury bills, to the Central Bank by the commercial banks.

(3) Increased Cash Reserve Requirements: An increase in reserve requirements of the member-banks also serves as an anti-inflationary instrument during inflation. It curtails the ability of the banking system in credit expansion. For e.g., if the Central Bank increases the legal reserve requirements from 10% to 15% of the demand deposits, the member-banks will be obliged to keep larger reserves with the Central Bank and to that extent their ability to create credit will be curtailed.

This instrument suffers from the following limitations:-

(a) If the commercial banks happen to have large surplus reserves, then even the raising of reserve requirements may not succeed in curbing credit creation.

(b) The ability of commercial banks to increase or replenish their cash reserves by selling government securities may lead to higher reserve requirements and make this instrument ineffective.

(c) A large inflow of gold due to the existence of export surplus will also increase the member-banks' reserves and make the policy of higher reserve requirements ineffective.

(4) **Consumer Credit:** This instrument focuses on curbing excessive spending by consumers during inflation. In advanced countries and now even in developing economies, installment purchasing plays an important role in consumer spending. Most of the durable consumer goods such as refrigerators, washing machines, etc., are purchased by the consumers on installment credit. However, during inflation to reduce consumer spending on consumer durable goods, firstly down payment is increased and secondly the length of repayment period is reduced.

(5) **Higher Margin Requirements:** Every commercial bank, before granting a loan to a businessman against collateral security keeps a certain specified margin, say 30% or 40%. For example, if the value of the security offered to the bank is ₹ 1,000 and the bank keeps a margin of 30%, then it will advance not more than ₹ 700 to the businessman. This margin is a cover against a fall in the value of the security. Thus, when at the instructions of the Central Bank, the member-bank raises the margin it discourages excessive credit. In other words, higher the margin requirement, lower the amount of the loan that the borrower can obtain from the bank. In this way the banks check undue monetary expansion.

(B) **Fiscal Measures:** The major anti-inflationary fiscal measures are:

(1) **Taxation:** During inflation it is essential to reduce the size of disposable income in the hands of the general public as the supply of goods and services are less in comparison to the demand for them. Thus, it is necessary to take away the excess purchasing power from the public in the form of taxes. For this the existing rates of taxes should be steeply increased and new taxes should be imposed on goods and services. Perhaps, the best anti-inflation tax is the personal income tax with steep rates and high surcharges. This would definitely reduce the disposable income in the hands of the public and check inflationary pressures.

Thus, (i) direct and indirect taxes should be raised to the maximum limits to reduce the disposable incomes; (ii) tariffs or custom duties should be reduced to increase imports and thus increase the supply of goods in the country; (iii) the tariffs on necessities of life and other items in short supply should be reduced to increase the supply of goods and services and check inflation.

However, a word of caution is that while increasing taxes it should not be to the extent that money incomes are highly deflated and provoke depression in the economy.

(2) Government Spending: During inflation effective demand increases. The increased private spending puts pressure on limited supply of goods and services available in the market. Thus, it becomes essential, on the part of the government to reduce its expenditure to the minimum and avoid greater pressure on limited supply of goods and services.

However, there are limitations in reducing of the government spending:

(a) In the war period, it is not easy for the government to bring down its expenditure.
(b) Heavy reduction in government expenditure may help to arrest inflation, but it may land the economy into recession in the long run.
(c) This policy may also clash with the long-term public investment programme.

(3) Public Borrowing: The objective of public borrowing is to take away from the public excess purchasing power which can be utilized by the people to exert pressure on limited supplies of goods and services.

Public borrowing can be compulsory or voluntary. When a certain percentage of the wages or salaries are compulsory deducted in exchange for savings bonds, it is compulsory public borrowing. With this the purchasing power of the public is blocked for a definite period and reduces pressure on the limited amount of goods and services. Generally, public borrowing is voluntary.

(a) It involves the use of compulsion which is generally not readily acceptable to the public;
(b) It results in discontent when applied to people who are not in a position to contribute easily.

(4) Debt Management: The existing public debt should be managed in such a manner that it reduces the existing money supply and prevents further credit expansion. The government functions as an instrument of anti-inflation. For the government to conduct debt-management, it is required to repay the bank held assets out of the budgetary surplus. The reason is that when the government securities held by the commercial banks are retired by the government out of budgetary surplus, then it would check the power of the banks to encash their securities and add to their reserves for credit expansion.

However, this instrument would be ineffective if the non-bank investors were unwilling to give up spendable money in exchange for government bonds. Secondly, the non-bank investors may use for purchasing the government securities idle and surplus funds which would not have been spent at all. This action on part of non-bank investors would also make the weapon ineffective.

(5) Over-valuation: When the domestic currency in relation to foreign currencies is over-valued, it would serve as an anti-inflationary method. (i) it would discourage exports and thus make available the goods and services in the country; (ii) it would encourage imports and again add to the limited supply of goods and services.

The limitation confronted is that when the other countries suffer from inflation, then the country concerned will have to overvalue its currency considerably to neutralize the inflationary effect of the rising cost of imports.

(6) Fixed exchange rates: Under fixed exchange rate currency regime, a country's currency is tied in value to another single currency or to a basket of other currencies. A fixed exchange rate is usually used to stabilize the value of a currency, in relation to the currency it is pegged to.

(C) Other Measures: Other anti-inflationary measures are:-

(1) Expansion of Output: The best medicine to cure inflation is to increase production. An 'inflationary gap' arises partly due to the inadequacy of output. However, there are two major hurdles in increasing the output. One is the attainment of full employment and the other is the problem of increasing costs. In the first case, once the full employment level has reached, there is no possibility of expanding further any production. In the second case, if costs increase, there is a possibility of prices rising too. But, inspite of these limitations, it becomes desirable to increase the production of those essential consumer commodities which are inflation-sensitive. To increase the output, some measures have to be undertaken like avoiding industrial disputes, import of raw materials, and increase in working hours, etc.

(2) Income and Wage Policy: During an inflationary boom, wages cannot be left free to chase prices upward, i.e., they have to be controlled to curb inflation. This can be done only if:

- Wage increases may be allowed to workers only if their productivity increases; but if wages increase without increase in output per worker then the producer raises the price of goods (it is inflationary situation) as his profit margin reduces.
- The Government during inflation should keep down the cost of living through its anti-inflationary programmes or then the high wages to workers would be justified.
- The Government can through its taxation policy or by its compulsory borrowings from public can take away a part of money wages to curb inflation.

(3) Stimulating Economic Growth: Other things being equal, if economic growth matches the growth of the money supply, inflation should not occur. A large variety of factors can affect the rate of both. For example, investment in market, production, infrastructure, education, etc., can all grow an economy in greater amounts than the investment spending.

(4) Price Control and Rationing: The aim of price control is to lay down the upper limit beyond which the price of a particular commodity would not be allowed to increase. However, two conditions are essential for effective functioning of price control:

- The Government should have enough stock of that particular commodity under its control.

- The demand for that particular commodity should be controlled through rationing; if it fails to do so then the advantage of the controlled price would be taken away by the richer section.

In general, wage and price controls are regarded as a temporary and exceptional measure, only effective when coupled with policies designed to reduce the underlying causes of inflation during the wage and price control regime. Artificially low prices often cause shortages and discourage future investment, resulting in yet further shortages. The usual economic analysis is that any product or service that is under-priced is over-consumed. For example, if the official price of bread is too low, there will be too little bread at official prices, and too little investment in bread making by the market to satisfy future needs, thereby exacerbate the problem in the long term.

However, in general the advice of economists is not to impose price controls but to liberalize prices by assuming that the economy will adjust and abandon unprofitable economic activity. Keynes, too, was not in favour of price control because it leads to the loss of consumer's freedom. Despite its limitations, this anti-inflationary tool seems to be indispensable to control the prices of at least the essential goods during inflation. However, price control and rationing cannot be adopted as a general policy.

(5) Cost – of – living allowance (Dearness Allowance): The real purchasing power of fixed payments is eroded by inflation unless they are inflation-adjusted to keep their real values constant. In many countries, employment contracts, pension benefits, and government emoluments (such as social security) are tied to a cost-of-living index, typically to the consumer price index. Salaries are typically adjusted annually in low inflation economies. During hyperinflation they are adjusted more often.

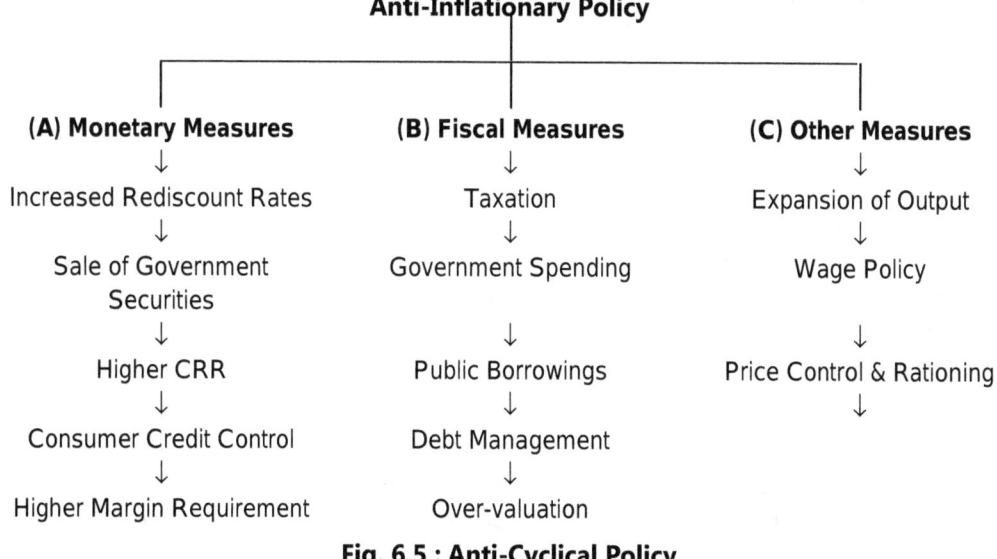

Fig. 6.5 : Anti-Cyclical Policy

(The **flow-chart** gives a quick glimpse of all the anti-inflationary measures discussed above.)

Measurement of Inflation

Inflation is the rapidly rising prices of goods and services caused to the increase in the supply money. Inflation arises when the demand for goods and services in an economy exceeds the supply of same. Inflation is a determinant in functioning of any economy.

Why is it necessary to measure Inflation? Inflation, when measured gives the economy the nature of inflation- mild or hyper and its effect on the economy.

Influence on Economic Welfare: Inflation has an effect on the economic welfare. So, it will serve as a target of the public policy. Therefore, for this reason, inflation measurement is pretty much important.

Influence on other Economic Figures: Since the computations are estimated by exploding the nominal values with a price index, measures of inflation has a clear effect on the construction of other economic figures such as Gross Domestic Product (GDP).

Effect on Economic Conclusions: Every now and then economic resolutions depend directly on the published measurement of inflation.

Hence, correct measurement of inflation is badly needed.

Contesting on the challenges faced, several economists have questioned the method of measuring inflation, to be faulty. The present day process being used in India has been the Wholesale Price Index (WPI), while several other developed countries adopt the Consumer Price Index (CPI) to calculate inflation.

Tools of Measurement

Consumer Price Index: (CPI) as the name suggests, this index shows the change of values of the consumers' goods and services. From this index, the change of prices of food materials, clothes can be obtained. Thus, it is a measure of price changes in consumer goods and services such as gasoline, food, clothing and automobiles. The CPI measures price change from the perspective of the purchaser. In short, it measures the price of a selection of commodities. In the present commodity price indices are weighted by the relative importance of the components to the "all in" cost of an employee.

Producer Price Index: (PPI) - This index gives the change of the selling prices of the producer who sell goods. To compute this index, the mean (average) of all the changes over a year is usually been taken. Thus, PPIs measures average changes in prices received by domestic producers for their output.

PPI differs from the CPI as price subsidization, profits and taxes may cause the amount received by the producer to differ from what the consumer paid. There is also typically a delay between an increase in the PPI and any eventual increase in the CPI. PPI measures the pressure being put on producers by the costs of their raw materials. This could be "passed on" to consumers, or it could be absorbed by profits, or offset by increasing productivity. In India and the U.S.A., an earlier version of the PPI was called the Wholesale Price Index (WPI).

Core Price Indices: Food and oil prices can change quickly due to changes in demand and supply conditions in the food and oil markets and hence it becomes difficult to detect the long run trend in price levels when those prices are included. Therefore, most statistical agencies report a measure of 'core inflation', which removes the most volatile components (such as food and oil) from a broad price index like the CPI. Since core inflation is less affected by short run supply and demand conditions in specific markets, Central bank rely on it to better measure the inflationary impact of current monetary policy.

There are two basic system of measuring inflation present today. While India adopts the prior method (WPI) which is considered to be lesser advanced. The demographics and structures of India don't permit it to adopt the second basis system of measuring inflation, i.e. CPI.

CPI presents several problems for India to shift from the current Wholesale Price Index. The Consumer Price Index is not viable to be used in India because there is too much of a lag in reporting the Consumer Price Index numbers. Another debate that contradicts the application of CPI is the fact that it is calculated on a monthly basis while the Wholesale Price Index is calculated on a weekly basis and it is the system which India adopts at present. However when the index for consumers is to be recorded than the CPI system rather than the WPI should be adopted.

To measure the inflation correctly, i.e. to get the accurate figure, certain things have to be kept in mind. *Firstly,* the type of the collection of market prices has to be decided; *Secondly,* attention must be given at the time of measuring the change of prices, and *lastly,* for calculating the sum total certain rules has to be followed to combine those changing figures.

Problems in Measuring Inflation.

Inflation is a measure of changes in the cost of living. Inflation is measured by using a weighted basket of goods and looking at the changes in price. However, in practice, there are many practical difficulties for measuring inflation.

1. Family Expenditure Survey does not include everybody. E.g. pensioners are excluded. Pensioners have different spending habits e.g. heating / bus travel account for a higher % of their expenditure. Young people will benefit more from falling prices of mobile phones and electronic goods. Therefore, the basket of goods may not be representative. Also, as it is updated once a year, it may soon become outdated for changes in spending habits.

2. Changes in Quality of goods. Changes in the quality of goods mean that price rises may not reflect inflation, but just the fact it is a different good. For example, computers have many more features than 10 years ago, so it is difficult to compare prices because they are effectively different goods. This is similar situation for many goods such as mobile phones and cars.

3. One off shocks may give a misleading impression. For example, a rise in oil prices will lead to higher inflation. But, this rise in prices may just be temporary. Tax changes have a similar effect.
4. Which Measure to Use? - CPI, RPI or RPIX. RPI includes mortgage interest payments. CPI doesn't. In 2009, with falling interest rates, RPI gave a negative inflation rate, whilst CPI was positive. Therefore, it is important which measure is used. The government's preferred measure is currently CPI.
5. People have different inflation rates. Rising electricity and gas prices may affect old people more than young people. Therefore, old people could have a higher inflation rate than the national average. This is important if pensions are index linked because their cost of living may rise more than prices causing a decrease in living standards.

Challenges (Developing Economy)

The challenges faced by a developing economy are many, especially when Monetary Policy is related with the Central Bank for bringing in price stability. There has been a universal argument these days when monetary policy is determined to be a key element in controlling inflation. The Central Bank works on the objective to control and have a stable price for commodities. A good environment of price stability happens to create saving mobilization and a sustained economic growth. The former Governor of Reserve Bank of India, C. Rangarajan, points out that there is a long-term trade-off between output and inflation. He further adds that short-term trade-off happens to only introduce uncertainty about the price level in future.

6.5 Deflation

Meaning and Causes

Deflation is a process that is exactly the opposite of inflation.

In the words of **Crowther**, *"Deflation is the state of the economy in which the value of money is rising of prices is falling."*

While defining deflation, Prof. Pigou has laid more emphasis on the difference between real income and money income. If real income is increasing at a faster rate than money income, prices are bound to fall.

According to Pigou, it is deflation:
(a) When the total output is constant but the money income is falling;
(b) If both, output and money income are falling, but money income is falling faster;
(c) If money income is stable but real income is increasing;
(d) If both are increasing but money income is increasing at a slower rate; or
(e) If output is increasing (real income) but money income is falling.

Similar to inflation, deflation is also explained differently by various economists.

The two points of view of deflation are that, reduction in the total quantity of money or reduction in the monetary income, leads to a fall in the demand.

Before we begin to explain the effects of deflation on the economy, it is necessary to define two terms which are often used in economic literature, i.e., 'Reflation' and 'Disinflation'.

When prices begin to fall and depression begins an attempt is often made to maintain prices by inflating the currency and credit in the country. These attempts to maintain or increase prices are known as 'Reflation'. 'Reflation' is done deliberately and is always pre-planned.

When an attempt is made to put a stop to rising prices, by reducing the total supply of money and credit in the country, it is termed as 'Disinflation'. This again, is done deliberately and while resorting to the reduction of supply of money and credit, care is taken to see that production and employment do not suffer. But, deflation affects production and employment adversely.

Effects of Deflation

It is customary to classify the effects of deflation on production and distribution in the economy as follows:

(1) Effects on Production

Due to deflation, the value of stocks and inventories decreases. Entrepreneurs suffer losses as the cost of production is high, but products are to be sold at lower prices. Similarly, traders and wholesalers also incur losses. The loss in luxury and durable consumer goods is large, as their demand falls and their production has to be reduced substantially.

(2) Effects on Distribution

(a) **Producers and Entrepreneurs:** Producers and entrepreneurs are adversely affected by deflation. Firstly, prices fall, but costs are 'sticky' and lag behind i.e., they remain high. Secondly, raw materials and other requirements are purchased or hired at higher prices and by the time finished products reach the market, prices have decreased. Thirdly, there is a continuous fall in the aggregate demand, because of which, traders, manufacturers and businessmen suffer losses.

(b) **Investors:** Those who invest in assets yielding fixed incomes, such as bonds, debentures, etc., are benefitted as the value of monetary returns on these assets go on increasing. But those who have invested in equity shares yielding dividends suffer losses, as they do not get any dividends because the purchasing companies do not make profits.

(c) **Wage and Salary earners:** The wage and salary earners and all others, whose income is fixed in terms of money, are benefitted. Their salaries and earnings remain more or less the same, but the value of money goes on increasing, hence they benefit. But when the rate of deflation is very rapid, manufacturing concerns close down, lock-outs are declared and this results in unemployment.

(d) **The Consumers:** Consumers, whose income remains unaltered, benefit, but those whose income is reduced or who are rendered unemployed are put to losses. In short, consumers find that their money income has a higher purchasing power, i.e., the value of money has increased.

(e) **Creditors and Debtors:** During deflation, creditors benefit and borrowers suffer losses. The borrowers have to pay in terms of higher purchasing power, as the value of money is high.

(3) Other effects:

(a) The value of money goes on rising when there is deflation. But as taxes remain unaltered, the burden of taxes goes on increasing and the tax payer is affected adversely.

(b) During deflation, the income of the people is reduced. So, even if the rates of taxation are what they were, the yield from taxes is reduced. This compels the government to resort to loans, at a time when the real burden of debts is more. Thus, the government is compelled to shoulder a greater burden because of deflation.

(c) The worst possible effect of deflation is the closing down of many manufacturing concerns, which renders several employees jobless. Thus, production is reduced and depression sets in.

(d) As there is a fall in the demand for loans, financial institutions and banks face difficulties.

(e) Due to economic depression, the pace of economic development comes to a standstill, all economic transactions shrink and there is large scale unemployment. With unemployment, the number of industrial disputes increases and there is an all pervasive dissatisfaction. Such a state of the economy is politically extremely disturbing. If the government is not in a position to overcome depression, the public opinion goes against the government.

Inflation Vs Deflation

Which is better, inflation or deflation? In the words of **J. M. Keynes**, *"Inflation is unjust; deflation is inexpedient. And of the two- deflation is worse".*

If *inflation* is rising price, falling value of money and overfull employment; *deflation* is the opposite of inflation, where prices are persistently falling. Deflation is a state of disequilibrium in which shrinking purchasing power tends to cause or is the effect of fall in the price level. Disequilibrium in the economy is caused by both inflation and deflation and both have an adverse effect on the economy in different ways.

Inflation is unjust because of the following reasons:

(a) During inflation, purchasing power is transferred from the poorer section to the richer and the gap between the two widens. In other words, it increases economic inequalities through its redistributive effects.

(b) Inflation is regressive in character, i.e., it imposes a heavier burden on the poorer sections of the community.

(c) An atmosphere of artificial prosperity is seen during inflation. Inflation feeds inflation. The price level rise upto great heights. This disturbs the working of the economy and the government is compelled to take certain steps that give rise to deflationary tendencies in the economy, i.e., falling profits, increasing unemployment, etc.

(d) Inflation demoralizes the people in the economy. It promotes speculative activities and diverts the productive activities to speculation.

(e) Prof. C. N. Vakil has compared inflation with *'invisible robbery'*. In his words, *"inflation may be compared to a robber. Both deprive the victim of some possession, with the difference that the robber is visible, while inflation is invisible, the robber's victim may be one or a few at a time, the victim of inflation is the whole nation, the robber may be dragged to a court of law, inflation is legal".*

Deflation is inexpedient:

Deflation is considered inexpedient due to the following reasons:

(a) Deflation is inexpedient because once it starts, it goes on gathering momentum and within a certain span of time the crisis becomes deeper.

(b) During deflation prices are reduced. This leads to reduction in production and ultimately, in the national income. With the decline in the national income the country becomes poorer than before.

(c) With production decline, deflation is marked by increased unemployment. This is because when the prices fall, profit margins decline and the businessmen close-down their establishments or cut-down the volume of production, giving rise to mass unemployment in the society.

(d) Deflation causes economic depression in the economy. Business becomes dull, production is reduced, money income contracts and the volume of employment go down, creating highly pessimistic conditions in the economy.

(e) It is not incorrect to say that deflation results in a complete ruin of the economy as the social, economic, political and moral consequences of deflation are vicious and highly undesirable.

Inflation Vs Deflation:

Of the two evils-inflation and deflation- deflation is worse. Lord Keynes considers inflation better than deflation on the following grounds:

(a) Inflation redistributes wealth in the favour of the richer section of the society, but in no way does it reduce the national income. On the other hand, deflation has an undesirable effect of reducing the national income of the country.

(b) Inflation is a situation of full-employment. However, deflation is socially undesirable as it leads to the reduction in the volume of employment.

(c) Moderate inflation may be good for a depressed economy, as it can serve to stimulate the economic development. Thus, mild inflation is better than deflation from the point of view of economic growth.

(d) Inflation, howsoever serious, can be controlled to a certain extent by implementing monetary and fiscal measures. On the other hand, deflation is difficult to check even after the application of monetary and fiscal measures. These measures become ineffective in checking the deepening depression. During depression, the businessmen generally lose confidence in the future of their investments and no amount of monetary expansion can restore that confidence. Fiscal policy fails to check the spread of depression in the economy.

Inflation has its dangers, particularly when it gets out of control and develops into hyper inflation, but according to Lord Keynes, deflation should be avoided at all costs.

Points to Remember

- The occurrence of alternating periods of prosperity and depression is generally referred to as a 'business cycle'. The British economists call it as 'trade cycle.'
- Business cycle is a 'wave-like' movement. It operates periodically. It is universal and all embracing. Business cycles are 'cumulative' in effect.
- **J. M. Keynes**, "A trade cycle is composed of periods of good trade characterized by rising prices and low unemployment percentage; altering with periods of bad trade characterized by falling prices and high unemployment percentages".
- **Various anti-cyclical policies are** (i) Monetary policy; (ii) Fiscal policy; (iii) Built-in-stabilizers.
- There is hardly any country in the capitalist world today which is not afflicted by inflation. Inflation, in the popular mind, is generally associated with rapidly rising prices which cause a fall in the purchasing power of money.
- A typical or standard business cycle is characterized by five different stages or phases- depression, recovery (or revival), prosperity (or full employment), boom (or overfull employment) and recession.

- The trade cycles, by creating cyclical fluctuations in business activity, do a great deal of harm to the smooth and orderly progress of society. Therefore, efforts should be made to check the operation of the business cycle. As regards the long waves (i.e. long business cycles), it is not possible to check them. Long waves are inevitable in a capitalist society. But something can definitely be done to mitigate the ravages of the short business cycle.
- The effect of inflation is not distributed evenly in the economy, and as a consequence there are hidden costs to some and benefits to other from this decrease in the purchasing power of money.
- Causes of Inflation: (i) Increase in demand; (ii) Fall in the supply of goods and services.
- **(a) Increase in demand is due to:** (i) Increase in public expenditure; (ii) Increase in Private expenditure; (iii) Increase in foreign demand; (iv) Reduction in taxation; (v) Repayment of internal debts; (vi) Population growth; (vii) Existence of Black Money; (viii) Deficit Financing; (ix) Cheap Money policy; (x) Rise in consumer spending.
- **(b) Decrease in Supply is due to:** (i) Natural calamities; (ii) Scarcity of the factors of production; (iii) Industrial disputes; (iv) Imbalanced production; (v) Operation of the Law of Diminishing Returns; (vi) Hoarding by merchants; (vii) Hoarding by consumers.
- **Effects of Inflation:**
    (a) Fixed income groups, for example, pensioners, persons living on past savings, interest or rent earners, small farmers, creditors, wage and salary earners are *losers*. Flexible group persons are *gainers*.
    (b) Production, savings, investments etc., suffer adversely.
    (c) Inflation is socially unjust, as it redistributes wealth in favour of the affluent classes.
    (d) Inflation is a serious danger to underdeveloped countries.
- **Control of Inflation**
    (a) Monetary Measures: (i) Increase in bank discount rates; (ii) Selling of Government securities; (iii) Increased cash reserve requirements; (iv) Consumer credit; (v) Higher margin requirements.
    (b) Fiscal Measures: (i) taxation; (ii) government spending; (iii) public borrowing; (iv) debt management; (v) over-valuation.
    (c) Other Measures: (i) expansion of output; (ii) income and wage policy; (iii) price control and rationing.
- Deflation: According to Crowther,"Deflation is that state of the economy, in which the value of money is rising or prices are falling".
- **Effects of Deflation:**
    (a) On Production: Businessmen suffer losses as the cost of production is high but prices of the products are low.

(b) On distribution: Flexible income group suffers due to fall in money income.
(c) Other effects: Income of the people is reduced, the pace of economic development comes to a standstill.

- **Inflation Vs Deflation**
  (a) Inflation is unjust; (b) Deflation is inexpedient.
  - Of the two evils – inflation and deflation – deflation is worse.

Multiple Choice Questions

1. Which of the following is not an essential characteristic of business cycle?
   (a) Recurrent in nature
   (b) cumulative in effect
   (c) Regular
   (d) All pervading in their impact.

2. Which of the following statements is not correct with regard to the assumptions of Hicks' theory of business cycles?
   (a) Changes in consumption and investment influence the equilibrium of the whole economy
   (b) Accelerator remains operative in all stages of an economic cycle, but multiplier becomes inoperative during depression
   (c) Ceiling to expansion is imposed by full employment
   (d) Autonomous investment increases at a constant rate even after reaching depression

3. Which of the following factors create demand-pull situation?
   (a) Increase in production
   (b) Increase in cost of production
   (c) Increase in money income
   (d) Increase in demand for cash balance

4. Which of the following measures will help in checking inflation?
   (a) Fall in Bank rate
   (b) Stability in exchange rates
   (c) Devaluation
   (d) Increase in public expenditure

5. Inflation is beneficial to which of the following sections of the economy?
   (a) Creditors
   (b) Consumers
   (c) Debtors
   (d) Investors in bonds and securities

6. Inflation is unjust because it –
   (a) Goes on gathering momentum
   (b) Increases unemployment
   (c) Helps the producers
   (d) Increases economic inequalities

7. The important monetary measures in the hands of the central bank include all of the following except:
   (a) Public revenue
   (b) Open market operations
   (c) Reserve ratios
   (d) Rediscount rate

8. As per Keynesian theory, economic fluctuations are due to changes in:
    (a) Disinvestment (b) Rate of investment
    (c) Autonomous investment (d) Warranted rate of growth
9. Nominal interest-rate is:
    (a) Adjusted for inflation (b) Not adjusted for inflation
    (c) Real purchasing power (d) Not market interest rate
10. Fiscal policy includes all except:
    (a) Taxation (b) Expenditure
    (c) Borrowing (d) Credit creation

Answers:

1 - (c), 2 - (b), 3 - (c), 4 - (b), 5 - (c), 6 - (d), 7 - (a), 8 - (b), 9 - (b), 10 - (d)

Questions

1. What is business cycle? Describe the various stages of a typical business cycle.
2. Describe the five stages or conditions of the economic system which, if put together in order, would contribute a standard business cycle.
3. What are the characteristics of trade cycles?
4. Distinguish between major and minor cycles.
5. What is recession? How does it differ from depression?
6. Discuss the various anti-cyclical policies.
7. How do automatic stabilizers help in combating fluctuations in business activity?
8. Explain how business cycles can be controlled?
9. Why is controlling trade cycles necessary?
10. Explain the various measures to control inflation.
11. Define inflation. What are the various types of inflation?
12. Explain the causes of Inflation.
13. How does inflation affect different sectors of the economy differently?
14. Why is measurement of Inflation essential?
15. What are the problems and challenges that occur during measurement of Inflation?
16. Explain the different tools of measurement of Inflation.
17. Illustrate with diagram the demand-pull inflation.
18. Explain in detail the Cost-Push Inflation. Are the two types of inflation, demand-pull and cost-push inter-related to each other?
19. "Inflation is unjust; deflation is inexpedient. Of the two, deflation is worse". Explain.

Bibliography

1. Principles of Macro Economics (4th Edition) Mankiw.
2. Macro Economics – M.L. Seth – Lakshmi Narain Agarwal, Agra.
3. Economics – Samuelson Nordhaus (18th Edition) – TATA McGraw-Hill Edition.
4. Macro Economic Analysis – Mrs. Kiran Jotwani, Dr. Mukund Mahajan – Nirali Prakashan.
5. Economic Analysis for Business Decisions. Mrs. Kiran Jotwani (MMM Semester I), Nirali Prakashan.
6. Managerial Economics – Geetika, Piyali Ghosh, Purba Roy Choudhury - Tata McGraw Hill Education Private Limited.
7. Managerial Economics. R. L. Varshney, K. L. Maheshwari, Sultan Chand & Sons.
8. Macro Economic Theory. M. L. Jhingan. Vrinda Publications (P) Ltd. 10th Revised & Enlarged Edition.
9. Managerial Economics- P. L. Mehta – Sultan Chand & Sons.
   (Analysis, Problems and Cases)
10. Economics – Lipsey & Chrystal (11th Edition) - Oxford (Indian Edition)
11. Business Economics – Prof. Vasudha Garde & Sunayini Parchure (Narendra Prakashan).
12. Macro Economics. Theory & Policy. H. L. Ahuja S. Chand & Sons.
13. Macro Economic Theory. M. C. Vaish (Wishwa Prakashan).

UNIVERSITY QUESTION PAPER
OCTOBER 2014

Time : 3 Hours   Max. Marks : 80

Instructions to the candidates :

1. All questions are compulsory.
2. Attempt any four from the rest.
3. Figures to the right indicate full marks.
4. Draw neat diagram where necessary.

Q.1. Write short notes on any FOUR :   [20]
- (a) Inflation.
- (b) Autonomous and Induced Investments.
- (c) Paradox of Savings.
- (d) APC and MPC.
- (e) Definition of Money.
- (f) Pigou's Equation of Cash Balance Approach.

Q.2. What is demand pull inflation? What are the factors causing it?   [15]

Q.3. Explain the working of the Foreign Trade Multiplier.   [15]

Q.4. What is a consumption function ? Explain the factors affecting it.   [15]

Q.5. Explain Keynes' Theory of Income and Employment in detail.   [15]

Q.6. Explain the Cash Balance Approach in detail.   [15]

Q.7. Define Macro Economics and explain its nature and scope.   [15]

UNIVERSITY QUESTION PAPER
APRIL 2015
(2013 PATTERN)

Time : 3 Hours   Max. Marks : 80

Instructions to the candidates :

1. Question no. 1 is compulsory.
2. Attempt any four from the rest.
3. Figures to the right indicate full marks.
4. Draw neat diagram where necessary.

Q.1. Write short notes on any four :   [20]

    (a) Savings function

    (b) Primary functions of money

    (c) Effective demand

    (d) Scope of macro

    (e) Factors affecting MEC

    (f) Characteristics of trade cycles.

Q.2. Define Macro-Economics. Explain its nature, scope and importance.   [15]

Q.3. Explain the Quantity Theory of Money in detail.   [15]

Q.4. 'Production creates a market for goods'. Elucidate.   [15]

Q.5. Elaborate on Keynes' Psychological Law of Consumption.   [15]

Q.6. Explain the investment function in detail.   [15]

Q.7. Discuss the objectives and tools of the monetary policy.   [15]

www.ingramcontent.com/pod-product-compliance
Lightning Source LLC
Chambersburg PA
CBHW081300170426
43198CB00017B/2866